THE HUMAN MEANING OF
THE SOCIAL SCIENCES

THE HUMAN MEANING OF

THE SOCIAL SCIENCES

Edited by

DANIEL LERNER

Meridian Books
THE WORLD PUBLISHING COMPANY
Cleveland and New York

H
35
L54

AN ORIGINAL MERIDIAN BOOK

Published by The World Publishing Company
2231 West 110th Street, Cleveland, Ohio 44102
First printing March 1959.
Sixth printing November 1965.

Contents

PREFACE

This book is the outcome of conversations with Jean-Marie Domenach, editor of the French review *Esprit,* in the spring of 1956. Like many humanists, Domenach had been puzzled by the rapid postwar growth and diffusion of Social Science. Unlike many literary intellectuals, who found no better use for their talents than to throw spitballs at the barbarians invading their territory, he set out to learn why Social Scientists were moving so swiftly—and apparently so successfully—into areas previously occupied only by Wise Men.

Domenach perceived that this process was at work throughout modern Europe, alike in France and the Low Countries, in Germany and Central Europe, in the Scandinavian lands, in Great Britain and the Commonwealth. Only the most retrograde and immobile European social order, as in Spain and Portugal, Southern Italy and Greece, seemed unaffected. The direct relationship between social change and social research was visible in every case. The more dynamic the country, the further had the new Social Sciences developed. On the Old Continent, indeed, the postwar pace was set by the effort to come abreast of American studies which, provoked by the war, had speeded advances in many fields.

Once the close connection between social change and social research is perceived, the recognition grows that Social Science is more than a peculiar new vocabulary. Its jargon, often baffling to laymen and outlandish to the literati, represents the effort to apply a new conception of man and society to the systematic study of phenomena never before subjected to rigorous empirical inquiry. Social science is a genuinely new way of looking at the world—replacing the successive methods of magic, religion, philosophy by the method of observation.

Under the rule of Social Science, there are no eternal mysteries—in its proper domain of human behavior—but only phenomena that have not yet been adequately observed. Nothing human is inscrutable; all behavior is amenable to inquiry. So from Le Play's persistent prying into the secrets of the family budget among European workers to Kinsey's intimate inquiries into the secrets of sexual behavior among American females, Social Science has continually ignored, evaded, or assailed conventional limits and tabus by asserting its right to know everything that seems worth knowing about the behavior of human beings. If this poses a threat to privacy, the risk must be weighed against the gain. We now *know* more about human behavior than has ever been known by any society recorded in history. The question: Is this gain worth the risk?

As there are no more eternal mysteries, in Social Science, so there are no more eternal verities. Social Science knows no once-for-all Truth, seeks no once-for-all Law. It deals, at bottom, with human values—what people want; and social institutions—what they receive. Values and institutions are continuously changing in the centuries since men acquired mobility. Once set free from their native soil, men were also liberated from their native status and their native self. Men who changed their address found it appropriate to change as well their place and personality. The son was no longer his father's shadow. He began to have "ideas" —what he wanted from life and how he proposed to get it being, usually, quite outside his father's traditional code. Social Science developed largely as a way of perceiving, evaluating, and correcting the frictions and tensions generated by the high rate of individual mobility and institutional change in modernizing society. The passing of eternal Truth and natural Law cost men the feeling of certainty and continuity that went with behavioral codes revealed and imposed by external authority. The gain was personal freedom, the vast enlargement of the autonomous private sphere that distinguishes modern life. Social Science provides guidance through the dilemmas and anxieties of free personal choice to replace the instruction in prescribed behavior of Truth and Law. The question: Is this gain worth the cost?

The answers to these questions seem obvious. Yet, Domenach was able to raise them in a form which reminded us of their profundity, viz., "The basic question is this: what, approximately, is the possible boundary between the known and the unknown, the analysable and the mysterious, in the theory and practice of the scientific study of man? What percentage can the research worker determine, and what percentage of liberty, consciously, or otherwise, does he recognize, or attribute, to man? This question does not necessarily lead to a dilemma: it may be that it is the most scientific research which, by fixing the limit of its determinations more accurately, finally respects liberty better, would establish the conditions of its development more firmly within its limits. But it is also possible that this rigorously 'scientific' conception may require cri·ˈ

cism, objections from other fields of knowledge—philosophical thoughts, literary expression . . ."

In this inquiring spirit Domenach posed some searching questions about the values, methods and uses of Social Science. As the American experience has been so large and varied, Domenach asked me to arrange a symposium in which American social scientists would respond to the queries that had been raised. The symposium was published as a special issue of *Esprit*. As it became evident that many Americans shared our interest in reconsidering some of the basic issues underlying Social Science, it was decided to recast the symposium in a form suitable for a larger American public. The present book contains the eight original essays, expanded and revised, together with two new essays addressed to questions of special interest to Americans that emerged from the symposium itself.

Clearly, not all of the questions raised by Social Science can be answered in this short space. We have sought, rather, clearly to formulate the central issues and appropriate ways of thinking them through. The introductory chapter defines the social setting in which Social Science can flourish. To understand that Social Science is a product, as well as a tool, of the modern democratic West is to see why it has come under such sharp attack from the new despotisms of our time and why its future in the vast underdeveloped world is uncertain. Social Science will grow with social democracy or, probably, not at all.

Two historical essays amplify these propositions, Glazer tracing the rise of Social Science in Europe and Alpert reviewing its rapid postwar growth in America. Three key issues that will govern future development are then given lucid exposition. Lasswell deals with scientific strategy, the rational use of observation to maximize the goal values of our science and its society. Shils deals with scientific ethics, focusing on the possible risks to private autonomy inherent in studies of personal behavior. Millikan then clarifies the complex issue of science and policy, setting out the conditions for wedding knowledge and power in the public interest.

The uses of Social Science in America today are illustrated for only two disciplines, space being limited, but they are the two whose impact upon individuals and institutions has been most pervasive. Samuelson tells us "what economists know" in a concise primer on economic forecasting, probably the applied Social Science which has most directly modified our conceptions of what American society is and, under certain conditions, can be. Frank shows how the many and varied infusions of psychology into our personal, personnel, educational, religious, business, military and governmental institutions have reshaped our social order.

We conclude with the prospects for Social Science in the great underdeveloped world, now modernizing at a ferocious pace. Here we call upon anthropology, the discipline with the longest sustained experience in studying the non-Western world. Kluckhohn, by linking "common humanity" with "diverse cultures," reformulates the Social Scientist's creed as he moves into research on the modernizing world. Margaret Mead, rich with the experience of modernizing Manus, shows how "reflective change" in primitive socities involves a rudimentary model of rational choice—the process of self-regulation through self-observation that we in the modern world have come to call Social Science.

DANIEL LERNER

CENTER FOR INTERNATIONAL STUDIES, M.I.T.
CAMBRIDGE, MASSACHUSETTS
NOVEMBER 1958

PERSPECTIVE

SOCIAL SCIENCE: WHENCE AND WHITHER?

Daniel Lerner

Every human community develops some mode of self-observation to record, and ultimately regulate, its own operations. Since its records of the past guide decisions and revisions in the present, self-observation builds continuity into a social system. As the fulcrum of continuity is variously located in different societies, so the things they need to know about themselves also vary widely.

Many tribes have kept genealogies, such records of blood-relationship being useful for maintenance of tribal laws on inbreeding and incest. Dynastic China kept chronologies, which are essential custodial records for a society infused with reverence for the past and the related practices of ancestor-worship. Modern industrial society keeps census data and other statistical records by which its massive populations, manifold operations, and ever-changing institutions can be comprehensively observed and continuously regulated.

The modes of self-observation vary so profoundly because what a society needs to know about itself is tied up with everything that society is and wants to be. While chronologies were useful records in dynastic China, which paid scant attention to the ways and welfare of its multitudes, they are merely mementoes in the rapidly modernizing society of Red China. Wanted now are "social statistics," the typical mode of self-observation in the modern world.

What use would genealogies and chronologies be, say, in mobile America, whose people rarely die in the same place where they were born? Such people do not spend their lives revering the past but planning the future. This change of personal style transforms the societal mode of self-observation. One needs to know not what great men of the past have done, but what ordinary men of the future may be doing. Without such information, rational planning of private or public activity is difficult. Decisions on whether to buy a house or wait, quit one's job or ask for a raise, send one's son to engineering or medical school, plan a vacation in Hawaii or Brussels—all such highly personal decisions are weighted in terms of what "most people" are doing and likely to be doing.

The mode of self-study characteristic of modern society —what we now call Social Science—evolved out of a rich tradition of observation and reflection. Social philosophy has engaged serious thinkers throughout western history. The place of man in his social order has posed problems as baffling for first-rate minds as his place in the natural universe. Through much of the Christian era, religious doctrine governed conceptions in both these realms and unified them. With the secularization of thought in modern times, theology in the grand manner gave way to more specialized inquiry under the titles of natural philosophy and social philosophy. As our complex, secular, national societies evolved, even philosophy changed its character. Natural philosophy gradually became natural history and finally natural science—this array of experimental disciplines we today call, simply, Science. Social philosophy, changing its ways later and slower, became Social Science.

1. Modern Society: The Setting for Social Science

The historical transformation of social inquiry from rational speculation to empirical research occurred, as part of the general conquest of philosophy by science, in nineteenth-century Europe. This decisive turn in intellectual history accompanied the institutional transformation which gave modern society its distinctive character. We have grown used to casual summaries of modernity as the product of exploration and invention, industrialization, urbanization, secularization. But this historical sequence worked itself out through millions of individual lives; many suffered, others prospered, while the western world was being reshaped in the modern image. By recalling the personal dramas of modernization, we gain some insight into the human meaning of the social sciences.

The key word is mobility—freedom to move. The Age of Exploration opened the New World, into which moved millions of people from the old worlds. The Industrial Revolution moved many millions more into towns, thereby chain-reacting into the urban revolution that has spread around the world and, in our time, marks the passing of traditional society from human history.[1] As people moved from fields to factories, from farms to flats, their daily round of life was completely transformed. Erik H. Erikson emerges from psychoanalytic study of the modernization of one very famous "peasant" with the conclusion: "Luther's childhood illustrates the fact that adherence to . . . an 'estate', such as that of peasant, cannot remain a reliable factor in one's inner sense of continuity unless one is involved in the common hardships, hopes, and hates of the estate. These alone keep an ideology relevant." [2]

Modern society transformed the hardships, hopes, and hates of the rural estates. In the traditional setting of rural isolation, a person grew up knowing every role and relationship in his environment. In most instances he knew every person in his village—and by knowing their names, houses and kinships, he thereby knew their "place" in his society. His own "place" was defined by birth: he *was* his father's son. This fixed all his primary (kinship) and virtually all his secondary (friendship) relations. This determined his abode and his work. In childhood he was trained to till his father's field with the same tools and by the same routines as his father; then he married and passed abruptly into adulthood, when he did what his childhood had trained him for. He expected nothing else and he experienced nothing else. He died young, in the same place where he was born.

The move to the city changed all this. Physical mobility, by giving a man freedom to change his location on the earth, perforce gave him freedom to change his "place" in the world. This entrained those vast changes in the traditional social order which we call social mobility. In a city the son no longer was, nor could be, his father's shadow. He had to "learn a trade" and "get a job"—with someone other than his father as teacher and employer. He had to learn to get along with strangers. Once outside the completely known universe of the village, new faces became an essential feature of his daily life—faces hired or fired at his factory, faces moving in or out of his tenement, faces passing his own in streets or stores or trolleys. The city was "a different world," full of novelty and surprise.

To cope efficiently with this new and strange world,

traditional man needed a new stock of personal responses and a new kit of personal skills—in short a new personality. Physical mobility, having supplied the conditions for social mobility, now posed the demand for *psychic* mobility. As a man could change his physical residence and social role, so he must be able to change his personal "style." But this involved nothing less than the alteration of one's inner identity. In the historic shift from the traditional to the modern "way of life," acquisition of psychic mobility introduced a most subtle and profound transformation into man's conception of himself and his environment.

In this new conception, a man's inner self is no longer fixed and immutable—and indeed inscrutable. The inner self is nowadays no *territoire sacré,* no bondage of terror between a man and his God, but rather a supple relationship between him and his fellows. In our more humane modern conception of personality, we no longer drive the deviant individual to the wall—under a volley of bullets, as once was done, or of ridicule. The terrifying view of the "village idiot" as one possessed by demons and an object of danger, which led to the most awful inhumanity against non-conformist behavior through the long centuries of traditional society (see Dostoevsky), has passed out of the modern mores. Since the late nineteenth century, the village idiot has been conceived, at worst, as the village "crank"—more usually, in England, "the eccentric"; in France, *"le numéro";* in America, "the character."

Under this more generous modern conception of normalcy,[3] deviant personality is not treated as diabolical impiety toward God, but rather as a failure of communication with one's fellow men—a malfunction of the inner mechanism. This is not a curse but an illness, hence it can be cured. We now regard a man's "self-system" as the dynamic organization of his internal relationships to the external world, subject to continuous rearrangement as his circumstances of life are altered. The mobile modern society imposed such a view of one's self as plastic, variable, and amenable to reshaping. In traditional village society, where a man's identity was defined once for all by being his father's son, a variable personality was unnecessary, was regarded indeed as a sign of "bad character." In the modern urban setting, where a man must constantly confront new persons or varied roles or strange situations, the capacity to rearrange his self-system on short notice is essential. He needs a wider and more varied stock of personal responses and an inner sorting mechanism that will operate rapidly and efficiently.

This has involved, historically, a new conception of the human ego, whose function it is to give a man a rational definition of his own identity. Through ego-identification a man relates himself to his family, his work, his community, his nation, his religion, his race, his culture, his politics. Modern men have active and variable relationships to all these elements in the world around them. Hence, one attribute of the modern personality is its more capacious inventory of ego-identifications, its larger sense of identity with secondary "roles" in social realms. The mechanism by which this was accomplished we call *empathy,* a basic personality skill in sorting one's stock of identities that equips a man for continuous rearrangement of his self-system.

In modern society, then, mobility has conveyed freedom to move in all the basic dimensions of a human life. Physical mobility released man from his native soil; social mobility freed man from his native status; psychic mobility liberated man from his native self. This process of human liberation worked itself out through the long centuries which followed the decline of medievalism. The titanic struggles whereby man acquired mobility are the story of Europe from the Renaissance and Reformation to the nineteenth century. In western Europe, a century ago, society had acquired those distinctive traits of modernity which made the growth of a social science indispensable.

2. From Europe to America: The Growth of Social Science

As the mode of self-observation evolved by dealing with the new human problems raised by the endlessly changing lifeways of modern society, social science developed primarily as an empirical, quantitative, policy-related *method of inquiry* (not as a system of beliefs). These three traits have grown together, from nineteenth-century Europe to contemporary America, in the continuing study of modern lifeways.

The great problems of the age issued from the newly uprooted and displaced class of industrial urban workers and their families. Removed from the subsistence relationships of agricultural life, and newly dependent upon their cash wages for livelihood, *how much* did these workers need to earn in order to maintain themselves? Employers wanted to determine this quantum. *How much* did they have to earn before there was a surplus left that could be taxed? Governments wanted to determine this quantum. *How much* did they have to save out of their wages every week to pay an unpredictable doctor's bill, to accumulate a daughter's dowry, to send a son through school? Workers wanted to determine these quanta. As modern society moved steadily onto a cash basis, the determination of such quanta became a critical need of private and public policy. The roots of social science lie in its responsiveness to these needs of modern society for empirical, quantitative, policy-related information about itself.

This explains the historic importance of Frederic Le Play in nineteenth-century France. Instead of writing philosophic treatises on the "New Society," Le Play devoted much of his life to the painstaking collection, classification, and analysis of first-hand data on over three hundred working class families in every European and several Asian countries. He produced comprehensive *monographies sociales* on these families, representing different industries and locales, of which the thirty-six most complete reports were subsequently published in his majestic *Les Oeuvriers Européens* (6 volumes, 1855). No ostrich empiricist, grubbing for facts in the desert sand, Le Play kept his eye constantly fixed on the larger issues of his time. By competent marshaling of weighted empirical evidence, Le Play confronted the great policy problems and the ideologies then being propagated concerning them. It was for this research that he was to win his great place in the history of social science.

The example of Le Play was vigorously recommended, by the *Saturday Review* in London, to "those who have charge of the welfare of England." One who responded was Charles Booth, a shipowner of Liverpool, who paid scant attention to the high intellectual claims of the newly-coined Sociology, but devoted much of his own time and money to the careful collection and statistical analysis of facts bearing on the critical problems of the new working class in Britain. His studies, modestly designed to show "the numerical relation which poverty, misery, and depravity bear to regular earnings and comparative comfort," were published in the monumental *Life and Labour of the People in London* (1891-1903). Their appearance undermined the moralizing ideologies which, in Victorian England, debated poverty as Good or Evil (and insanity as diabolical) but ignored the facts of the matter. There was no arguing

Booth's precise statement of the "numerical relation"; nor could mere ideology withstand his striking maps which represented, in shades of color, the exact distribution and degrees of poverty in London. Booth was named to the Royal Commission on the Poor Law. Subsequently, his volume of statistics on the aged poor (1894) led to revision of old-age pensions (1899). By wedding research to policy more directly than Le Play had done—thus exhibiting what the French love to call *l'empirisme anglosaxonne*—Booth gave empirical, quantitative, policy-related research a great push forward.

This line of social inquiry appealed to the temper of Americans and the needs of their rapidly-changing society. The social service pioneers especially provided a vibrant reception for empirical research in America, as in the *Hull-House Maps and Papers* (1895). Booth's method of direct systematic observation was adopted also by a new school of sociological journalists—who came to be called, by the epithet of Theodore Roosevelt, "the muckrakers." While muckraking later declined into routine journalism, its early practitioners were serious and competent students of current realities. The work of Ida Tarbell and Lincoln Steffens stimulated the growth of American social research in the first decades of this century.

The academic fraternity systematized reformist journalism and bolstered social-service activism, their concerted efforts often showing the way to new laws and new institutions for observation and correction of social ills. Studies of labor exploitation led, through minimum wage and social security legislation, to the modern methods of "industrial relations." Reports on urban misery led, through slum clearance and public housing, to urban redevelopment and city planning. Exposure of consumer exploitation led, through pure food and drug legislation, to regulation of fair trade practices. The New Deal, which appeared to be a government of social scientists in its early years, codified these conceptions and institutionalized them in an array of "alphabetical agencies." Some of these passed with the depression crisis (NRA, WPA, PWA). Others became a permanent part of the machinery of American government (SEC, FHA, SSA). These agencies conduct continuous research in key sectors of American society and take (or recommend) appropriate action where violations or malfunctions appear. The New Deal codified a relationship between social research and social policy which had developed through preceding decades under the regime of both major parties. The role of social scientists in the Democratic administration of Woodrow Wilson, particularly during the wartime period, is well known. Less widely noted is the fact that the two major surveys, *Recent Economic Trends* and *Recent Social Trends*, were commissioned by the Republican administration of Herbert Hoover.

Social research has become an indispensable instrument of public policy, regardless of party, in the complex urban industrial society of modern America. The problems defined by Le Play have preoccupied American sociologists since the pioneer generations from L. F. Ward to R. E. Park. Among the leaders of the current generation, Talcott Parsons has systematized data on family roles and Robert Angell has codified our knowledge of cities; S. A. Stouffer and P. F. Lazarsfeld collaborated in a monographic report on the family in the depression; R. K. Merton has made empirical studies of urban housing and occupations. These matters are under continuous study also by public and private agencies, to which the universities annually supply a corps of researchers. Oriented in the perspectives and trained in the methods of social science, these students occupy posts in education, in government, in business, and in the multitudinous array of civic and social-service agencies which guide a substantial portion of the nation's private and public affairs. Such organizations as the League for Industrial Democracy, League of Women Voters, Planned Parenthood League, Civil Liberties Union, World Affairs Council, Better Business Bureau—to name a random half-dozen of the several thousand voluntary associations that function in American society today—are usually directed and staffed by persons who were exposed to the social sciences through their higher education.

The growing corps of social researchers has extended the tradition of candid and comprehensive observation into virtually every important phase of contemporary American life. Sexuality and piety, work and wealth, leisure and health—all these varieties of human behavior are brought under informed scrutiny and often systematic study. These developments have been possible only in a society that placed a high value upon continuous self-improvement through self-study. Otherwise the prying into personal lives which such studies require would not be tolerated. Nor, in a society committed to an absolute myth, which laid down The Truth once and for all, would empirical inquiry into the way things really are serve any useful purpose. Social science flourishes only in a society which seeks to improve itself by learning where it needs improving.

This raises some questions concerning the future of the social sciences in the world. During the past generation, they have come under very heavy attack from the new despotisms of the twentieth century. As part of their counter-offensive against the libertarian foundations of modern democracy, the Fascist, Nazi, and Communist regimes have officially outlawed and intellectually deformed the social sciences as we have known them.

3. Modern Despotism: The Challenge to Social Science

The functioning of a society can be studied by consulting either the elite or the mass, the governors or the governed. But from these two sources of enlightenment stem two quite different modes of social inquiry, which entail different concepts, methods, and uses. The two modes are contrasted in the research traditions of democratic society as against modern despotism.

The totalitarian view has been clarified by Svend Ranulf, the late Danish sociologist, in a remarkable little book on *Hitler's Struggle against Objectivity*.[4] Nazism's conflict with objective knowledge has been paralleled in every revolutionary despotism of this century. The most striking case, of course, is the system which Soviet Russia elaborated from its German philosophic heritage of Marxism. While the physical sciences (those which produce high energy acceleration of nuclear particles, for example) have been over-indulged, the social sciences in Russia have been straitjacketed. There is an *official* Sociology of the Soviet state—namely, the comprehensive ideology derived from Marxism—but there is no empirical sociology.

Social research, which requires direct observation and objective recording of reality, is the natural enemy of *all* ideology. Ideology *prescribes* a preferred future—the way the world ought to be made to be. Research *describes* an actual present—the way things, in fact, really are. In the long run, research which reveals the ever-changing facts about a society is bound to undermine the fixed doctrines of any ideology. Accordingly, the Soviet state, with an official ideology to defend, banned social research and replaced it by *agitprop*—agitation and propaganda. Whereas the function of research is to test social theory by observation of reality, the function of *agitprop* is to make reality appear to conform to *The Ideology*. One does not consult the man who wears the shoe to learn where it pinches; one tells him that it must pinch now in order to fit better later —or that it doesn't really pinch at all. Under the regime of *agitprop* one consults the governors and instructs the governed.

The rule of research in democratic regimes, where the governed *must* be consulted and by none more solicitously than by their governors, operates quite differently. The process is illustrated by the remarkable growth, over the past three decades, of what is called *attitude research*. This mode of consulting the governed, for the instruction of their governors, developed integrally with the spread of democratic institutions. Again, the historical source is in France. It was Jacques Necker, charged with raising state revenues under the *ancien régime,* who declared that a favorable public opinion was indispensable to a minister of finance—who must "associate the nation, as it were, in his plans, in his operations, and even in the obstacles that he must surmount." Necker fitted deeds to words by his major innovation of publishing the official fiscal statement (*compte rendu*)—so that government policy could be appraised by the public. The profound implication for political democracy of such concern with public opinion was not lost upon his contemporaries. Count Vergennes wrote in a confidential report to the king: "If M. Necker's public opinion were to gain ascendancy, Your Majesty would have to be prepared to see those command who otherwise obey and to see those obey who otherwise command." [5]

The connection between political democracy and attitude research developed rapidly in America, where, in the famous overstatement by de Tocqueville, "the will of the customer is the only limit." Since World War I, attitude research has invaded every field of social inquiry. Political analysts do voter research, economic analysts do consumer research, mass media analysts do audience research. All of these use the basic concepts and techniques of attitude research developed by psychologists and sociologists (largely in the newer joint discipline called "social psychology"). More than half of the American annual expenditure on all types of social research—in business, government, universities—is now spent on attitude research. So crucial, for our mode of self-observation, is information about the will of the governed.

In the modern despotisms, attitude research is regarded as irrelevant and irreverent. In Fascist Italy and Nazi Germany, such studies would have run counter to the official theory and practice of governance. Totalitarian "intelligence" about the governed is produced through the covert channels of the *Apparat*. Attitude research is subversive, in a despotism, because it encourages people to believe that their opinions matter. Such false expectations can only lead to conduct that is not "correct." Totalitarian use of public communication does not clog the channels with the public opinion of the governed but keeps them resonant with instructions from the governors.

The despotic process is most fully developed in the Soviet Union. There, despite recent spectacular successes in the physical sciences from which flow the highly visible technologies of production and destruction, the social sciences remain meagre and intimidated—in the crucial areas of research, indeed, virtually nonexistent. There, despite the intense and competitive focus on American production, little attention is given to the pioneering researches that have gone beyond primitive incentive systems (Stakhanovite piece work) in sustaining American world leadership in productivity. Absorbed by their spartan phase of rising industrial production, the Soviets have not yet reached the humanizing phase of rising civilian consumption. In this distinctive phase of truly participant modern society, each person must figure not only as a unit of economic output but as a source of social inputs—in his roles as the cash customer and the voter, the attitude-holder and the opinion-giver. As the citizenry of western society became participant, democratic institutions were evolved and new kinds of information about the participants (those who wear the shoes) were needed. To cope with this participant process, attitude research is the most efficient mode of self-observation yet devised.

But attitude research does not exist in the USSR, and the basic social sciences which nurture attitude research are inert. Sociology has never been permitted, we noted, since Marxism is the official Soviet "science of society." Psychology has been confined largely to neuro-physiology, particularly the elaboration of Pavlovian conditioning called reflexology. Of the great psychological advances made in the West since 1917, there is little resonance in the USSR. Understanding human behavior seemed irrelevant for an elite committed to change it willy-nilly. Psychological tests, when the sons of rich *kulaks* scored too high to suit Marxist preferences, were dismissed as bourgeois inventions for preserving the *status quo*. Exorcised also were standard intelligence tests when their findings—that children from the impoverished minor nationalities scored, as might be expected, lower than others—ran counter to the official proclamation that all Soviet nationalities were "equal."

Banished as well, under the Stalinist dispensation, was attitude research—when the act of asking people questions appeared to invite reconsideration by the governed of issues on which the governors had already pronounced the "correct" attitude. An article published in 1931 concluded that the contributions of psychologists to political indoctrination of the New Soviet Man had been totally useless. Thereafter, interest in psychological research and its broad social applications deteriorated rapidly. Whereas Soviet psychologists in 1930 had three journals to publish their work, by 1935 they had none. In 1936, the scope of psychological research was explicitly restricted by a decree of the Central Committee of the Communist Party. After two decades of steady decline, the Moscow Psychological Institute in 1957 counted fewer than 1,000 psychologists in the USSR—as compared with over 15,000 members of the American Psychological Association (which is only a fraction, however large, of all the psychologists in America).[6]

The official ban on sociology and restriction on psychology obviated any development of social psychology— the new discipline whose growth since 1918 has been central to the rise of behavioral research in the West. As a result, the USSR has lagged across the full range of the social sciences, notably those modes of self-observation which elucidate group behavior in the societal setting.[7] This runs counter to much popular imagery which depicts psychologists, for example, as slightly diabolical characters, badly needing haircuts, whose laboratories are used to cook up truth serum or shock syrup or other mysterious concoctions (usually pharmaceutical) for making people say and do things against their will. On such a view, the Soviets —with their rituals of "self-criticism," confession, and brainwashing—are assumed to be the master "scientists" of human behavior.

The true situation is just the reverse. Precisely those studies popularly associated with "mass manipulation" in a democracy have been frustrating and useless to (and ultimately repressed by) the governors of Soviet society. A little reflection indicates why this is so. To "manipulate" a population in the despotic sense—by imposing the will of the governors—requires no social research. Information on the will of the governed is irrelevant. One needs to know, first, what the will of the *governors* is; this can be determined by a meeting of the Central Committee or the Politburo or, quite often, by a word from The Man in The Kremlin. Then one needs a channel for disseminating the known will of the governors among the relevant masses of the governed; this is done through the official monopoly of the mass media and through the *agitprop* apparatus of the Party. Finally one needs a coercive instrument to "correct" those deviants who did not receive, understand, or obey the instructions; this is done through the secret police and the *control* apparatus of the Party.[8]

4. The Democratic Commitment:
Knowledge for Betterment

Despotic control of a population thus operates in tidy and efficient fashion, compared with which democratic "manipulation" is an exceedingly complicated affair. Since democratic governors cannot impose their own will by fiat, but must consider the will of the governed, they require information on public attitudes and expectations that is hard to get by cabinet meetings or common-sense procedures. Hence the steady diffusion of social science as a mode of self-observation under democratic governance.

To perceive the integral connection between social science and social democracy is to see the historic relationship of knowledge to power in a new and encouraging light. There has developed in the modern West a deep fear of being "manipulated"—of the invasions of privacy which seem inevitable in a widely participant society. This shows itself in "propaganditis," an allergy to public communications, especially from official sources but also from commercial techniques like "motivation research" and "subliminal advertising." It shows in our acute sensitivity to the charge of "conformism," which evokes stern denunciations of "the other-directed organization man in the gray flannel suit." It shows in our anxiety about machines and their alleged potential for total control over human behavior—the "1984 syndrome."

These worries are natural and healthy among a generation that has witnessed the spread of new-style despotism around the globe and the growing centralism of government at home. But they veer toward psychopathology and social disorganization when based upon the notion that central administration and despotic rule are identical. This derives from a faulty connection between knowledge and power— the idea that knowledge about our social behavior abridges our personal freedom—and leads to a spurious linkage between social science and political control. That the allegedly most manipulative of these sciences, social psychology, was found useless and even dangerous by the Soviet governors suggests that the reverse linkage would be more nearly correct.

Nothing in the social sciences increases the capacity to manipulate an individual against his will. To the extent that there is new knowledge of this type, its science is neurophysiology and its technique is pharmaceutical. The central tendency of social science is rather to increase man's capacity to manipulate his own social environment. Social statistics tell us nothing about any individual but a good deal about the environment in which all of us as individuals live. To know the size of our population at any moment, and its probable size a generation hence, does not speed a single death or stop a single birth; but it does provide a better basis than any Politburo discussion for estimating the number of houses, schools, hospitals, roads needed to provide for all individuals alive, now and then. To know the maximum unemployment that can be sustained by an economy without excessive strain does not cost a single person his job; but it does provide the information needed to plan tax rates and unemployment regulations so that those without jobs can be adequately supported.

These examples indicate that the social sciences tend, not to restrict personal liberty, but rather to expand the domain of free choice by clarifying the rational alternatives. This is strikingly the case with attitude research. The purpose of consumer research, for example, is to find out what the customer wants so that he can better be served. Even motivational research, often regarded as iniquitous invasion of a person's deepest secrets, provides information that can only be used—insofar as it provides useful information at all—to satisfy more customers more fully. The argument that attitude research betrays a person's secrets, exposing him to manipulation by others, is often reversed in the special case of audience research. There, the fear is that social science helps to satisfy people's desires *all too well.* Audience research is criticized on the grounds that it makes the mass media "pander to the public." Radio, television, movies, picture magazines are said to be—in the perpetual popularity poll—captives of their audience ratings. On this contention it is the manipulator who, by learning what people want through audience research, is manipulated.

The same critique is often made of political leadership in a democracy—that the governors are captives of the governed, who rule through the ballot box. Attitude research is said to aggravate this alleged evil by reporting the will of the governed continuously and clearly on a wide range of issues. The complaint against this mode of self-observation—exemplified in public opinion surveys and pre-election polls—comes to this: that it makes the will of the governed more difficult to evade or ignore. But this, presumably, is just what all of representative democracy—with its elaborate checks and balances to ensure a government of "laws not men"—is designed to make more difficult. If the idea of "a decent respect for the opinions of mankind" is not a pious fraud, then any method which clarifies the will of the governed is a valuable tool of democratic governance. This, despite the limits imposed upon the elective leadership that cause anguish in moments of crisis, is the democratic commitment. The task of social science—and here none are quicker than social scientists to insist that fulfillment lies in the future—is to prove worthy of its mission.

5. *Modernizing Lands: The Testing Ground of Social Science*

If we take the view that social science operates to make authoritarian manipulation harder and not easier—that this mode of self-observation is useful only in societies which equip the participant citizenry to contain the official power centers—then we see why social science has developed hitherto only in the western world. We see, too, why it makes small appeal to leaders of the underdeveloped lands. In these large areas of the world, where the drama of modernization is now being re-enacted, governance perforce tends to be authoritarian. It is not necessarily despotic. But the principal check on despotism yet evolved in the underdeveloped world is the personal charisma of The Leader—his capacity to persuade (so that he need not coerce) the populace to do what *he* considers good for them. This flies in the face of the cherished democratic preference for government by "laws not men." But the main alternative to the rule of personal charisma, in this phase of rapid modernizing, is probably the reign of terror.

This is so because genuine political democracy can operate efficiently only in a genuinely participant society. Modern society is participant in that it functions by "consensus"—freely given consent to a common "ideology." The ideology sets forth a transpersonal code of values in terms of shared secondary symbols. This enables persons who do not know each other to engage in political controversy and yet, under the rule of consensus, to reach common decisions often enough to permit stable governance. The historic achievement of participant social organization occurred in lands where most people go through school, read newspapers, receive cash payments in jobs they are legally free to change, buy goods for cash in an open market, vote in elections which actually decide among competing candidates, and express opinions on many matters which are not their personal business.

Especially important, for the "Participant Style," is the enormous proportion of people who are expected to "have opinions" on public matters—and the corollary expectation of these people that their opinions will matter. It is this subtly complicated structure of reciprocal expectation which sustains political consensus. Western people learned to "have opinions" as their opinions, when expressed and shared, came to influence what happened in their world. In this modernizing process, the persons whose opinions mattered were also the newspaper readers, the cash customers, the voters. The participant style of life involved simultaneous engagement in all the major social sectors—market, arena, forum, polls.

The conditions for participant society do not yet exist among the impoverished, illiterate, inert peoples of the underdeveloped lands. To make the transition from the routinized, immobile lifeways that have been their lot throughout history, they need a large and growing corps of transitional individuals—urban, literate, money-handling, media-consuming, opinion-forming persons. But such persons cannot be produced in sufficient quantity by societies which make only marginal and piecemeal approaches to modernity.

The transition is especially hard in the face of the population explosion occurring around the world today. The growth of cities, factories, schools can hardly keep abreast of rising births and longer lives. Many underdeveloped lands produce more urban literates each year, but few can reduce the proportion of rural illiterates in the total population. A population whose birth rate quickly engulfs every gain of modern technique within a swollen tide of ancient needs must, as the Red Queen told Alice, run all it can to stay in the same place. "If you want to get somewhere else, you must run at least twice as fast as that!"

This is what the modernizing lands are trying to do—run twice as fast as they can. What the West evolved as a consistent style of life over centuries, the underdeveloped areas now seek to accomplish in years. But the components and sequences of the Western model of modernization have global relevance. Everywhere, increasing urbanization has tended to raise literacy; rising literacy has tended to increase media exposure; increasing media exposure has "gone with" wider economic participation (per capita income) and political participation (voting). The same basic model reappears in virtually all modernizing societies on all continents of the world, regardless of variations in race, color, creed. The new modernizers would do well to study the historical sequence of Western growth.

But these societies-in-a-hurry have little patience with the historical *pace* of Western development. Moreover, they want to do it their "own way." Wanted are modern institutions but not modern ideologies, modern power but not modern purposes, modern wealth but not modern wisdom, modern commodities but not modern cant. It is not clear, however, that modern ways and words can be so easily and so totally sundered. Underlying the variant ideological forms which modernization took in Europe, America, Russia, there have been certain behavioral and institutional compulsions common to all. These historical regularities some leaders now seek to obviate, trying instead new routes and risky by-passes.

Consider the view exponded by Colonel Nasser, whose great personal charisma is confronted by viciously circular problems of modernizing a society that appear impervious to any short-term strategy. Says Nasser:

> "It is true that most of our people are still illiterate. But politically that counts for far less than it did 20 years ago. Literacy and intelligence are not the same thing. Radio has changed everything. Once the villagers had no knowledge of what was happening in the capital. Government was run by small coteries of people who did not need to take account of the reactions of the people, who never saw a newspaper or could not read it if they did. Today people in the most remote villages hear of what is happening everywhere and form their opinions. Leaders cannot govern as they once did. We live in a new world."

Nasser's statement, as he doubtless knows better than most observers, raises more questions than it answers. How does the enlargement of the opinion arena work out in a society that is not yet genuinely participant, where the bulk of the population still lives in rural illiteracy? Can leaders short-cut the historic course of modernization by "involving" their people ideologically before they are involved sociologically? Can the involvement in apocalyptic politics of these illiterate and impoverished pseudo-participants really produce anything more durable than a new brand of chaos? Does Nasser's decision to give radio propaganda primacy over political economy really lead to modernization? To put these questions in more general form: How can these modernizing societies-in-a-hurry maintain stability while rapidly acquiring mobility? In lands where people have opinions before they have jobs and cash and literacy— in short, before they have a stake in the society's efficient operation—whence will come the compulsions toward *responsible* formation and expression of opinion on which a free participant society depends?

To deal adequately with such questions will require better understanding than we now have of the factors which maintain personal and institutional equilibrium under conditions of rapid social change. In the "new world" of which Nasser speaks there is, beyond the rhetoric, an array of new factors which alter the scope and limits of social change familiar to students of modern Western society. The meanings of "an income" and "a vote" and "an opinion" are, and likely will continue to be, different from their historic meanings in the West. Ballots cast in a single-option plebiscite are construed as votes, remittances from kinfolk employed in other lands as income, vocalization of assent to radio directives as opinion.

But modernization, even under tight controls, works its magic in ways not always foreseen by political leaders. The listener to a state-controlled opinion directive (labelled "news") *also* hears the sound of a cultured voice aranging words according to a formal syntax of exposition unknown to the story-telling universe of oral communication in which he grew up. The receiver of remittances, even though these reflect no independent effort or personal merit, nevertheless develops a sense of cash. The voter in a plebiscite, even though his ballot makes no significant difference, nevertheless develops a sense of power—and is likely, sooner than a person who was never invited to cast a ballot, to demand a real vote.

These are crucial problems of modernization with which charismatic leaders of underdeveloped lands must deal—in Egypt as in Ethiopia, in India as in Indonesia, in China as in Chile. Can the social sciences help to find useful solutions of these crucial problems? Economists are already at work on the planning of economic development. Sociologists are already involved in the complicated studies upon which can be based the series of social statistics needed for planning and surveillance of economic development. Political scientists are already at work on problems of public law and administration, whereby the relationship between governors and governed in the modernizing lands will be defined and codified.

But this much social science exists in every society moving toward urban and industrial institutions—including the USSR. The real test of social science comes when the urban-industrial matrix begins to evolve those distinctively participant lifeways of modern society. For the unique function of social science—as a method of inquiry into the social process whereby its operations are continuously recorded and regulated—can only come into play after the psychopolitical die is cast. If the rulers prefer to govern by the tidy simplicity of coercion, avoiding the complex ambiguities of consensus, they will require nothing more than some rudimentary system of social auditing. If they opt for widespread participation under the rule of consensus, then the full conceptual and procedural range of social science—including attitude research—becomes relevant.

Whether despotism or democracy, or some new variant,

will gain the modernizing world in the second half of our century remains to be seen. Despotism is rather clearly ascendant at present, and likely to remain so in the near future—as presaged by the pattern of military take-over established in Egypt, Syria, Iraq, Lebanon and repeated in Burma, Pakistan, the Sudan. But many of these despots show signs of benevolence and some have issued firm declarations of intention to democratize. Some such declarations are written in *Newspeak*—that Nasser's constitution proclaims Egypt to be a democratic republic does not alter the fact that it is a military dictatorship. But the continuing power of the democratic idea is shown by such verbal tokens of allegiance. Elsewhere, as in Nehru's India, it has begun to shape consensual values and participant institutions. If the democratic idea survives the crisis of our time, then Social Science will spread around the world in the next century as it spread through the West in the last century.

The great current issue for Social Science is how to increase democracy's chances for survival in our time. One part of this task is to improve continuously the intellectual quality and social utility of its own products. The other job is to spread the skills and habits needed for intelligent consumption of its products. Both the benevolent despots and the harassed democrats who now rule the modernizing lands will be encouraged to face the complexities of participant lifeways by demonstration that modes of self-observation are available which can help them try mobility without undermining stability. Social scientists, both West and East, have made a start in this direction.[9] There is a long hard way to go. But it is surely worth the effort.

NOTES

[1] Daniel Lerner, *The Passing of Traditional Society: Modernizing the Middle East* (Glencoe, Illinois: Free Press, 1958).

[2] Erik H. Erikson, *Young Man Luther: A Study in Psychoanalysis and History* (New York: W. W. Norton, 1958), p. 52.

[3] See Georges Canguilhem, *Essai sur quelques problèmes concernant le normal et le pathologique* (Paris: Société d'Editions, 1950).

[4] Svend Ranulf, *Hitlers Kampf gegen die Objektivät* (Copenhagen: Ejnar Munksgaard, 1946).

[5] See Hans Speier, *Social Order and The Risks of War* (1952), pp. 327-332.

[6] For a good overall summary, from which the foregoing information is drawn, see: R. A. Bauer, "Our Big Advantage: The Social Sciences," *Harvard Business Review* (June 1958), pp. 125-136. A more detailed study is Brian Simon, ed., *Psychology in the Soviet Union* (Stanford University Press, 1957).

[7] Arvid Brodersen, "Soviet Social Science and Our Own," *Social Research* (Autumn 1957), p. 253.

[8] On the Bolshevik system of manipulation, see: Philip Selznick, *The Organizational Weapon* (N. Y.: McGraw-Hill, 1952).

[9] See the special issue on "Attitude Research in Modernizing Areas," ed. D. Lerner, of the *Public Opinion Quarterly,* vol. XXII (Fall 1958).

RETROSPECT

THE RISE OF SOCIAL RESEARCH IN EUROPE [1]

Nathan Glazer

Contemporary sociology in America—and sociologists everywhere, rightly or wrongly, consider that it is in America that sociology is most highly developed—is a discipline defined more by its special methods of research than by either its conclusions or its subject matter.[•] The sociologist today—whether his field of interest is the com-

One may argue against this point that, although neither a special subject matter nor special conclusions (laws) now characterize sociology, its *approach* to social questions, rather than its *methods* of research, is uniquely distinctive. This approach does have certain characteristics. The emphasis on concepts such as "social mobility," "social roles," "social norms," "reference groups" is, at the moment, sharply characteristic of most of American sociology. It would be necessary to trace the history of these concepts in any complete account of the origins of contemporary American sociology. However, rather more attention has been given to the development of these concepts than to that of the particular methods of research, which represent a more radical break with the general history of social thought. Since this most striking element has received the least attention, I have chosen to concentrate upon it here.

43

munity, criminology, marriage and the family, world politics, social classes, housing—is a man who asks people questions and then statistically analyzes the answers to them. If he does not ask the questions himself, he hires someone else to ask them; or, if not that, he analyzes the statistics gathered by those who *have* asked questions— census-takers, social workers, and others. At any rate, at the base of today's typical social science, there are usually questions addressed to ordinary people, and their answers, arranged in statistical tables.

All this is perhaps obvious, and yet why this has come to pass, and what has resulted and may result for our understanding of the problems of society as a result of this approach is not at all obvious—not even to sociologists. They, searching for the origins of their discipline, tend to seize upon the most respectable forebears they can find. August Comte, author of the term itself, is thus considered a father of sociology. The American fathers of sociology are considered to be men like Charles H. Cooley, Franklin Giddings, Lester Ward, Albion Small, and Thorstein Veblen. Karl Marx, Georg Simmel, and Max Weber are considered among the chief German exponents of sociology. Emile Durkheim is perhaps the single most influential figure for American sociology—since he affects, by the example of his study of *Suicide*, what sociologists *do* rather than what they *say*. All these men made contributions to the creation of contemporary sociology. Yet few of them ever drew up a questionnaire, and those that did based nothing important in what they said upon them.•

• Marx drew up a questionnaire; so, for some early work, did Max Weber. We will consider Marx's questionnaire later. As for Weber, it is sufficient to note that his questionnaires and empirical research are not the basis for this influence in the field.

Durkheim came closest, at least, in one important work he made use of masses of figures based on others' questions, and it is revealing that it is he who should play the largest role in contemporary sociology.

It is understandable that a new intellectual discipline should look to its thinkers and their ideas for the source of its uniqueness: yet to do so obscures what is most distinctive about sociology, even what is most valuable about it, and tends to spread confusion about its character and aims, a confusion that sociologists themselves are often incapable of dissipating. It is possible to find in the sweeping ideas of Comte and Marx the sources of contemporary sociology—sociology is based on ideas as well as operations —yet I believe more relevant sources are to be found in men of quite different character and purpose. Present-day sociologists have more in common with the earnest men of the early nineteenth century, mainly in England, who painfully built up a picture of social reality, detail by detail, than with those strong-minded thinkers, disdainful of such details, who wanted to tear down worlds and build quite new ones. We will understand contemporary sociology better by considering the phenomenon of the men who wanted to measure everything than by remaining fixed on those who wanted to destroy or rebuild everything.

Regardless of which route we take, we come back to the same starting point, the first half of the nineteenth century. It was about then that a new way of studying man and society began to develop. The "science of man" or the "science of society" had been often proposed, predicted, and even announced since the first great successes of modern science in the sixteenth century. Spinoza, Hobbes, Locke, Hume, Saint-Simon, had all thought of themselves as in some way "scientists"—for did they not approach human and social problems in the same spirit in which physical scientists approached the problems of the non-human world? And yet, from the point of view that concerns us here—namely, the development of the special methods of social science—the work of these men is no different from that of, say, Aristotle or Thucydides or Plato. For all of these great thinkers, over a stretch of two thousand years, the relation between facts and theories in discussing social problems was roughly the same—and completely different from that of contemporary social science. Whether one considers Aristotle or Montesquieu, one will find history and existing social life considered as simply a storehouse of examples to illustrate presumed truths. The notion that it might be possible to survey systematically *all* the facts bearing on some generalization may have been suggested here or there, but it certainly played little or no role in influencing those who concerned themselves with social problems. For two thousand years we will find little change if we consider only *why* certain assertions are made: evidence, if it is presented at all, exists in the form of illustration. More significant, there is no notion of *creating* any evidence beside that of existing sources by, for example, asking questions directly of people —of people, that is, not as authorities but as sources. People serve sociologists, we might say, as the atoms, the smallest behavioral units, from observation of which a view of reality might be built up.

From the beginning of the nineteenth century, I believe, a remarkable change in viewing man and society began to make itself felt. The change was not that these subjects were now to be approached independently of the dictates of morality, religion, and authority, and in a scientific spirit, this had already been proposed and done by many social philosophers and, although a necessary prelude to what was now to happen, was quite different from it. What was truly new was the rise of a belief that the world, the social world around one, was not *known*, and that its reality could not be grasped by reading books, listening to learned men, or reflecting upon the facts of one's experience. It began to be felt that the collection of scattered observations from writers, combined with the casual observation of social life as one saw it in the ordinary course of one's activities, could not possibly tell one what was true and important: it was necessary to collect all relevant facts, to consider the grounds on which one accepted these as facts, and, in the end, to test social knowledge by professionally investigating what had previously been casually observed. We may speak of an age of doubt, affecting not *truths*—these had been doubted since the Renaissance, and before —but *facts* simple empirical realities. Facts, if previously doubted, had not been considered important enough to matter.

Thus, the Enlightenment figures were really not interested in establishing the details of the lives of primitives; it was sufficient to use these details as reported, true or false, to attack the general points of view they disagreed with. Now, this new concern with the factuality of very small details may itself have been misguided, but it was the origin of contemporary social science.

We can give many examples of this new concern with simple, trivial facts in the social world. Thus, the first censuses in modern history come at the end of the nineteenth century. Whereas the United States census of 1790 may reflect not, the new concern but only the requirements written into the constitution, there is no question that the English census of 1801 did reflect a widespread desire to know definitely how many Englishmen there were, and whether the population was increasing or declining. The causes of this new desire to establish facts definitely we will discuss later: here we merely wish to document the fact that it existed, and was felt as new.

The rise of the new term and discipline of "statistics" is itself revealing of the new concern with facts. It was first used, one authority asserts, by a German, Gottfried Achenwell, in the middle of the eighteenth century (but he was no statistician);[2] its first use in France dates from 1789; in England, it was first used by Sir John Sinclair, who was engaged in preparing an enormous *Statistical Account of Scotland* (1791-1799)[3]—itself representative of the new desire to know definitely. The rather weak efforts to collect figures in the eighteenth century became a torrent in the early nineteenth. The new spirit was indicated, however, not by the simple collection of figures—which, for example, is what Achenwell seems to have done—but by a serious concern with *how* they were to be collected, with their correctness, and this was to be established by *technique*, by a direct involvement in the process of collection.

Here by far the most important figure was Adolphe Quetelet (1796-1874), a mathematician and astronomer of Brussels, on whom devolved, as was natural in that relatively unspecialized age and in a small country, much of the necessary scientific work of the kingdom of the Netherlands (and later Belgium). By the end of the 1820's he was deeply involved in the problems of collecting good census figures, and dealing with such practical matters as the form of schedules, kind and quality of enumerators, kinds of questions to be asked, methods of tabulation and presentation, and so on.[4] He was also concerned with extracting laws from these figures—but again, we must distinguish him from such figures as Marx or Comte. Quetelet's laws were not the result of thinking about the received "facts" of history and general observation—they arose directly from facts which he had gathered himself, or if not, which he could evaluate and criticize on the basis of his experience in gathering similar facts. And his facts were not the relatively arbitrary detritus of history coming into the hands of social philosophers—*they were all the facts relative to some generalization:* all the suicides in a certain country for a series of years, all the births, all the deaths, all the crimes (if we define crime as that which comes to the attention of the police). Crude and simple and perhaps silly as these laws were, they *were the first based on all the facts that they attempted to explain,* as against those other laws, of Marx and Comte and other thinkers, which were based only on a sparse and non-systematic selection from the universe of relevant observations of those examples which fitted their thesis.

It is interesting to note Quetelet's relations with the system-builders. Comte was quite outraged at Quetelet's use of the term "social physics" to refer to the regularities (Quetelet called them laws) that he had discovered in statistics of crime, punishment, births, deaths, etc. A footnote referring to Quetelet in Comte's *Cours de Philosophie Positive* is interesting as indicating the temperament of a system builder:

The expression [social physics] and the no less dispensable one of positive philosophy were formulated seventeen years ago in my first works of political philosophy. [Comte refers here to a work of the year 1822; he was writing in 1838.] Although they are therefore quite recent these two terms have already been to some degree spoiled by the vicious attempts at appropriation by various writers. . . . I must above all note the abuse, in connection with the first term, by a Belgian savant, who has adopted it in these last few years [Quetelet's book, *Sur L'Homme*, subtitled *Essai de Physique Sociale*, had appeared in Paris in 1835] as the title of a work composed simply of statistics.

Marx has a more kindly reference to Quetelet in an article in the *New York Daily Tribune* for 1853. But if he is kinder, in this reference, it is only because he can misuse some figures of Quetelet's as to the remarkable equivalence of certain crime statistics for France and Philadelphia as a club to attack all "bourgeois" society.[5]

Quetelet was influential in the establishing of the Statistical Society of London (later the Royal Statistical Society) in 1834,[6] for Quetelet was tutor to Prince Albert before he married Queen Victoria, and it was undoubtedly because of this influence that the Prince Consort became, in 1840, the patron of the London Statistical Society.

This Society and the Manchester Statistical Society, which was founded a short time before,[7] represent at its most developed the new attitude to social data. They were self-conscious about their role: to replace ancient and sterile controversies with definite facts. Thus, we may read in the first issue of the *Journal of the Statistical Society of London* in 1838:

It is indeed truly said that the spirit of the present age has an evident tendency to confront the figures of speech with the figures of arithmetic; it being impossible not to observe a growing distrust of mere hypothetical theory and *a priori* assumption, and the appearance of a general conviction that, in the business of social science, principles are valid for application only inasmuch as they are legitimate induction from facts, accurately observed and methodically classified.[8]

The immediate interest of the societies was the condition of the new masses in the cities. Organized, as they were, by men who were close to the new industrial interests (there were bankers and industrialists, as well as professional and gentleman scholars among them), they were concerned at times to demonstrate that the effects of industry and the cities upon the workers and their children was not as fearful in all respects as the landed interests, and their propagandists, insisted.[9] But their concern was only partially apologetic: they had an honest interest in reform; and, beyond any other interests, they were concerned with science, with gathering facts, independent of the arguments they could serve. They had a deep belief in the saving power of the fact as against the theory.

The Manchester society had a stronger element of reform interest. The first annual report of the society asserts: "The [Society] owes its origin to a strong desire felt by its projectors to assist in promoting the progress of social improvement in the manufacturing population by which they surrounded." [10] And yet they immediately launched themselves, not into the work of reform, which they attempted under other auspices, but into serious and extensive efforts to describe exactly, by their own activity and the use of paid agents, the condition of the poor.

The London society, under the influence of more academic figures, of whom Malthus was the most prominent, was less reform-minded. Its object was described in a motion by Malthus as "the collection and classification of all facts illustrative of the present condition and prospects of Society." [11] Its prospectus, drawn up by the historian Henry Hallam, asserts: "The Statistical Society will consider it to be the first and most essential rule of its conduct to exclude carefully all opinions from its transactions and publications—to confine its attention rigorously to facts—

and, as far as it may be found possible, to facts which can be stated numerically and arranged in tables." [12]

The London Society began with the project of a great questionnaire or interrogatory, which was designed to get vast numbers of figures, on all sorts of questions. Thousands of copies were distributed; as with a number of other grand projects designed to get all the definite facts at once, this failed.[13] The returns were poor. But the society, like that in Manchester, conducted a number of special investigations. It too made use of "paid agents"—the first professional interviewers, perhaps.[14]

We see at this time a growing number of individuals interested in the collection and study of figures based on direct observation and interviewing, but, more than that, we find for the first time the growth of a cadre of individuals capable of undertaking this interviewing and observation work. The census of 1841 in England was the first in which the enumeration was conducted—at the suggestion of the London Society—by special agents. Until then the enumeration had been the work of the overseers of the poor. In 1841, and regularly thereafter, the London Society advised the government on its censuses.[15]

Perhaps the most important element in creating this cadre of people who professionally gathered facts on the state of society was the rise of a factory inspection system in England, connected with the beginning of factory legislation in the first few decades of the nineteenth century. The investigations into the conditions of the working population which preceded and followed the passage of acts controlling the hours and conditions of labor of children and women, and then workers in general, are generally familiar from the copious quotations in Engels' *Conditions of the Working Class in England in 1845* and Marx's *Capital*. What is less familiar, and indeed still insufficiently studied, is the methods by which this information was gathered. Sizable staffs—at least for those early years—were collected for the purpose of interviewing employers, local clergymen, other local authorities, and the workers themselves. These early reports are enormously valuable repositories not only of the facts they were intended to uncover but of information on the social character of the working classes, their language, their values, their attitudes, their way of life.

For one study, conducted between 1840 and 1842, we read that the employers filled out "tabular forms" so the commission could get a complete record of the numbers of children employed, and the conditions under which they worked, and that no less than twenty "sub-commissioners" were used to investigate conditions at first hand and take evidence. They did more than question witnesses: "The Commissioners, in order that they might be the better qualified to report on [the mines] thought it desirable that some of their body should see a few instances of underground labour, and make themselves acquainted with the nature of it, by personal observation." A number of them became sick as a result of their work.[16] And when we read of conditions in the mines, where men had to work in seams two feet high or less and characteristically worked naked, in intense heat, and in the days before electricity (we do not speak of the children, down to four years of age, who assisted them, or the girls who dragged away carts of coal, attached to them by chains, on hands and knees), we see that although this effort at first-hand investigation into a close approximation of Hell could not be considered heroic, it certainly was rather different from reading books—even parliamentary reports—in a library or a comfortable home. In any case, until these reports were written, there were simply no accounts of such labor.

Just how these inquiries were conducted, by whom, and

what was the further role of the men who conducted them, are subjects which could all bear further investigation. In any case, it is here that we must look to find an important group of forefathers of the thousands of interviewers, enumerators, first-hand investigators who today form the largest body of workers in the field of social science.

Our concentration on England in this story till now may seem arbitrary: was not the same thing going on in France and in Germany? We may say with some confidence that the major lines of empirical, first-hand investigation of social problems, and even of statistical reporting based on first-hand inquiry, were developed in England. At any rate, the English experience is by far the most important. In France, despite the great interest in the problems of the new industrial order, we find many fewer and far less intense inquiries.[17] Although Germany was in the forefront of statistics-gathering nations, the German historian of statistics writes: "No other country gave such early and extensive publicity to its statistics as Great Britain," [18] and we have seen to what extent the development of these statistics was necessarily based on first-hand investigation. England, the first great industrial country, was also the country in which the contemporary social scientific approach to problems had its origins.

On the other hand, the French concern, as indicated in the utopian socialists, with what we may call total reform—as against the English concern with partial reforms—did lead to more than grand schemes, utopian planning, and general theories. In the work of Frédéric Le Play (1806-1882), a graduate of the *École Polytechnique*—as was Auguste Comte, which may perhaps suggest there is more than analogy in the term "social engineering"—we have one of the first major empirical undertakings, *Les Ouvriers*

Européens (1855). By a careful and exacting analysis of the income and expenditures of workers in different countries, Le Play tried to give a quantitative picture of social life and the way it varied.

Le Play had decided that the best insight into the structure and problems of any society was an exacting study of an average family; and he had decided that the best way to study the family was by way of an exact account of its income and expenditures. There is a certain naïveté in the assumption that the family is sufficient for the understanding of a certain society or stratum of society, and that other elements of society—organizations other than the family—required no such exacting system of investigation. And we might point out that it was Le Play's strong commitment to the traditional patriarchal family as the necessary healthy building block of contemporary society that led him to ignore other things, as against the more eclectic English social investigators who studied more widely. However, his commitment to this type of study did lead him and his followers into the difficult task of studying the family *au naturel,* so to speak. They had to gain the confidence of simple people, establish *rapport,* and get people to be specific and concrete about things they had not thought about. Thus they had to face all the difficult tasks involved in first-hand social research. Although his followers continued his work, and extended it somewhat, they had a concern with their own variety of social reform too strong to allow them to develop a really powerful interest in developing empirical research techniques. However, the empirical work of Le Play and his followers stands—as any good empirical work should—as valuable material independent of the social views of his school. An early volume of the *American Journal of Sociology* (1897) translates his instructions for the study of the family: there had been no marked advance in this area for forty years.[19]

Germany seems less important for our story than France and England. It was in the forefront of statistics-gathering nations. And in the work of Ernst Engel (1821-1896), who "drew his first inspiration for social economics from Le Play and for statistics from Quetelet," [20] we have a very important early example of the effort to derive laws from the sum of first-hand observations, that is, statistics. Engel's law, as to the increasing percentage of income spent on food as income declined, was derived from Le Play's material and, more significantly, from the new statistics that were being gathered ever more rapidly. This law, and others suggested by the new statistics, played an important role in stimulating further statistics-gathering and analysis in the effort to refute, refine, or defend them. And yet, for our special perspective—the development of empirical approaches—this German experience does not seem to offer much that is new. We do not find there the same passion for first-hand observation that we find in Le Play or in England.

About the same time that Le Play was at work on *Les Ouvriers Européens,* Henry Mayhew was engaged in his studies of the London poor, first published in two volumes in 1851, which he later resumed in 1856. I refer to Mayhew —even though he was primarily a journalist—because he fits into the line of personal investigators and because, in his attitude to his subject, we discover views characterizing all this early work and helping to explain some problems in the development of empiricism. It is striking, if one opens Mayhew, to discover that he seriously believes the street-folk (peddlers, laborers, performers, prostitutes, etc.) of London to be of a different race. Quoting ethnologists, he points out that:

Almost every tribe of people who have submitted themselves to social laws, recognizing the rights of property and reciprocal social duties, and thus acquiring wealth and forming themselves into a respectable caste, are surrounded by hoardes of vagabonds and outcasts from their own community. . . .

It is curious that no one has as yet applied the above facts [concerning the relations between settled peoples and those who surround them] to the explanation of certain anomalies in the present state of society among ourselves. That we, like the Kaffirs, Fellahs, and Finns, are surrounded by wandering hordes . . . paupers, beggars, and outcasts, possessing nothing but what they acquire by depredation from the industrious, provident, and civilized portion of the community— that the heads of these nomads are remarkable for the greater development of the jaws and cheekbones rather than those of the head—and that they have a secret language of their own . . . for the concealment of their designs: these are points of coincidence so striking that, when placed before the mind, make us marvel that the analogy should have remained thus long unnoticed.[21]

This point of view was not uncommon. Certainly until the 1850's, and for some decades thereafter, large sections of the working classes and lower classes of England lived under conditions that were so strikingly different from those of the "respectable" that it was difficult to believe there was any relationship between them. This gap encouraged as well as inhibited investigation. Curiosity alone, the same curiosity that led travelers to new lands and the study of new peoples, made the poor an important subject of study —leaving aside the fact that their conditions of life were obviously of far more relevance for the state of England, and even the lives and fortunes of the well-to-do, than those of distant savages. However, as Mark Benney has pointed out,[22] this gap was also so great that it inhibited direct personal inquiry by the middle classes. It was unthinkable that respectable ladies should go among the poor, and hardly thinkable that respectable gentlemen should. For even aside from one's prejudices, there was a real fear of physical attack or of contracting some horrible disease —fears not all ungrounded.

Thus the more intensive and systematic investigation of the working and lower classes depended on raising them, to some degree, from the incredible conditions under which they lived. This was the work of the 1850's and 1860's, when the Factory Acts began to work more and more effectively, when education began to spread among the lower classes, when private philanthropy became more extensive and better organized, and when the increasing political power of the working classes, and particularly their partial enfranchisement in 1867, demanded that somehow the two nations should now become one. One step in doing this was to find out what the other nation was like.

The best account of this new period—and indeed the most important book, to my mind, for an understanding of the rise of the contemporary social scientific approach—is Beatrice Webb's *My Apprenticeship*. Beatrice Webb describes the rise of her interest in social problems, and the unique vantage point afforded to her by the Potter family (she was Beatrice Potter) and its connections to further this interest. Although the most distinguished visitor to her home was Herbert Spencer, two other distinguished Victorians who played a central role in the development of social science were often there. One was Francis Galton, whose discoveries in correlation were to be largely responsible for moving social statistics from the level of simple enumeration to that of a scientific tool of great precision and value. The other was Charles Booth, who with his own fortune, acquired from industry, was to conduct, beginning in the 1880's, the first great empirical social scientific study, an investigation into the conditions of life among all the people of London. Through the influence of these men and through the further influence of middle-class philanthropists and reformers who ran the charity organizations and worked among the poor, Beatrice Potter gradually developed the feeling that she must see for herself what the objects of her interest and concern were like. The general problem of the rise of an industrial proletariat moved such men as Comte and Marx to the formulation of large general ideas, which soon began to lead a life independent of social realities; it moved Beatrice Potter and Charles Booth to a direct involvement with the human beings who made up the problem, and to the attempt to ground any general statement about the poor and the working classes on direct acquaintance with them—not a chosen segment alone, but, as far as special techniques made possible, all of them.

In Beatrice Potter's case, the first step was an attempt to see for herself:

It was in the summer of 1883 [she writes] that I took the first step as a social investigator. . . . What had been borne into me during my book studies was my utter ignorance of the manual-working class, that is, of four-fifths [*sic!*] of my fellow-countrymen. During the preceding London season I had joined the Charity Organization Committee and acted as one of its visitors in the slums of Soho; but it was clear to me that these cases of extreme destitution, often distorted by drink and vice, could [not be] regarded as a fair sample of the wage-earning class. . . . How was I to get an opportunity of watching, day by day, in their homes and in their workshops, a sufficient number of normal manual-working families to enable me to visualize the class as a whole; to understand what was meant by chronic poverty and insecurity of livelihood; to ascertain whether such conditions actually existed in any but a small fraction of the great body of the people? Were the manual workers what I was accustomed to call civilized? What were their aspirations, what was their degree of education, what their capacity for self-government? [23]

Mrs. Webb had distant relatives who were manual workers, and by visiting them she was able to get her first sustained contact with the respectable working class. In time, she got to know other workers: by becoming, for example, a rent collector for a house put up by philanthropists in a poor section of London. Many other people were of course doing the same thing. The settlement house movement was beginning in England, and at this time it meant just what the term indicates: that middle-class people "settled" among the workers and the lower classes. By this time it was possible for a young lady of the upper-middle classes to go among the lower classes; the first shock of urbanization and industrialization had been absorbed. What distinguished Mrs. Webb from other middle-class philanthropists and reformers who came into direct contact with the poor, however, was that she was a social scientist. Her first interest was in authenticated knowledge of the reality of the working class: not what a reformer or revolutionist, each speaking in the basis of partial knowledge, said, but what the situation, on the basis of a first-hand acquaintance with all the facts, actually was.

But how was one to know "all the facts"? It was this that Charles Booth attempted. If he could not find out all the facts about four million people by himself, he could closely examine those who knew them—in London these were the school inspectors; and he could check upon what they said by going to live among the poor himself, as he did. In time, the development of statistics suggested that it was unnecessary, in order to survey the entire universe, to examine every member of it: one could select a sample and find out more economically what Charles Booth had tried to discover by laboriously considering millions of individual cases. The purpose of Charles Booth's investigation of London in the 1880's and 1890's was to find out facts and to test generalizations that seem to us so simple and obvious as to need no investigation at all. Booth wanted to find out how many poor there were—for the actual extent of poverty and misery was a real subject for debate in England in the 1880's (just as the actual number of people in England was a subject for debate a hundred years earlier). And he wanted to find out what the causes of this poverty and misery were. For, obvious as the answer may be to us now, at the time the most remarkable ideas were current as to the causes of poverty and misery. Beatrice Webb writes:

> The belief—it may almost be called an obsession—
> that the mass misery of the great cities arose mainly,
> if not entirely from spasmodic, indiscriminate and
> unconditional doles, whether in the form of alms or

in that of Poor Law Relief, was, in the 'sixties and 'seventies, the common opinion of such enlightened members of the governing class as were interested in the problem of poverty.[24]

And at that time it was no simple matter to investigate how many poor there were and why they were poor. The census asked no question about income or rent. And then, just what was "poverty"? Booth's approach was incredibly elaborate, and yet perhaps there was no other way of going about the matter at that time. He spent many, many hours with the school visitors, who visited every family having school children, finding out the circumstances of each family's life. He got people to study each of the major trades of London: average rates of pay, amount of employment, conditions of labor. He summed up enormous quantities of data, dealing, in the end, with literally millions of people. He divided the people into various "classes" simply on the basis of their income and the way of life that income made possible. And he described vividly the conditions of each of the classes by way of representative families within them. He thus gave a graphic picture of the quantity of misery in London that surpassed in authority and conviction any journalistic account.

I think the descriptive task alone was worth while, in view of the conditions of the time. Everyone knew, however, that misery existed; sophisticated causes of its analysis had been made; was it not sheer make-work to document it so elaborately? I think not; for it was largely owing to this detailed examination, which was concerned not only with quantities but, as far as it could be determined, causes, that Charles Booth was, to my mind, more correct about the effective causes of the misery of his time than, for example, was Marx.

These matters may appear so obvious to us as to need no investigation, but this is because at one time they were investigated. To Marx, the cause of poverty was obvious— it was capitalism—and he and his followers thus found it impossible to explain the increasing prosperity of the working classes throughout the nineteenth century.[25] To Booth this was by no means proved: "The *a priori* reasoning of political economy, orthodox and unorthodox alike," he wrote in 1887, "fails from want of reality. At its base are a series of assumptions very imperfectly connected with the observed facts of life. We need to begin with true picture of the modern industrial organism. . . ."[26] And indeed he eventually emerged with a modest diagnosis of the causes of a large part of the misery he uncovered, a diagnosis which was to be instrumental in helping to moderate this misery. He argued that "The disease from which society suffers is the unrestricted competition in industry of the needy and the helpless," and that the answer was for "the state to nurse the helpless and incompetent . . . and provide for those who are not competent to provide for themselves."[27] Indeed, the removal from competition for jobs of the aged, the sick, the handicapped, those who were too young, and other categories of the poplation, by means of state support for them, has undoubtedly played a significant role in increasing the income and the comfort of those who continue to compete, despite the existence of private capitalism—an outcome that was completely outside the range of policy alternatives that Marx, who was unquestionably more brilliant than Booth, envisaged as possible in capitalist society.

If one looks at some of the first important early research undertakings in American sociology, one sees the quite direct influence of Booth. Thus, the *Hull-House Maps and Papers* of 1895 bases itself directly on Booth: "The great interest and significance attached to Mr. Charles Booth's maps of London have served as warm encouragement. . . ." [28] The same color scheme is used to differentiate degrees of poverty, but here another group of major "natural categories" (this is Chicago, not London) must be introduced alongside the classes, the ethnic groups. W. E. DuBois' *The Philadelphia Negro*,[29] a particularly fine work of 1899, is also specifically indebted to Booth, down to the colors of the maps.

Of course, other influences were also at work in developing the empirical trend: the social reform interest was particularly great, as one may see from glancing at the early volumes of the *American Journal of Sociology;* there was also a strong influence from young economists who had studied in Germany and, influenced by historical studies there, emphasized direct empirical research rather than theory.[30] To trace all the influences in the rise to a central position of a concern with first-hand, empirical research in the United States is, however, too large a task for this paper, and we will bring our historical account to a close with the end of the nineteenth century.

We have commented briefly in this essay—much too briefly, for this is a first sketch where a portrait is wanted —on a number of influences in creating a point of view and a method of work. The point of view, we have argued, is a new one: it is one that challenges not only opinion but fact in the social sphere and, further, insists on the importance of small, exact observations. The method is one in which first the factuality of a tiny detail is established; and then a mass of details is summed up to say something important. This, at any rate, is the ideal. Very often, as we know, the mass of small, exact observations has remained only a collection of trivialities and the summation has not led to any profundity. But at other times this point of view and method have had brilliant successes, and certainly its development has not come to an end.

But why, we may ask, did all this come to pass? Why did not people remain satisfied with generalizations based on illustrations—with, in effect, the approach of social philosophers, whose individual achievements have certainly been greater than that of any practitioner of the method of first-hand investigation, precise description, and statistical analysis? We can detect many factors which led to this break in the study of the social world. There was the model of the natural sciences, for one thing, and the different ways in which this influence made itself felt. For example, it made itself felt in the demand for a rational system of laws, expressed by Jeremy Bentham in England, which had some effect in creating the system of parliamentary investigations. It made itself felt in the rise of the ideology of social engineering in France, expressed by Saint-Simon and Comte —the notion of a rational reconstruction or stabilization of society. Whether expressed through liberal or conservative thinkers, the scientific tradition inevitably involved the method we have described.

In addition to the influences of science and certain strands of thought influenced by it, we may detect the influence of the development of the national state and its need for facts and figures. The needs of the state often coincided with the demands of reformers, and the result was bodies of empirical data and masses of statistics. The modern state in the nineteenth century seemed to need far more data than European states had previously required. Kings and republics had always been interested in the quantity of their revenue, but seem to have been very often indifferent to the numbers of their inhabitants. This may have been because, in relatively static societies, both the number of inhabitants and their status, it was assumed, did not change. The constitution of the body politic was "known." But as societies began to change ever more rapidly, it became clear that traditional knowledge and assumptions could not hold. First people became interested in the numbers of inhabitants, then in their conditions and behavior, and ever greater volumes of statistics were gathered, for purposes of administration, to guide legislation and simply for public information. The state had wider and wider functions; societies were more and more complex; and thus more and better facts were needed.

But now we must emphasize the significance of these large sounding changes on social consciousness in general, aside from any influence they may have had on state functions. For it is my strong impression that among educated people in the early nineteenth century, one of the major causes of the drive toward exact knowledge of the society around them was the fact that society had changed so radically that people were at a loss to understand it. During the nineteenth century there was an enormous growth of cities and an enormous growth of a city proletariat. London and Paris were of course already large in the eighteenth century, but they were nevertheless cities that remained known or knowable to their observers. The social classes and different groups within them were traditional classes and groups—merchants, artisans, porters, dignitaries, nobles, poets, and musicians. These cities were then perhaps less different socially from the great cities of the ancient world and the middle ages than they were from what they were to become in the course of the nineteenth century, as vast masses of peasants streamed into them to become transformed into the city proletariat.

If we envisage a literary man of the mid-seventeenth century walking through London or Paris, I think he would not find much that he could not, from his own experience, in some way grasp or understand. In one way or another, and even if at distant remove, the city population were all people with whom he had contact, and he would not do badly if he were to set himself to writing characters of the butcher, the baker, the liveried servant, the carter, etc.

With the rapid development of the industrial revolution, the great growth of population, and the very rapid growth of cities, a new class began to grow rapidly in the city, and this produced a strong feeling among the educated that they were surrounded by a reality they did not understand. The working class, limited to contact with itself alone, unrelated except by a series of impersonal agents to the middle and upper classes or to any educated or cultured person, appeared, and was, frightening. It appeared, and was, exotic and foreign. We read in English parliamentary reports of children who had not heard of Jesus Christ at the age of fourteen, of the almost complete disappearance of any traditional religion among the new working-classes, of an almost complete breakdown of traditional patterns of sexual control.

The developments of the later eighteenth and early nineteenth centuries thus transformed the familiar scene of the city into a strange jungle, which cried out for exploration and safaris—what was Charles Booth's study but that?—aimed at discovering not the secrets of Africa but the mysteries of London. (The model of modern exploration and ethnography, developing in the middle of the nineteenth century, must also have played a role in suggesting the exploration of Western cities.) Before this time the lower orders of society had been just that—lower orders—and it was sufficiently clear, to the ruling and educated classes, who they were and how they were ranked.

The new masses of industrial civilization presented them-selves as quite new. The new methods of empirical sociology arose, I believe, in an effort to grasp a new world, to which traditional thought and observation gave no guidance.

Empirical sociology is thus in its origins oriented not only toward social problems but also toward the new and exotic arising in the midst of old societies, for it was the new classes, become exotic because they were so little traditional, that gave sociology its first subject matter. In America, too, as empirical sociology developed in Chicago and other centers, it emphasized the working classes and more particularly the marginal, problematic, and exotic elements among them or drawn from them. In Chicago sociologists studied hoboes, criminals, boys' gangs, taxi-dancers, prostitutes—and only later more normal occupations. The immigrants and the Negro were from the beginning the most prominent concern of American sociologists —both elements created social problems, but they were also (and this is one of the reasons they *were* social problems) strange and foreign to the middle-class observers and reformers.

It was thus not purely an intellectual development—the influence and example of science—which led to the challenging of received pictures of social reality: it was the fact that the reality itself had changed rapidly and drastically, and there was no traditional guide to it. In time, a discipline that was developed to study the masses turned on the classes which sponsored it. The methods developed to study illiterate factory labor were to be turned on the employers of labor by a now independent class of social investigators. So we now have, growing out of a kind of investigation which once concerned itself only with the poor and the miserable, accounts of businessmen, professional classes, politicians, statesmen. The origin of these methods of research is perhaps one reason why they are capable of arousing such discomfort in those who are subjected to them.

There were thus, I believe, good reasons for the rise of methods of research which today still astonish and amuse literary man, humanists, and historians. Of course, history is never a justification: these methods must be justified by their results, and concerning these there is a wide field for argument and discussion. The history of these methods —and this essay is only an exploratory sketch, which suggests what may be, rather than establishes, the case—may, however, well play a role in this discussion.

NOTES

[1] I am particularly indebted to Mark Benney, who sent me a very full letter with many of the details of his own researches on this same question, and who directed me to sources of which I would otherwise be ignorant; and to Lewis Feuer, with whom I have had many discussions of the problems raised in this article, and who has freely shared with me his extensive knowledge of these matters.

[2] August Meitzen, *History, Theory, and Technique of Statistics,* Supplements to the Annals of the American Academy of Political and Social Science, March 1891, p. 23. See, on Achenwell, comments by George Sarton, "Preface to Vol. xxiii of Isis Quetelet," *Isis* 23, 1935.

[3] Leslie Stephen, *The English Utilitarians* (London: 1900), Vol. I, p. 80.

⁴ In connection with the early censuses of Holland (1829) and Belgium (1832) "he gave careful consideration to the collection of data, both as to the blank forms to be used and as to the nature of the questions to be asked, to the tabulation and forms of presentation of the material, to methods of averaging and summarizing data, and to the criticism, both of the sources and the results of the investigation. . . . [He held there should be] inquiry into the influences under which the data are collected and the nature of their sources." Frank H. Hankins, "Adolphe Quetelet as Statistician." *Columbia University Studies in History, Economics, and Public Law,* Vol. 31, No. 4, 1908, p. 42.

⁵ Hankins *op. cit.,* gives the reference to the footnote here translated: *Cours de Philosophie Positive,* Volume IV, p. 15, (4th edition) Paris 1877. Sarton, *op. cit.,* was not aware of any comment of Comte on Quetelet. For the Marx reference, see Karl Marx, *Selected Writings in Sociology and Social Philosophy,* T. B. Bottomore and Maximilien Rubel, Eds., London, pp. 229-30.

⁶ *Annals of the Royal Statistical Society,* 1834-1934 (London: 1934), pp. 7-9.

⁷ T. S. Ashton, *Economic and Social Investigations in Manchester,* 1833-1933 (London: 1934), p. 3.

⁸ *Ibid.,* p. 3.

⁹ *Ibid.,* p. 17-18.

¹⁰ *Ibid.,* p. 13.

¹¹ *Annals. . . . ,* p. 10.

¹² *Ibid.,* p. 22.

¹³ *Ibid.,* pp. 31-33. The extent to which this enthusiasm for facts—sheer facts—went is sometimes startling: "A letter was read from Mr. Mackenzie, Secretary to the National Philanthropic Association, suggesting that an endeavor be made to discover the quantities of horse-dung deposited daily in the streets of the Metropolis, and Mr. Fletcher was requested to reply thereto to the effect that the Council have not at their disposal any funds of the Statistical Society applicable to such an investigation as that which is proposed and they do

not consider it advisable to take the credit or responsibility of expending the Funds of others upon it; but that they will be very glad to receive any paper on the subject amongst those which are constantly being submitted to the Society and give to it the place in the Society's transactions and publications which its relative merits and importance may demand." From a Council minute, 1850, quoted *ibid.*, p. 79.

[14] *Ibid.*, pp. 79, 241, and Ashton, pp. 20, 21, and elsewhere.

[15] Annals. . . . , pp. 45-46, and elsewhere.

[16] *Children's Employment Commission. First Report of the Commissioners. Mines* (London: Her Majesty's Stationery Office 1842), pp. 2, 3, and 5.

[17] Hilde Weiss, "Die Enquete Ouvrière von Karl Marx," *Zeitschrift Fur Sozialforschung,* Vol. V, 1936, p. 78.

[18] Mietzen, *op. cit.,* p. 63.

[19] See Dorothy Herbertson, *Frédéric Le Play* (London: 1950); and the volumes of the journal published by his followers, *La Science Sociale,* from 1886 on.

[20] *Ibid.*

[21] Henry Mayhew, *London Labour and the London Poor* (London: 1851), Vol. I, pp. 1-2.

[22] Personal correspondence.

[23] Beatrice Webb, *My Apprenticeship* (London: Penguin Books, 1938), pp. 175-176.

[24] *Ibid.,* p. 227.

[25] Marx once prepared an enormous questionnaire, 25,000 of which were distributed to French workers and socialists in 1880, for the purpose of collecting information on the conditions of the working class, but—according to one interpreter—also designed to increase class-consciousness among the French workers: see Weiss, *op. cit.,* and Bottomore and Rubel, *op. cit.,* pp. 203 ff. Its usefulness as an information-gathering device and Marx's insight into the characteristics of workers may be gauged from a sample question: "13. Give details of the division of labour in your industry." There is no record of any of the questionnaires having been filled out and returned.

[26] Booth, in 1887, quoted in Webb, p. 270.

[27] Booth, 1902-3, quoted in Webb, p. 301.

[28] *Hull-House Maps and Papers,* by Residents of Hull-House, N. Y., 1895, p. 11.

[29] "The Philadelphia Negro" in *Publications of the University of Pennsylvania Series in Political Economy and Public Law,* 14, 1899.

[30] Richard T. Ely, *Ground Under Our Feet* (New York: 1938), pp. 154-155, 167 ff.

THE GROWTH OF SOCIAL RESEARCH IN THE UNITED STATES [1]

Harry Alpert

The outstanding organizational characteristic of social science research in the United States is its decentralization. It pervades all major sectors of the economy and the society. The federal government, state and local governments, colleges and universities, industrial organizations, commercial and business firms, private foundations, research councils, and independent research institutes, both profit and nonprofit—all participate in varying degrees in the financial support and actual conduct of social science research. The strength of this system derives, in my judgment, from its very diversity. The multiplicity of organizations which support and conduct research insures healthy growth by sustaining diversified channels for exploration of new areas and untried methods. Private foundations, for example, are available for support of research in controversial areas which could not be supported by public agencies. The latter, conversely, support research in social auditing which often exceeds the scope of private institutions.

Accurate figures on the actual expenditures for social science research by the various sectors of the economy are difficult to obtain. I trust that the data here presented will be interpreted as estimates indicative of general magnitude and not as firm statistics. The total national effort in social science research, both basic and applied, involves annual expenditures of approximately $215 million. The following table indicates roughly the sources of funds:

Table I. SOURCES OF FUNDS FOR SUPPORT OF SOCIAL SCIENCE RESEARCH IN THE UNITED STATES

Source	Annual Rate	Per cent
Federal government	$ 55,000,000	25.6
Private foundations	15,000,000	7.0
Colleges and universities	5,000,000	2.3
Industrial and commercial organizations	137,000,000	63.7
Other (independent institutes, State and local governments, etc.)	3,000,000	1.4
Total	$215,000,000	100.0

The distribution is somewhat different when viewed in terms of the cost of the research actually performed by these various types of organizations. Rough indications of the magnitude of the annual expenditures involved in the social science research conducted by these agencies are presented in Table II.

Comparison of the estimates in Table I and Table II indicates that: (1) more than three-fifths of the total national activities in social science research is supported by and conducted by industry and business; (2) the federal government provides about one-fourth of the funds

Table II. ANNUAL RATES OF EXPENDITURES FOR SOCIAL SCIENCE
RESEARCH PERFORMED BY VARIOUS TYPES OF ORGANIZATIONS
IN THE UNITED STATES

Performing Organization	Annual Rate	Per cent
Federal government	$ 38,000,000	17.7
Private foundations	2,000,000	0.9
Colleges and universities	35,000,000	16.3
Industrial and commercial organizations	137,000,000	63.7
Other (independent institutes, etc.)	3,000,000	1.4
Total	$215,000,000	100.0

available for social science research but conducts a little
more than one-sixth of the total through its own facilities;
(3) colleges and universities contribute just over 2 per
cent of the separately budgeted funds for social research
but actually expend a sixth of the total on research that
they themselves perform; (4) institutions of higher education are dependent upon the federal government and
private foundations, and to a lesser extent upon industry,
for support of the research they conduct.

Among the more prominent of the federal government's
intramural activities in the social sciences—that is, research
conducted by federal agencies with their own facilities and
staffs—are the mass statistical data-collections by such
agencies as the Bureau of the Census, Bureau of Labor
Statistics, Agricultural Marketing Service, the National
Office of Vital Statistics, and the National Health Survey;
the analytical work in business, labor, and industrial economics by the Department of Commerce and Department
of Labor and other agencies; socio-environmental studies
of health and related health research by the Public Health

Service, the Department of Defense, and the Veterans' Administration; educational and social welfare research by several constituent units of the Department of Health, Education, and Welfare; social science investigations in personnel and training problems and related fields conducted by the Army, Navy, Air Force, and other agencies within the Department of Defense; the agricultural economics and rural sociology programs of the Department of Agriculture; and the studies in international relations and foreign areas by the Office of Intelligence Research of the Department of State and other intelligence agencies.

The extramural social science research supported or sponsored by the federal government through grants, contracts, and other arrangements with colleges and universities, commercial and industrial organizations, and other agencies qualified to conduct social science research covers a wide range of disciplines. Social psychology, sociology, anthropology, social statistics, mathematical social science, social psychiatry and social medicine, and agricultural economics are all active areas of government support. Certain large segments of the social sciences remain for the most part outside the domain of government extramural sponsorship. Political science and economics (outside of agricultural economics) and certain areas of sociology are not supported on an unclassified, extramural basis, although federal agencies, as indicated above, conduct research in these fields intramurally.

The extramural social science supported by the federal government is, in very large measure, applied research and tends to be related to the specific missions of the agencies supporting the research. Research pertaining to defense, health, education, rehabilitation, rural welfare, and the agricultural economy predominates. Only one federal agency, the National Science Foundation, is devoted exclusively to the support of basic research. It has recently initiated a modest program of support of fundamental research in the anthropological, economic, and sociological sciences and in the history and philosophy of science.[2]

The social science programs, both intramural and extramural, of the private foundations also tend to be applied research. Some of the larger foundations, such as the Ford Foundation, the Rockefeller Foundation, and the Carnegie Corporation of New York, are dedicated primarily to the promotion of human welfare and international peace. Nevertheless, they recognize the importance of basic as well as applied research and generally support both types of activities. These "giants" among the private foundations have general programs in the social sciences. Others, such as the Wenner-Gren Foundation for Anthropological Research, concentrate on a single discipline.

Research in general constitutes but a small part of the over-all program activities of foundations. Foundations usually maintain rather small research staffs of their own. Their major activity, as far as research goes, involves support of the work of institutions of higher learning and independent research institutes and even, on rare occasions, government agencies. Their funds are made available to research groups either by direct grants or through support of the programs of such intermediary agencies as the Social Science Research Council and the American Council of Learned Societies.

As expected, industrial and commercial research is almost exclusively practical and applied, although basic social science research programs have been established in the past few years by Bell Telephone Laboratories and General Electric Company. Research in business and industry includes opinion and attitude surveys, marketing research, media analysis, industrial relations research, economic analysis, studies of employee relations and morale, personnel and organization research, psychological testing, and related research activities.

By far the largest sums are spent for opinion and attitude surveys and marketing research. It is estimated that survey and marketing research activities, mostly by and for industry and business, involve annual expenditures of $125 million, or more than half of the national cost of all types of social science research. Most of these funds are spent by commercial organizations on behalf of business and industrial clients, including the mass media and advertising agencies.

The universities and the nonprofit research organizations attached to them, such as the Institute for Social Research at the University of Michigan, the National Opinion Research Center at the University of Chicago, the Bureau of Applied Social Research at Columbia University, and the Center for International Studies at the Massachusetts Institute of Technology, are the nation's main intellectual resource for the conduct of basic research in the social sciences. Most universities cannot support such research from their own funds separately budgeted for this purpose and depend largely on grants and contracts from government agencies, private foundations, and industrial and commercial organizations.

The universities are involved in applied research not only through the institutes already mentioned but also through agricultural experiment stations, bureaus of business and economic research, bureaus of state and local governmental affairs, and similar institutions.

Individual investigators pursuing research as part of their normal academic responsibilities but not identified with research organizations or institutes are also an important source of original, creative research at colleges and universities.

This rapid survey of social science research in the United States, *circa* 1958, presents only a static picture of the current situation. Much that has been described here is a product of World War II and of the postwar era and represents novel developments both with respect to the magnitude of the funds involved and the types of problems and disciplines supported. The events of the war on both the military and civilian fronts, and the problems of postwar readjustment as they affected the nation and the individual, provided the social sciences with dramatic opportunities to demonstrate their practical value and essential role in modern society. As a result, social science research firmly established its legitimacy as a fundamental contributor to our national life. Government, private foundations, and industrial and commercial establishments all participated in this development.

World War II was undoubtedly the major catalytic event leading to the expansion of the federal government's programs in this field. Even as late as 1940, the government's activities in the social sciences were confined largely to the collection and analysis of statistical information. The roots of later developments in the government's social science programs, however, were discernible in the 1920's.[3] The appointment by President Herbert Hoover of a research committee on recent social trends provided significant White House endorsement of a major social science enterprise. Further impetus for governmental support of the social sciences came in the thirties from the practical programs of the New Deal. The Department of Agriculture, in particular, expanded its research activities in a wide variety of social disciplines and assumed the leadership in introducing the sample interview survey as a basic social science tool and as an instrument of governmental policy. The accomplishments of the Department's Division of Program Surveys prepared the way for the subsequent use of the interview survey in the Office of War Information, War Production Board, Office of Price Administration and other war-time agencies. Valuable data were obtained on people's desires, needs, problems, opinions, behavior, knowledge, reading and comprehension, and motivation.

Both military and civilian agencies were quick to exploit the potential contributions of the social sciences to significant problems of national security, welfare, and defense. A brief review of illustrative uses of social science during World War II lists eight examples of problem areas in which important research accomplishments were achieved: soldier orientation and morale; analysis of command problems, particularly among Negro troops; more efficient use of psychiatry through the development of effective brief screening devices; venereal disease control; analysis of the American soldier's problems of adjustment, combat performance, and response to mass communications; evaluation of Japanese morale; estimation of war production requirements; and regulation of prices and rationing.[4] To this list may be added the media analysis activities of the Office of War Information and the Foreign Broadcast Intelligence Service; the propaganda studies of the Library of Congress, Department of Justice, and various intelligence agencies; the surveys of war bond purchases and other evaluations of the effectiveness of drives; the testing of the public comprehension of governmental information materials, including rationing and price regulations and tax forms; and research on national character and other problems related to a better understanding of the behavioral characteristics of foreign peoples.

It is interesting to note that prominent among those testifying before a congressional committee in 1945 on the contributions of the social sciences in World War II were officials of the Office of Strategic Services. Political science, economics, statistics, history, social psychology, sociology, anthropology, and geography were all identified as basic social sciences which contributed significantly to the intelligence activities of O.S.S.[5]

Many of these war-time activities were, of course, discontinued with the cessation of hostilities. But the social sciences had demonstrated their capacities and had built up knowledge and methods which remained useful and applicable. Thus, the immediate postwar period showed a healthy continuation of many of the social science research programs, especially in the defense agencies. The Office of Naval Research, created shortly after the war, supported research on manpower problems, personnel and training, group morale, organizational structure, and related social psychological and sociological areas. The Army continued, in abbreviated form, its studies of opinions and attitudes of American soldiers. The new Department of the Air Force, proud of the accomplishments of the Aviation Psychology Program, organized units to undertake and support research in problems of selection and training, manpower, leadership, human relations and morale, and psychological warfare. When the Research and Development Board was established in the Department of Defense it included a Committee on Human Resources.

At the same time, as part of a broader pattern of support of the physical and life sciences, the federal agencies began to develop programs of extramural support, either through grants to colleges and universities or through contract arrangements with specially created research institutes such as the Operations Research Office of The Johns

Hopkins University and the Human Resources Research Office of George Washington University. In addition to the defense agencies and the traditional support of agricultural experiment stations by the Department of Agriculture, the National Institutes of Health, especially the National Institute of Mental Health, became a major source of social science support. Later, other units of what is now the Department of Health, Education, and Welfare, such as the Office of Education and the Office of Vocational Rehabilitation, developed extramural support activities. Finally, in 1954, the National Science Foundation began its modest program of support of basic social science research.

The postwar period has been one of steady growth of governmental activity in the social sciences, in terms of both the number of agencies involved and the amount of money spent intramurally and extramurally. But this general picture should not obscure the fact that individual social science programs in particular agencies have had their ups and downs, ins and outs. I have elsewhere referred to this as the process of starts and fits: an activity gets started and then is curtailed or discontinued when some congressman or general throws a fit.[6] The Division of Research of the Housing and Home Finance Agency, the excellent survey research unit of the Veterans' Administration, the Air Forces' Human Resources Research Institute at Maxwell Field and its Personnel and Training Center at Lackland Air Force Base are but a few examples of research units which have experienced difficulties. Despite the "on again, off again" character of these programs, the general record of government support indicates an increasing appreciation of the social sciences as a valuable national asset.

The record of private foundation support of social science research is also one of steady progress in the face of shifting program emphases and discontinuance of activities in midstream. Just as government agencies abolish research units from time to time, so the Ford Foundation, for example, recently decided to discontinue its Division of Behavioral Sciences. But here again, the over-all record involves substantial support of diversified programs of social science research.

In fact, prior to World War II, the private foundations were by far the major source of social science support, and in many areas they were perhaps the only financial resource to which social scientists could turn. Even with the increasing role of the federal government in the social science field, the private foundations have remained a dominant factor in support of research in areas involving political and moral sensitivities and public controversy.

Some years ago, when the private foundations were being investigated by a congressional committee, Dean William I. Myers of Cornell University prepared a statement setting forth some contributions made by the social sciences with private foundation support.[7] Among the activities mentioned were national income studies; analyses of fluctuations in incomes and employment; historical and statistical studies of financial and credit markets; aptitude testing and personnel selection; research on questionnaire and interviewing methods; area studies; human relations in industry; public administration research; and mental health. Other research areas supported by private foundations include international relations, problems of aging, research in foreign areas, group dynamics, education, social psychiatry, public health, race relations, and civil liberties. Three important milestones in American social science, it is generally agreed, are Gunnar Myrdal's *The American Dilemma, The American Soldier* volumes officially known as "Studies in Social Psychology in World War II," and

The Authoritarian Personality and related volumes in the "Studies in Prejudice" series. All three research activities received substantial support from private organizations.

Finally, a brief word may be added regarding social science research conducted for industrial and commercial establishments. Here the emphasis is predominantly practical and immediate, but such research may lead as well to important theoretical and conceptual contributions. Thus, many of the communications research studies of the Bureau of Applied Social Research at Columbia University, although commissioned by publishing firms, mass media organizations, and drug companies, have yielded new knowledge on the informal processes of communication and on the influence patterns in community life.

The first area of social science research to command the attention of American industry and commerce was economics. Many banks established research bureaus, and such organizations as the Chamber of Commerce encouraged economic analyses. Economic research has continued to receive industrial and commercial support, but in recent years increasing attention is being directed toward the social, cultural, psychological and other noneconomic aspects of our economic life.

Specific examples of research which American business and industry are supporting include analysis of market potentials; the testing of new products; copy testing; evaluation of effectiveness of advertising and selling campaigns; readership surveys; content analysis; consumer behavior and consumer expectations studies; motivation research; attitudes of workers toward the job; the public's attitudes and opinions toward the industrial or commercial organization; attitudes toward foremen and other supervisory personnel; analysis of communication networks; effectiveness of organizational structures and supervisory patterns; population movements; and many other related problems bearing on the efficient production, marketing, and consumption of goods and services.

The social sciences have obviously established a firm, albeit modest, place for themselves in the life of the nation. By their continued contributions to knowledge about and understanding of human behavior and by their demonstration of their practical usefulness to national welfare and security as well as to the nation's economy, they will undoubtedly continue to improve their role and status in the social fabric of the nation.[8] As Julian Huxley once remarked, "We need have no fear for the future of social science . . . By the time that the profession of social science, pure and applied, includes as many men and women as are now engaged in natural science, it will have solved its major problems of new methods, and the results it has achieved will have altered the whole intellectual climate. As the barber-surgeon of the Middle Ages has given place to the medical man of today, with his elaborate scientific training, so the essentially amateur politician and administrator of today will have been replaced by a new type of professional man, with specialized scientific training. Life will go on against a background of social science." [9]

NOTES

[1] The valuable assistance of Bertha W. Rubinstein of the U. S. National Science Foundation is gratefully acknowledged.

[2] See H. Alpert, "The Knowledge We Need Most," *The Saturday Review,* Vol. XLI, February 1, 1958, pp. 36-38.

[3] A. H. Dupree, *Science in the Federal Government* (Cam-

bridge, Mass.: The Belknap Press of Harvard University Press 1957), p. 335.

[4] Russell Sage Foundation, *Effective Use of Social Science Research in the Federal Services* (New York: Russell Sage Foundation, 1950).

[5] *Hearings on Science Legislation (S. 1297 and Related Bills)*. Hearings Before a Subcommittee of the Committee on Military Affairs, U. S. Senate, 79th Cong., 1st Sess. (Washington, D. C.: Government Printing Office, 1945 and 1946). See chart facing p. 900.

[6] *American Sociological Review*, Vol. 22, October 1957, p. 618.

[7] W. I. Myers, "What the Social Sciences Are," Statement presented to the Select Committee of the House of Representatives to Investigate Tax-Exempt Foundations and Comparable Organizations, in *Hearings* Before the Select Committee to Investigate Tax-Exempt Foundations and Comparable Organizations, House of Representatives, 82nd Cong., 2nd Sess., (Washington, D. C.: U. S. Government Printing Office, 1953), pp. 141-149.

[8] For a general picture of American social science and a comparison with social science in the U.S.S.R., see R. A. Bauer, "Our Big Advantage: The Social Sciences," *Harvard Business Review*, Vol. XXXIV, May-June, 1958, pp. 125-136.

[9] Quoted in B. Barber, *Science and the Social Order* (Glencoe, Illinois: The Free Press, 1952), pp. 249-250.

ISSUES

STRATEGIES OF INQUIRY:
THE RATIONAL USE OF OBSERVATION

Harold D. Lasswell

Any item of descriptive knowledge may bear significantly upon the life of man. Nevertheless, it is too much to expect that a finite intelligence is capable of enclosing past and future within a single vision and of validly estimating the importance of every detail for the whole of human experience.

The foregoing propositions are beyond the realm of serious dispute. For our present purpose it is enough to draw the solitary implication that when properly interpreted they do not invalidate the idea of strategy in intellectual life.

The idea of strategy does not depend upon omniscience. Rather, the motives that culminate in strategy are bred of the necessities generated by limitation. We are trapped in the corridors of the present at the very moment of their recession into history. Our choices refer to the future and affect the modalities by which the future is entered, endured, and modified.

If, on the one hand, necessity forbids an assured prevision of the future, necessity also requires that we provide ourselves with expectations concerning the shape of things to come. From the earliest reaching out of the infant to the most sophisticated general staff plan lies a chain of adventure in the making and retouching of images of the future.

It is more characteristic of humanity to suffer the consequences of too many, too detailed, and too inflexible expectations than to cringe before a void. Hence there is a sense in which the sciences of society make their principal contribution by moderating the grip of yesterday's practices upon today's assumptions about tomorrow. In their way, the costs of clinging to something too long are as devastating as the cost of clinging to nothing at all.

The Incremental Growth of Knowledge

Historians of science are impressed by the incremental character of knowledge. There are, of course, reservations upon this statement. It does not necessarily apply to the whole life span of a civilization or, for that matter, to a "time of trouble."

The strength of the reservations does not demolish the point that the accumulation of knowledge has "settled" or brought about the reformulation of many controverted issues. Consider "racial" differences. Self-serving declarations that were once plausible have given way under the impact of data obtained from every relevant branch of investigation, not excluding the recorded performance of men, women, and children when given tests of aptitude, including native intelligence. A similar fate has befallen the self-congratulatory myths once so confidently grounded upon the admittedly spectacular attainments of Graeco-

Roman and Egyptian civilization. The archeologist, who specializes in "the testimony of the spade," has brought about a more just evaluation of the past by disclosing the formidable achievements of Tigris-Euphrates and Middle American civilizations. These re-assessments are relatively easy to accept today in the light of results obtained by social anthropologists who have been working among the submerged peoples of Asia, Africa, the Americas, and the Pacific. From them we learn how many societies have exhibited spectacular creativity in particular segments of culture.

I have referred to the incremental growth of descriptive knowledge of man and his ways. It is not too difficult to identify some of the factors that account for this. In modern times, especially, systematic social studies figure in the universities. Social and psychological theory is taught, and whatever is taught finds appropriate channels of communication. It is also made subject to standardizing influences.

The distinctive instrument of communication at the level of advanced instruction and research is the seminar. No matter where the seminar was first introduced, there is no question that within the last century and a half it has come to dominate the scene everywhere that advanced study is the rule. This applies as fully in Japan as in the Americas, the Soviet world, or Western Europe.

The rise of the seminar and the habilitation of research and training in the sciences was part of the awakening of the universities to the new empirical curiosity of man in the modern age. At first the physical sciences lived a half-life partly inside and partly outside the universities. The scientific societies were invented outside the traditional bastions of learning as a means of encouraging the new outlook. Although scientific societies never lost their reason for being, they declined in relative importance as the universities came to provide a hospitable setting for empirical inquiry.

A partial explanation, then, of the cumulative character of systematic knowledge is the fact of its professionalization. This brought with it an imposing armory of devices to ensure cumulation. As inquiry itself became a stable form of social activity, it fell into the hands of a congregation of specialists whose members are exceedingly sensitive to their position in relation to the entire field of knowledge and to other knowledgeable figures. As an aid to intellectual and social geography, "maps" are drawn. These maps show "fields." Indeed, map makers appear to have invented fields.

Map makers have rarely been free of that form of myopia that appears to be the result of overfocusing upon what is immediately before one's eyes. That which is close is perceived as relatively grandiose; all else, including other myopiates laboring in distant fields, seems to sink into the background. Hence a number of maps carry rather specialized labels which are not modestly affixed to the foreground but purport to designate the whole panorama of social and psychological relationships. By competitive industry and ingenuity every science thus becomes "queen" of the hive —the name may be social philosophy, sociology, psychology, political science (or what not).

Besides playing a role in bolstering the self-esteem of map makers, systematic delineations never fail to disclose "gaps"; namely, uncultivated territory potentially open to occupation and settlement by an industrious thesis writer, research assistant, or associate. It is the discovery of "gaps" that transforms into a comprehensive enterprise the cumulative accretions that confer so much bulk upon the central core of descriptive knowledge.

There is a gap whenever the laws of "contract," of "tort," or of "crime" that prevail in the legal system of modern Paraguay or ancient Korea have been incompletely described; or when the social structure of contemporary Afghanistan or mediaeval Thailand is sketchily known; or when the ideological backwash of Europe throughout Africa is poorly recorded.

Of more technical importance, perhaps, are gaps of a methodological character. With the development of modern methods of conducting brief interview surveys, country after country has been brought into the orbit of continuous scientific sampling. The advent of portable sound recording instruments and of photography—in black and white or color, still or in motion—has given impetus to the study of languages and of oral literature throughout the globe.

We must not ignore a gap of another and more subtle kind. The discovery of a new set of formative factors discloses new scholarly terrain. Recall, in this connection, the vogue of the Troeltsch-Weber hypothesis about the liberating impact of Protestantism upon the spread of capitalistic economics. Or the recurring preoccupation with Durkheim's conception of *anomie* as a crucial factor in the alienation of human beings from the web of human association. Or the more recent disclosure under the impetus of dynamic psychopathology of the differentially disrupting impact of middle-class ideology—especially when combined with the one-child family—upon the healthy growth of personality.

The Scientist's Sense of Choice

From the vantage point of the intellectual historian or the summarizer of current trends it may appear that emerging zones of knowledge are quite foreseeable. The individual scientist, on the contrary, usually entertains a different perspective. Two divergent poles of emphasis are typical. At one pole the principal theme is the chance event. One's career is experienced as a strand of beads strung at random. Chance appears to have cast the die toward this or that university, toward auditing the lectures of one professor, toward reading a crucially enlivening page. Fellowships, prizes, appointments: these practical recognitions and means of assistance came at psychological moments.

At the other pole of self-perception is the sense of affirmative choice, the exhilaration of insight, pursuit, selectivity, attainment. The bobbing cork feels marvelously alive as a self-guiding creature. Not everyone has experienced a moment of piercing illumination comparable with what happened to Charles Darwin when he read Malthus. Yet it is in no sense unique to find that great moments of intellectual creativity have been concentrated within a brief time span. A not unrepresentative instance is the invention of three great organizing conceptions for the study of prehistory: The Stone Age, The Bronze Age, The Iron Age. Christian Thomsen came upon these seminal categories when, as a young man, he re-assigned the antiquities in the Museum at Copenhagen. One recalls the quickened sense of understanding when Le Play came to recognize the formative role of the lanes of travel in human affairs. Of such instances, indeed, there is no end.

The Criteria of Choice: Scientific

When we examine the criteria that have exerted a decisive influence upon the choice of programs of inquiry we come first to the most evident: scientific considerations themselves. Every student is more or less strategically situated in relation to the existing gaps in the current map of knowledge.

Some gaps, as said above, are relatively routine. They

show up where available information about a "case" is deficient, whether the case is a total society, a social structure, an interest that intersects class lines, a personality, a level of crisis (or intercrisis), or a distribution of human or physical resources.

When the gaps are more technical they challenge the research worker to extend the range of application of new procedures for the obtaining and processing of data. In the social and psychological sciences we have witnessed an unprecedented expansion of the repertory of instruments at the disposal of investigators. Among economists, for instance, the development of index numbers for the study of prices and goods has disclosed the finer structure of a modern economy. Thanks to the appearance of modern modes of summarizing the content of communication, it has become feasible for political scientists to investigate in detail the flow of politically significant news and comment. Wherever the interplay of personality and social context is under study, researchers have at their command a number of tests (or testing methods), many of which were inspired by the freeword association technique of Jung and the prolonged free association technique of Freud.

The most exciting gaps, as a rule, are suggested by the current theoretical models of the economy, the political arena, or of some other institutional process.

If he is cautious enough to stay within the permissible limits of originality, restricting his explorations to the gaps recognized to exist in the immediate vicinity, the scholar is at least assured of professional acceptance and a residue of respected contributions at the end of his career. There are, it is true, up-thrusting and doubting minds who fail to perceive the mellow beauty of the adjoining wasteland and who are willing to stake everything upon the chance of discovering, if not a new world, at least a new subdivision.

There have been few such successful adventurers; several, if not many, are self-chosen, and few survive the quest or the verdict of colleagues and successors. It sometimes appears that professional ethics operate as a code of self-limitation against contributing to the embarrassment of colleagues by discovering too much that they themselves might have found out.

However, it is not to be overlooked that the tension between the *conventional* and the *functional* affords an opportunity for the exercise of a considerable measure of originality. The conventional role of a specific social practice or institution is continually redefined by the daily erosion of the social process. By employing appropriate methods of study it is often practicable to discover the new significance of an old form. An inner equilibrium of factors can be exhibited that accounts for the relative stability of the new pattern. Changes that cannot be explained on the basis of internal factors may become intelligible when examined within the environing context of practice and institution.

Let us select an example from the study of modern property institutions. Adolf Berle and Gardner Means explored the decision-making process within the modern corporation and drew a telling distinction between the conventional meaning of "ownership" and the functional differences that had grown up within conventional practice. Some forms of "ownership" have in fact become divested of the function of management; they function solely as claims to income. Berle and Means inquired into the factors that appear to account for these modifications—causes with which we cannot concern ourselves here. They also undertook to assess the effect of changes in the institution of property upon other economic and social practices. The scientific result of the inquiry was to provide a more dependable, if more complex, model of an advanced economy than had been available hitherto.

It is typical rather than exceptional to find that conventionally labeled institutions do not in fact perform the function that the label implies. If the function continues, it may no longer dominate. It is conventional to speak of every prescription printed in a statute book as "law." In a functional sense, however, such prescriptions may differ enormously from one another in relation to the context. Some printed prescriptions are regarded as obsolete, or so obsolescent that no court deigns apply them. At the same time, other clauses of the code are expected to be lived up to, and a deviant is practically certain to become the target for sanctions whose character is severely deprivational. Are both sets of prescriptions part of the legal institutions of the community? Whatever conventional usage may be, it is evident that no social scientist can allow himself to be misled into treating such disparate phenomena as comparable. He will disclose by appropriate methods of research the functional as well as the conventional role of the written rules. In executing this research he will find it essential to employ a set of conceptual tools capable of distinguishing significant differences in function. No doubt he will separate a "pretended legal prescription" from a "law." The latter may be defined as both "authoritative" and "controlling." It is expected to apply and in fact does apply.

What are the appropriate criteria for the selection of functional categories? A system of classification is needed that is capable of being used to observe and compare any social context with any other. Now, the items of culture in any society, civilized or not, are innumerable. Social scientists stop cataloguing the thousands upon thousands of cultural details not because they exhaust the subject but because they exhaust themselves. The problem is selectivity. If the whole context is to be covered, the scientist must employ a generalized model of the whole. The observer needs to take responsibility for a basic list of categories that he uses in referring to every context. If he fails to work with such a definite and exhaustive list, his results lack internal consistency and become unreliable for comparative purposes.

One way to develop a set of workable categories for functional study is to select a series of "outcomes" representative of situations of interest to the comparative scientist. One category of outcomes can include "fighting," "peace-making," "voting in an election," "voting in a legislature." We refer to these as "decision" outcomes. Another eligible set is "buying and selling goods and services for consumption," "lending and borrowing," "saving." These outcomes are "transactions." And so on.

The social process as a whole is an endless chain of human interactions divisible into "outcomes," "pre-outcomes," and "post-outcomes." The specific practices that occur are the "culture patterns." We speak of outcomes as "values," meaning that for methodological purposes we treat them as the basic frames of reference. Obviously it is a matter of research and not of definition to ascertain the degree to which these outcomes are sought by particular individuals or groups. Everyone knows that individuals and groups are likely to differ from one another in the intensity of their pursuit of wealth (favorable transaction outcomes) or power (favorable decision outcomes) or of any other value. By keeping his terms constant, it is possible for the scientist to compare the degree to which various "value outcomes" are "evaluated" by any person or group.[1]

Since any social context is in process of change, inexhaustible opportunities exist for disclosing the shifting "fit" between the patterns by which a situation is conventionally defined and the function actually performed by a pattern.

It is evident that scientific work of the Berle-Means type differs from some traditional conceptions of science by giving great weight to time. Berle and Means generalized a theoretical model in the spirit and method of the scientific enterprise. But they were not trying to uncover *invariant* relationships. They were interested in the discovery of "generals," not "universals." They took it for granted that the working model of the American economy which they demonstrated will, in all probability, have many points of similarity with a model that is validated for a later phase of American history. But this is to be found out by research, not asserted by definition. And Berle and Means assumed that their model will coincide in many respects with theoretical constructions that can be validated for other modern industrial economies. This, too, is to be found out.

The desire to discover universal laws of society after the manner of physicists and chemists has provided one of the continuing motivations of psychologists and social scientists during the modern era. Up to the present this enterprise has been a source of much frustration, though it has produced many valuable by-products in the shape of "generals" and especially of observational methods. The experimental psychologists, for instance, have more or less unintentionally produced results whose importance for knowledge is less the "law" than the "instrument." The experimenter may have been concerned with discovering the universals of shape perception, which he proceeded to do under the controlled and simplified conditions of the laboratory. But his main contribution to the study of the social process may have been in the inadvertent development of a procedure capable of being adapted as a brief test for ascertaining the distribution of various personality forms in society. The factors affecting the frequency of personality forms according to culture, class, interest (and other categories) are of the greatest relevance to the development of working models of the social context.

Criteria of Choice: Policy Orientated

The discovery of time almost as a by-product of the scientific enterprise directs attention with great emphasis to the connection between scientific and other criteria in the choice of scientific problems. It is evident that the social and psychological scientist has at his command a means of affecting the policy of every organized group and indeed of every individual acting on his own behalf in society. Research is part of the "intelligence function" of the community, whether the research is planned, executed, and reported by an unattached scholar or by universities, organs of government, political parties, pressure groups, business corporations, church associations, or other organized bodies.

It is perhaps worth underscoring the point that considerations of policy need not be limited to the short range opportunisms of a market research project or a survey of the distribution of attitudes concerning corporate policy among middle and lower echelons of management or the labor force. Without casting aspersions upon the possible effect of such results upon business policy, I am interested in the following propositions:

1. Long-range problems can be selected for research programs.

2. The results of long-term research are potentially significant for any decision maker in society.

3. It is especially important for a society that aspires

toward freedom to make use of the understanding and in-- sight that can be provided by research results.

A few comments:

1. It is a matter of long-range importance whether modern man-machine combinations can be given forms compatible with the needs and aspirations of man. Researches in "industrial sociology," for instance, are already providing data relevant to this problem.

It is of long-range importance whether large hierarchical patterns of organization can be organized and managed in ways that hold in check the well-known tendencies toward "bureaucratism." Already some experimental innovations in government and business are challenging traditional assumptions in this domain.

It is of continuing significance to discover by what modes of organization and operation it will be feasible to hold antidemocratic tendencies in check inside mass political parties and other large private associations. We generally recognize that the prospects of popular government depend upon the vitality of the system of unofficial controls.

It is of continuing significance whether individuals and organizations engaged in performing the intelligence function in society can become accurate, alert, comprehensive, and honest—and remain so. This is the problem of a free and responsible press and of a free and creative university and educational system.

It is of continuing importance in democratic politics whether individuals and organizations who profess an ideology of freedom can maintain unity of interpretation and depth of conviction through the years.

It is of great relevance whether the potential creativity of human beings is discovered and developed at optimum periods of life.

It is important to anticipate the social impact of forthcoming developments in the physical, biological, and technical sciences and to discover the means by which drastic new innovations can be introduced at least cost in terms of all values.[2]

2. I shall say little about the proposition that governmental or private decision makers, acting collectively or separately, may be affected by the results of research. The potentiality, at least, is beyond debate.

3. Observation shows that man has little experience in mastering large scale operations for the sake of optimum self-expressiveness. More knowledge, coupled with more exploratory daring, is needed because the solutions offered by the past—are past.

Even among the scientists of a free society there have been misgivings about taking policy considerations frankly into account in the selection of research programs. Part of this reluctance must stem from a more or less unconscious distrust by the scientist of his own integrity. Evidently the specialist is apprehensive of his capacity to withstand the temptation to make dishonest observations, to suppress unfavorable findings, or to neglect or distort theoretical points.

Now it is important for everyone to wrestle candidly with his moral as well as his skill limitations. At the same time, one may doubt the justification of imposing the precautions of the morally immature upon the code of the scientific community as a whole.

Many of the most illuminating contributions to knowledge have been made with full awareness of the controversial character of the policy implications that would, in all probability, be drawn from the new insight. Furthermore, these contributions were made simultaneously to advance the state of the science and to clarify the available range of policy alternatives. Given a high level of professional competence and an open forum, scientific and lay, it was possible to carry on a serious scientific assessment at the same time that policy controversies were in full cry.

A famous instance was the theoretical innovation introduced by John Maynard Keynes a generation ago. Keynes stayed within the recognized rules of method in the building of a theoretical miniature of an economic system. Instead of continuing to account for the continuation of mass unemployment under private capitalism as the result of "frictions" interfering with the inherent capabilities of the system, he took the important step of changing the theoretical image. Keynes revised the model of the private economy to include a tendency, under stated conditions, to perpetuate rather than to overcome mass unemployment. He thereupon drew attention to a series of policies which, if adopted by the governmental sector of society, would bring about the restoration of full employment.

My recommendation is that colleagues in the social and psychological sciences shed whatever inhibitions they may have about taking the full range of value considerations into the reckoning as they plan and supervise scientific work. It should perhaps be said explicitly that in many circumstances the scientific vision will obliterate other matters from the mind of the practicing scientist. There are moments—and there may be years—in a career when the vision of new theoretical models or the fascination of perfecting a new instrument of observation or of completing the description of a hitherto neglected case may absorb every available quantum of energy.

But these moments are not necessarily protracted throughout the entire span of professional activity. Very often there is ample margin to concentrate upon the historical situation and to become sensitized to the trends making for or against continuing or more fully realizing one's preferred system of social values. Looking into the possible and probable lines of future development, it may be highly rational to anticipate emerging situations and, as a scientist, to conduct a program of inquiry that promises to illuminate the consequences of various alternatives of action that will eventually be open to individuals and to society.

Indeed, the scientists of society may come to feel a sense of responsibility for outlining and conducting a continuing appraisal of the changing relations of conventional and functional processes in the whole context of national and ultimately of global development. A comprehensive appraisal can provide essential information about the value outcomes, pre-outcomes and post-outcomes of any institutional practice. In this way a stream of knowledge may become available on the basis of which a higher level of disciplined rationality becomes possible for all who have access to this information.

Studying the Future:
The Idea of a Social Planetarium

I have been emphasizing the forward looking character of thought that has to do with policy. All choices refer to future events, whether the choice relates to the program of inquiry to be pursued by the scientist or the policies to be adopted by the nation on behalf of national goals.

Our traditional patterns of problem solving are flagrantly defective in presenting the future in ways that contribute insight and understanding. A bare enumeration of these limitations will give meaning to the task of improving social and individual practice in this area.

First of all, our approach to the future is *insufficiently contextual.* We are accustomed to extrapolate population trends or other special trends into the future. But there are relatively few occasions on which the flow of coming developments is seen in its wholeness.

Second, the methods by which the future is presented *do not foster vivid perceptions*. It is well known that a trained imagination is necessary before one can perceive with full vividness the significant events referred to in a table of figures, a map, or a chart. Our perceptions of current and past events are facilitated by the context provided by the concreteness of news stories, anecdotes, and personal observations. By contrast, the charts, graphs, and tables that refer to the future lack support. This is a problem especially for nonspecialists, since, if laymen are to grasp the meaning of a technical communication, they must rely upon equivalencies with common experience.

Third, presentations are often *lacking in transition*. Very often the potential future is described at a cross-section in time with no attempt to relate the cross-section to the state of affairs at present. This is especially common when rather "Utopian" proposals are put forward. Although the Utopian character of the recommended policy calls for particular attention to problems of strategy, problems of transition may be left out.

Fourth, *alternatives are disproportionately treated*. Even when scientists are asked to project population, production, investment, and centralization estimates, they often fail to give sufficient weight to important alternatives. Nothing is easier for intellectuals than to develop a "line"; the "line" includes a tacitly recognized range of permissible divergences of opinion. It is not unusual for postulates to gain support that have been subjected to very little criticism. Attention tends to be diverted from unorthodox assumptions. By default, therefore, alternatives receive disproportionate treatment.

I shall not carry the indictment further: the question is whether anything affirmative can be done about existing practice. What I propose can be quickly grasped by analogy to the planetarium, which was developed for the purpose of popularizing astronomical knowledge. I renew the suggestion of a social planetarium.

A principal advantage of the planetarium technique is contextuality. It can provide a total environment for an observer stationed anywhere on the earth or anywhere in the solar and galactic systems. The heavens move, and arrangements can be made for the observer himself to move. Such an experience brings scattered items into a whole pattern. Applied to the confused and uncertain publics and sub-publics of our time, the social planetarium can provide a shared experience of the past and potential future. It is probable that such unifying experiences can do much to restore sanity and consent where anxiety and withdrawal have begun to prevail.

The planetarium technique is especially well adapted to the fostering of vivid perceptions, since the subject is surrounded by a meaningful setting. The planetarium does not confine its appeal to the "reading response" of the target audience, or even to the "looking response." It is within the range of technical possibility to modify the setting in terms of barometric pressure, temperature, water vapor, olfactory, or other psychophysical characteristics.

The presentations are not only *in* time; they can pass *through* time. The observer can be conducted from where he is now to where he can go tomorrow—and the day after. By beginning where the audience is now, the time-phasing of the experience can carry everyone through a process of step-wise anticipation. Existing perceptual images can be challenged and modified in such a way that the novel future possibilities can be grasped. Participants are liberated from the perceptual caves of the present.

The planetarium technique makes it feasible to give proportionate weight to alternative versions of the future or the past. Suppose that professional economists are split into "Keynesian" and "anti-Keynesian" versions of how mass unemployment is generated and sustained. A series of rooms can be devoted to experiencing the past (and impending future) according to version A. Then a series of rooms can present version B. It is impossible to escape from some degree of selectivity; the problem is to guide attention selectively toward an image of relatively high—and low—consent among the most qualified thinkers in society at a given time.

The planetarium technique can be effectively employed as a means of strengthening every pattern of thought that enters into an act of decision. It is convenient to identify five such patterns:

Goals:	The clarification of values.
Trends:	The consideration of historical sequences in which developments have appeared, and have diffused or restricted.
Factors:	The scientific examination of theoretical and descriptive models of the social process.
Projections:	Hypotheses about the sequence of significant future occurrences.
Alternatives:	The policy alternatives to be invented, evaluated, selected, and applied.

Fundamental to all decision making and execution are the overriding value goals (the preferred outcomes) to be realized by policy. In a very approximate sense it is true that most people in the United States accept the ideals of our system of public order (life, liberty, and pursuit of happiness, or, more generally, the ideal of a free society in which values are widely, rather than narrowly, shared). But there are many differences among us in the interpretation of ideal declarations. Rational decisions are aided by a process in which it is clear what specific interpretations are adopted for working purposes. Here the explicitness of planetarium technique lends itself to the needs of policy judgment.

In connection with the goal values of public life it is not to be forgotten that vision fades from one generation to the next and from crisis to crisis. Statements of principle come to have a ritualistic role; they lose fertility as a means of furthering the growth of society. The setting of struggle and insight in which social ideals had their origin is lost to view.

The planetarium technique provides an opportunity for keeping ideals alive from one generation to the next. It becomes unnecessary to rely upon rhetoric alone when means are at hand to enable individuals to experience symbolic reproductions of historic occasions.

The extrapolation of the past obviously calls for knowledge and depiction of past trends. To extrapolate is to draw a curve into the future along the trajectory of recent trends. This technique is a useful aid to the discovery and timing of incompatible developments. It may be that two nations have been growing in the same direction; two business corporations may be expanding in the same market; two political doctrines may be winning the support of "neutral" communities. What happens when they come together?

If decision makers are to arrive at a critical assessment of the factors that account for the spreading or the restriction of nations, corporations, and doctrines, they need access to whatever scientific knowledge there is. Now it is no simple matter to apply past laboratory findings to the interpretation of future developments. In the laboratory, conditioning factors are controlled. In weighing the future, the task is to foresee the cluster of factors whose occurrence will influence the outcome. An advantage of the planetarium procedure is that scientific knowledge can be exhibited and employed critically in estimating the probable course of future developments.

It is a rational assumption that a vivid and contextual presentation of the future increases the likelihood that new policy alternatives will be invented; and that these alternatives will prove to be relatively efficient means of strengthening social values at optimal levels. At the same time, the gaps exhibited in our historical knowledge will influence the course of research on the past. The scientific community will undoubtedly become aware of gaps between theoretical models and situations; direction will be given to scientific work. And no doubt new instruments of investigation will be devised to meet new needs.

Suppose we indicate more concretely some applications of the social planetarium idea. Assume the theme is how regional planning can transform the New York area in the next several decades. We may move along a catwalk through a series of chambers where hypothetical changes can be viewed decade by decade. Alternative conceptions can be presented in adjoining chambers. Halls can be large enough to accommodate audiences that listen to broadcasts of critical commentary. Individual enclosures may permit an individual to sit comfortably and concentrate upon a film that deals in detail with one set of functional problems (such as the disposal of radioactive waste) or with one locality.

The exhibits will not accomplish their purpose if they do not clarify the connection between the visible changes in the physical aspect of the region and the social context as a whole. There must be a sense of "who does what with what effect"; or, to say the same thing another way, "who gets what values at what cost and how." The flow of human interaction in homes, schools, businesses, media of communication, government offices, hospitals and playgrounds, churches, and festivals must be described.

Some model environments may be very elaborate, such as anticipation of a colonizing expedition to the moon or to a planet within the solar system. Opportunities may be given to enter a deep-sea environment under suitable safeguards. In all these situations it will be necessary to make sure that the social scene is made intelligible to audiences of many levels of preparation. Ideally the presentations should be graduated to the interests of children, teenagers, young adults, middle adults, and the aged. Attention can also be given to functionally specialized audiences.

One of the most important functions in the decision process of a community is that of appraising the effectiveness of past community effort. The social planetarium can be employed to report such self-appraisals to the community. Private agencies of competence and prestige can take responsibility for appraising activities. (In the field of public health, for instance, the job can be especially well done.)

In principle, every community can build its own social planetarium where stress is put upon local objectives, local history, and local prospects. A significant feature of such presentations should be the articulation of smaller with larger contexts. New Haven needs to be seen as a component of New England, of the New York metropolitan region, of the Northeastern States, of the United States, of the Atlantic community, and so on, up to and including the globe as a whole. In this way the linkages of human affairs can be spelled out in ways that clarify the interconnectedness of life.

The social planetarium is a means of giving importance to institutions that in many places are struggling feebly for public recognition. I refer, for example, to art museums, museums of local history, and museums of natural history. The contextual frame of reference—the orientation toward the future and toward decision making—is a "shot in the arm." It makes the past pertinent to the present and the future.

In many circumstances, no doubt, it will be expedient to amalgamate the social planetarium with a program that encompasses all the museums and related cultural resources of the capital of the locality, city, region, nation, or the transnational areas involved. Great cultural centers and subcenters can be built according to a comprehensive plan. In Washington, D. C., the National Gallery of Art, the Smithsonian Institution (and certain other agencies) are major components of any general program of the kind we have in mind.

The social planetarium technique can be adapted to the task of instruction and research at every level. Consider its implications for education in the social sciences. All the decision institutions of society can be paralleled in special seminar rooms: the Supreme Court, the principal committees of the Congress, the White House, the Federal Commissions (equivalent agencies at local, State, and international levels), the national political party committees, the chief committees of the major pressure organizations, the management committees of the principal profit-making

corporations (including the mass media), the key committees of nonprofitmaking corporations (e.g., universities,
colleges, hospitals, churches).

Each seminar room (or sequence of rooms) can be
equipped with charts, maps, and other equipment designed
to present the past and future at specific cross-sections.
Instruction will consist in the critical evaluation (and
preparation) of this material. As gaps are discovered, new
scientific and historical problems suggest themselves.

Gradually society can be changed until people learn
to live as much in imagination of the future as in remi-
niscence of the past. In such a configurative setting—a setting that never comes to rest, though it never crumbles
into chaos—individual choices can be made at a respectable
level of rationality.

The future of the social planetarium idea depends upon
those who control it. In the beginning it is important for the
scientific community itself to take command and to make
use of the nonpartisan or multipartisan potentials of society. In this way the institution may make an optimum
contribution to the rational development of science and
policy.

The principal beneficiaries of such a program will be the
champions of human dignity. The champions of human
indignity do not need new strategies of inquiry or of action.
They have done well enough without them.

NOTES

[1] For further detail see H. D. Lasswell and A. Kaplan, *Power
and Society: A Framework for Political Inquiry* (New Haven;
Yale University Press, 1950). The social process is charac-

terized as "man" pursuing "values" through "institutions," using "resources." Eight value categories are used: power, wealth, respect, well-being, rectitude, skill, enlightenment, affection. These are roughly equivalent to the study of government, economics, social class, social biology, religion and morals, occupations and professions, education and public information, family. Any value may be a scope value for any value used as a base by a strategy of manipulation.

[2] See H. D. Lasswell, "The Political Science of Science: An Inquiry into the Possible Reconciliation of Mastery and Freedom," *American Political Science Review,* Vol. L, 1956, pp. 961-979.

SOCIAL INQUIRY AND THE AUTONOMY
OF THE INDIVIDUAL

Edward A. Shils

I

The humanistic contemplation of man has traditionally arisen out of observations gathered in the course of the daily business of life. Having its point of departure in living human beings, it sought no vantage point other than that of ordinary intercourse. Humanistic scholarship confined itself to the analysis of the lives and works of men and women no longer living. Both these modes of the study of man raised many ethical problems, such as the respect due to might and glory, the hierarchy of virtues, the reverence owed to traditional institutions and beliefs, and the value of originality and individuality. When the range and procedure of humanistic study were extended to cover what has come to be called social science, to these problems were added new ones.

Those angular and reluctant heirs of the traditional humanistic study of man, the present-day "humanities," have taken over only part of this inheritance, the inheritance of humanistic scholarship. They have dealt and still deal with the "objectivations" or expressions of the spirit, created in the past and even in the present and having an existence separate from their creators. In the main their materials have not come from living contemporaries, and even where they have, the product of the spirit has been sufficiently discrete from the person who created it that no direct contact with the author has been necessary. Even the study of living languages requires only a minimum of personal contact. The application of psychoanalytic and sociological ideas to the conventional humanistic subject matters has only raised again the older problems.

That branch of the study of man which inquires concretely into man's conduct in society and his actual beliefs, has increasingly tended, ever since its first modern stumblings, toward immediate contact with the sentiments and actions of living human beings. True, there are substantial parts of the study of man today to which this does not apply—for example, economic theory, much of sociological theory, the analysis of economic growth, large parts of comparative religion, and numerous others which use printed and written official documents, officially gathered statistics, published or unpublished, written records of organizations, legal and administrative documents, published books and periodicals, manuscripts, etc. The larger trend, however, has been toward the diminution of the proportion of effort devoted to the study of such sources. The study of man has shifted increasingly toward the assembly of data by direct, deliberate, and orderly observation and by interviewing, which enters in growing measure into spheres of sentiments and intimate personal relations which have traditionally been studied only by retrospection, reflection, and the analysis of discrete works with an objective existence of their own. It is not primarily the novelty of the subject matter that has brought about the change. Essays and maxims on friendship and love, biographies of the dead, editions of the personal correspondence and journals of persons whose life was over, historical reconstructions of the motives and intrigues of politicians and ecclesiastical dignitaries were by no means uncommon, but they were as far as traditional humanistic scholarship went in this sphere. The events studied were either definitely in the past or they were, if contemporaneous, usually studied at a distance from the principals, and above all from their private sphere.

Where, as in the United Kingdom, the direct approach of modern social science was developed in the study of living aborigines or of the lower social and economic classes of one's own society, serious issues did not arise. In the first place, these inquiries did not enter very deeply into the private sphere of their subjects; they confined themselves largely to external economic matters and to publicly observable actions. There was a restraint on curiosity, deriving from the puritanical ethos of the culture from whence the investigators came. There was, furthermore, no obvious problem in intruding on the privacy of savages or workingmen, particularly those at or near the poverty level, because, at bottom, the investigators did not feel that they shared membership in a common moral community with the persons investigated. They possessed no secrets which were sacred to the investigators; they possessed no secrets whose penetration could be expected to arouse discomfiture among the investigators or the circles in which they moved. The situation was little different in the United States. The first large-scale inquiries based on interviewing dealt with slum dwellers, Negroes, immigrants, juveniles on the margin of delinquency, persons with dubious moral standards, *et al.*—people regarded as not possessing the sensibilities which demand privacy or the moral dignity which requires its respect. Moreover, the investigators were inhibited in their curiosity by the wider culture and by the traditions of their discipline.

The shift to the study of the "respectable" classes came later and in a different atmosphere. Hence, the tradition of direct confrontation of the subject through interviewing became firmly established before there seemed to be any moral problem. This new tradition was, moreover, encouraged by the belief, sometimes held by the investigators or those who conceived, supported, and guided the research, that the results would be applied in the improvement of the welfare of the class of persons being studied. The chief problem of this technique of research therefore appeared to be the overcoming of "resistance" to being interviewed, i.e., resistance to the disclosure of private matter.

Nonetheless, the creation of techniques for the direct observation of living persons and contemporary institutions, the deepening of intellectual curiosity about the motives and the very tissue of social life, the diminution of inhibitions on intrusiveness into other persons' affairs, and the concomitant formation of techniques for perceiving these deeper and subtler things have precipitated problems of ponderable ethical significance. The ethical values affected by contemporary social research are vague and difficult to formulate precisely. They refer mainly to human dignity, the autonomy of individual judgment and action, and the maintenance of privacy. (To a lesser extent and in a different aspect, they involve the sacredness and majesty of authority and the security of the state and community from external enemies.)

The value of privacy is derived from our belief in the sacredness of individuality.

The sacredness of individuality in the conventional religious sense is based on the belief that men are a special category of God's creatures, having in them a breath of divinity or being capable of absorbing into themselves and of being absorbed into divinity. The so-called secular view omits the element designated as divinity, but retains nearly everything else. It is the sentient, mindful human being whose experiences are not just transient events in time and space but are elements gathered up in memory and transformed by the powers of the mind into a coherent, judging, choosing, discriminating, self-regulating entity, conscious of its selfhood. In its individuality, the human organism develops an ego, a complex bounded system into which the past is assimilated, the future envisaged and sought, and the present made the object of discriminating decisions in which are contained assimilated precipitates of past experience and judgments and choices about the future. Individuality is not, however, just a cognitive system or a system of cathectic (loving and worshiping) orientations. It is constituted by the feeling of being alive, consciously and continuously, by the existence of responsiveness which is part of a highly integrated system. Every response of individuality bears the mark of the uniqueness of the system, which is self-creating and self-sustaining. Individuality is a system with its own rules of directions and rest. This mindful, self-regulating core of the life of a human organism is what is sacred, and it is that which constitutes its individuality. It is this that makes man into a moral entity capable of entering into relationships of personal love and affection, capable of becoming wise, capable of assuming responsibility for his actions and acting on behalf of a civil community.

It is the possession of individuality that renders a human being capable of transcending his individualism in love and friendship and in responsible membership in a civil community. He can, however, transcend his boundaries if he possess and retain them; the transcendence must be discriminating and guided by standards and sensitivities which are integral to the individual. Obviously, there are limitations to the self-regulatory power: the organism within which individuality has its seat brings determinants, and the dispositions and capacities developed in interaction with the early social, primarily familial, environment likewise create a framework which it is not easy to leave behind. Moreover, the weight of cultural tradition, the needs of cooperative undertaking, and the maintenance of social order on a wider scale impose restrictions on the self-regulatory powers of individuality. But they never extinguish it, and the stronger, the richer, and the more elaborate the individuality, the more it can assert its self-regulatory powers. Individuality requires actual autonomy, not only the freedom of action, freedom in the outward movement of the individual, but also immunity from intrusion into areas where the center of selfhood resides. There must be both freedom to move outward and autonomy *vis-à-vis* intrusions or efforts to influence the inner sphere. The sphere of privacy is built up from memories and intentions, by standards, tastes, and preferences, which are constitutive of self-consciousness and which an individual would share only with an intimate, and voluntarily, if he were to share them at all. He might not be in a position to share these elements of his self because he is insufficiently aware of them, even though they are of constitutive significance for the structure of his self-consciousness. But whether he is aware of them or not, their disclosure must be entirely voluntary and deliberate; otherwise his autonomy is infringed upon. Disclosure of the content of the inner realm of individuality should be based on some knowledge of why the disclosure is elicited and a reasonable assent to the reasons for eliciting them.

Modern liberal society is the parent of individuality. It could not develop in a society in which there is no freedom to explore, to experience, and to judge, and in which the individual need not bear some of the responsibility for the consequences of his judgment. The emergence of individuality and the attendant demand for freedom are accompanied, however, by sensitivity and openness to the individuality of others. From this arises one of the problems which modern social research techniques do not create but only complicate.

The individuality of other human beings arouses curiosity; it arouses the desire to be in some sort of contact— whether it be entirely cognitive or cathectic can be left aside at this point. It generates a demand for intrusion into privacy far more powerful than the trivial gossip at a distance which is characteristic of less sensitive phases of human development.

The respect for privacy has taken its place in the constellation of values of modern liberalism. It is, however, a relatively recent addition. It rested for a long time among the undrawn implications of the liberal position and came to the forefront only with the growth of individuality and its appreciation, and the development of a more widespread personal sensitivity. However lately arrived on the scene, it is now fully incorporated. Like the other values of modern liberalism, it is subject to the affinities and the antimonies of every elaborate *Weltanschauung*.

The respect for privacy rests on the appreciation of human dignity, with its high evaluation of individual self-determination, free from the bonds of prejudice, passion, and superstition. In this, the respect for human dignity and individuality shares an historical comradeship with the freedom of scientific inquiry, which is equally precious to modern liberalism. The tension between these values, so essential to each other in so many profoundly important ways, is one of the antimonies of modern liberalism. The ethical problems with which we are dealing here arise from the confrontation of autonomy and privacy by a free intellectual curiosity, enriched by a modern awareness of the depth and complexity of the forces that work in us and implemented by the devices of a passionate effort to transform this awareness into scientific knowledge.

This essay is an effort to explore and to make explicit some of the problems which arise from this confrontation. It does not claim to be more than a first approximation, with respect to both the issues raised and the standards by which they should be treated. It tries to indicate, in a tentative way, some of the general standards which should enter into the sociological and psychological investigator's response to these problems, rather than to promulgate specific rules. Where principles are in conflict, only the exercise of reasonable judgment, following reflective consideration of the issues, is in order. Moralistic rigorism would be injurious to the crucial values of liberalism and above all to our self-understanding and our self-control. Callow scientism would be even more pernicious.

II

In contemporary sociology and social psychology and in those branches of social inquiry influenced by these two disciplines, it is generally thought desirable that our knowledge of human thought and action should rest primarily on information gathered by looking at and listening to living human beings in the immediate presence of the investigator.

These procedures are called interviewing and observation; the latter includes both "participant" and manipulative (experimental) observations as well as the more conventional type of detached observation. Interviewing consists in eliciting information about the self, about past activities which occur outside the interviewer's range of observation, and about other persons with whom the interviewed person has been in contact.

Interviewing seems, at first glance, to be, ethically, the least problematic of social science techniques. It seems to leave the subject's autonomy intact, and although it does enter into his private sphere without the legitimation of intimacy, it does so only with his consent. It is impossible to interview a person without his consent and willing co-operation. By meeting this requirement of autonomous action, one of the major ethical obstacles to social research is apparently overcome. Manipulation of an adult person denies his autonomy by deceiving him, i.e., by depriving him of his power of reasonable decision, and by directing his action toward an end alien to his own consciousness; it is therefore ethically reprehensible. Consequently, an interviewer who requests the prospective interviewee's permission to conduct an interview, giving in the course of the request some explanation of the intent and nature of the inquiry, therewith avoids manipulation and the moral onus associated with it.

Immediately one begins to scrutinize this proposition, it loses its simplicity and becomes more difficult to accept at face value. What is an "explanation of the intent and nature of the inquiry"? Is a perfunctory explanation which is enough to get the interviewer's foot in the door, adequate? Is a general explanation which truthfully covers the early part of the interview sufficient, if the latter part of the interview, once good rapport has been established, moves far beyond the original assertion of aims? Can explanation be omitted as long as assent is obtained on other grounds?

Sociological investigators certainly do not always inform their interviewees of the true intention of their inquiries. Some deliberately falsify their roles as sociological investigators and tell less than the whole truth or something quite other than the truth in order to avoid arousing resistance to the disclosure of the information sought. In interviewing on controversial questions, some interviewers simulate agreement with the expected attitudes of the interviewees; others falsify the intentions of their research, claiming, for example, to be working on housing needs while actually seeking to observe family life or leisure activities. The simulation of "warmth" is widely recommended in manuals of research techniques, and it is probably also widely practiced.[1] These practices are often inexpedient from the point of view of gaining the cordial cooperation of the interviewee, particularly at later stages of the inquiry when further cooperation is required. Sometimes their spurious explanations or misleading identifications embarrass the research worker and even impede the further progress of the inquiry. They are also occasionally damaging to the dignity and the public regard of social research, as well as being morally offensive by their mendacity and their pettiness. Yet their very triviality is their salvation; most of these misrepresentations are really peccadillos. They seldom harm the interviewee, who is often pleased with the experience of being interviewed. Nonetheless, quite apart from these latter considerations, which are entirely secondary, all this is improper, in principle, because it elicits information by deception.

Social scientists, whose disinterested quest for knowledge certainly must be acknowledged, may claim the privilege of *permitted* entry into the private sphere. Privacy, like free-dom, can be restricted for good reasons, but it is essential in our outlook that the diminution should be voluntary and retractable. Just as a free man has not the right to sell himself into slavery or to establish an irremovable dictator-ship, so the *particular* privacy which an individual sus-pends by making *particular* disclosures to another (in this case, the interviewer) must be reinstated by the treatment which the disclosed private information receives. The *particular* confidences must be respected; they must not be transmitted in their *particular* form to anyone else; they may be introduced into the public sphere only by gen-eralization and anonymity.[2] This protection is provided when there is no disclosure of its *particular* private contents to anyone else, i.e., as long as personal identities are com-pletely and securely obliterated. In the main, this is the usual practice of sociological investigators.[3] A few in-vestigators actually go so far in their respect for the privacy of their interviewees that they submit a draft of their research report to the persons on whose confidences they have drawn. This enables them to ascertain whether they have disclosed anything which their interviewees on subsequent thought have decided they would like to with-draw or would, at least, like to see withheld from further diffusion.[4]

The mere existence of consent does not exempt the social scientist from the moral obligations of respect for another's privacy. Nor does the fact that priests, lawyers, and physicians and psychiatrists receive the confidences of other persons automatically resolve the issue for the social scientist. The priest receives confidences as part of a scheme of cosmic salvation to which the confessing person is committed; the lawyer receives them because the con-fiding person needs his aid in coping with an adversary under the law; the physician and the psychoanalyst receive them because they offer the prospect of a cure to troubles of body and mind. The social scientist has, according to the traditions of our intellectual and moral life, nothing comparable to offer. To intrude into privacy solely for the sake of a contribution to the general understanding of man's nature and society's is unprecedented in history.[5] The conflict between an aspiration to contribute to knowledge and some sacred attachment is not new in history; what is new here is the kind of knowledge sought and the mode of its acquisition, and the particular sacred value with which it comes into conflict. The tension of the present conflict is aggravated by the quality of the claim to enhance our stock of understanding; it is a claim which must be put forward with great circumspection; especially in the present situation, it is no justification for the infringement of an important right of the individual.

The moral problem is somewhat lightened by virtue of the statisfaction that being interviewed gives to many persons. Unburdening oneself, especially to a stranger, often gives considerable psychological satisfaction. Then, too, among the neglected and the forgotten of our great societies, an interview is a cornucopia of attention and conviviality. All of these points make the intrusion into the privacy of interviewees more supportable, but they do not eliminate the problems it engenders. We would not be justified in interfering with a person's right to choose his friends or his occupation just because he has pronounced feelings of dependency, and our disapproval of prostitution does not depend on whether the prostitute finds it unpleasant; no more are we justified in forgetting that privacy is a right conjoint with freedom and that its voluntary suspension, although it presumably promotes social science, does so through a morally opaque occasion.

It is essential that the research worker recognize that he himself and the person he is studying both live in an identical moral realm. But why should the interviewer treat the interviewee as within his own realm? Are not the observance of the usual decencies of courtesy, such as attentiveness, and the expression of gratitude for cooperation, sufficient? I do not think so, and my doubts are connected with a fundamental position regarding the function of social science.

Social science is a science about human objects. The effort to make our knowledge of human beings scientific imposes discipline, detachment, and orderliness of procedure and the effort to formulate that knowledge in coherent and explicit propositions. It cannot, however, transform the nature of the subject matter, which must always remain human beings to whom the interviewer has moral obligations. In eliciting information from an interviewee, and even prior to that, the interviewer has the obligation to respect the interviewee's autonomy. Deception is contrary to this obligation.[6]

Moreover, the knowledge gained by social research, if it is to find application in a democratic society, must have the function of self-clarification, of increasing self-awareness. In other words, if it has any use, it is used by being shared by those "on" whom it is "used." Now, although it might well be questioned whether it is desirable for an individual to be as clear about his motives as a psychologist or sociologist could make him, or for an institution to understand itself "completely," there can be no doubt that if social-scientific knowledge is to be "used" in a liberal democracy, it must be "used" through being shared, by the formation of rational opinion in the wider public.

What is true of the consumption of social-scientific knowledge is true also of its production. The sharing of the interviewee's knowledge with the interviewer entails the sharing of obligations that comes from common membership in society, which in its turn is incompatible with the manipulation of the interviewee by the interviewer with superior knowledge. This is why the indispensable detachment of the social research worker from his subject matter must be combined with membership in the same moral realm with the subject matter. For this reason, the interviewer is obliged to explain to his interviewee not only his own personal goal, e.g., to complete a thesis, but also the cognitive intention. Questions ought to be justified by the explanation of what the answers will contribute to the clarification of the problem being investigated. Naturally, it is not necessary that each particular question should be so explained, but groups or types of questions asked in an interview should be explained in this way. I appreciate the difficulties that stand in the way of observance of this standard, and in many cases the interviewee himself will not care to have the explanation. Often the interviewee would not be able to understand the intentions of an elaborate piece of research, and furthermore, the limited time which the interviewee is willing to grant might be excessively consumed by the explanation. The standard is nonetheless valid and should be adhered to at least as a guiding principle if not as a specific stipulation.

III

Not all interviewing approaches the interviewee simply as an informant about his own experiences and the experiences of others with whom he has been in contact. This complicates the situation. Much interviewing is intended to lead to observation. It is often an attempt to manipulate the subject into "revealing" aspects of himself which he does not knowingly articulate. Questions are often asked not because of the genuine interest of the investigator in the manifest content of the answer but because of his interest in the overtones of the answer, in the disclosures of experience, sentiment, and mood which occur inadvertently and in which the interviewer has not initially avowed an interest. The interviewee is manipulated into disclosing aspects of himself that have not been openly solicited. This is an important feature of projective tests, which are manipulative interviews that seek to elicit manifestations of dispositions and sentiments of which the interviewee is presumably unaware. In responding to the test, he produces responses, of the content of which he must be ignorant, not only because he has not perceived them in his own thought and conduct or because he lacks the technical knowledge adequate to their interpretation but also because their assessment is done outside his presence. Projective tests almost by their nature must go beyond the informed assent of the person tested, and they go moreover into areas generally conceded to be private. Indeed, if they did not aspire to penetrate beyond the willingness of the interviewee to disclose himself, there would be no justification for them.

The same applies to the participant-observer technique which was once highly esteemed and still has many practitioners in sociological research. It seems to me to be susceptible to considerable ethical abuse. It is wrong for an inquirer ostensibly to take up membership in a community with the intention of conducting a sociological inquiry there without making it plain that that is what he is doing. His self-disclosure might occasionally hamper research he is conducting, but the degree of injury suffered does not justify the deviation from straightforwardness implied by withholding his true intentions. (Furthermore, since sociologists, like most other people, have a certain strength of moral scruple, their subsequent interviewing and observation in the group or community are likely to benefit from having an easy conscience.)

There is, in principle, nothing objectionable about much of the observation of the conduct of other persons. Life in any case is unimaginable without it; it is inevitable as long as human beings live together. It is, moreover, the source of reflective wisdom, and those who do not practice it at all abstain only because they are morally or intellectually defective. The observation which is part of the normal course of life, however, usually is not sought on false pretenses. It is integral to the process of interaction, and when it is focused on actions in which the observer has no immediate part, it is directed to actions which the persons observed perform in the pursuit of their own ends. The observations of everyday life are conducted in relationships which have arisen out of intentions other than observation. The observer has not created the relationship merely for the purpose of observing the other person; to the extent that he has done so he is guilty of manipulation, which, however frequent, nevertheless remains morally obnoxious; nor does it lose its obnoxiousness by virtue of its triviality or harmlessness.

Observation which has within it a large element of manipulation—and this is also common to certain kinds of interviewing and participant—observation and to most projective tests—seem to me to be morally questionable on two grounds. First, on acount of the wrongfulness of manipulation itself, and second, on account of the private nature of the subject matter of the disclosures which the manipulating interviewer tries to precipitate. It is an effort to intrude, without a person's consent or his knowing cooperation, into the reserved sphere of his individuality.

IV

Observation which takes place in public or in settings in which the participants conventionally or knowingly accept the responsibility for the public character of their actions and expressions, for example in a parliamentary chamber or in a university seminar or in a public meeting or in a restaurant, a bar, or a café or on the street, is different from observation which seeks to enter the private sphere unknown to the actor. The person who takes on himself the responsibilities of public life has to some extent made a large part of his action public property, although in the case of the mixed public-private situation, e.g., the restaurant, the moral right of privacy should limit the freedom of observation.[7]

The open sphere—the sphere in which the individual by his career has committed himself to publicity—is a legitimate object of observation, as it is of interviewing. The right to observe and to interview in this sphere is justified by the postulate of each individual's responsibility for the actions he undertakes in public places and in public roles. What of the conduct the participants believe to be private to themselves, and would even like to keep secret? The answer depends on whether the action is properly in the public domain. Even though he tries to keep it private or secret, the politician who takes bribes as well as the one who does not, and the administrator who favors a kinsman as well as the one who does not, cannot rightfully claim that his privacy is invaded if a newspaper reporter or a university research worker observes his professional actions or obtains the relevant information by interviewing him or another person about them. On the other hand, the quiet conversation of two friends in a restaurant or bar, the spontaneous intercourse of a family within its own home, the confidential discussion of a governmental committee, or the deliberations of a jury are for a variety of reasons not equally in the open sphere, or in the open sphere at all. In each of these, important events occur which are certainly relevant subject matter for the analyses of the sociologist and the social psychologist. Yet are they justified in entering this sphere through observation?

The propriety of their entry rests in part on the extent to which they do so with the knowing approval of the persons observed. If the social scientists observed what occurred in the relationship but did so with the knowledge and permission of the participants, then the intrusion into privacy can be justified by the assent of the observed. Privacy and even secrecy are positive rights, but the obligation to respect them may properly be suspended by the deliberate decision of the participants whose privacy is in question.[8] Moreover, as long as the knowledge was sought solely for the sake of increasing our general intellectual understanding of human conduct, the moral objection is held within bounds. Likewise, if it is impelled by considerations of public good (and not public curiosity).

But, although there might be some uncertainty regarding the propriety of entering, by permission, into the private sphere, there seems to me to be no doubt at all about the impropriety of unauthorized entry when the persons are observed in situations which they legitimately regard as private to themselves, as persons or as a corporate body. The development of new mechanical devices for observation, such as small soundless motion picture cameras, small, unnoticeable microphones, and other undiscernible sound-recording equipment, has precipitated a very urgent issue, and one on which social scientists should take an unequivocal position. They cannot, on any grounds, approve observations of private behavior, however technically feasible, without the explicit and fully informed permission of the persons to be observed. Such an intrusion into privacy could be justified only as an emergency measure necessary for the maintenance of public order, or the protection of the society as a whole, if it might otherwise be severely threatened.[9] The growth of sociological and psychological knowledge scarcely falls into this class of emergencies, because the real and immediate benefits which it can bring are so small and problematic.

Although the jailing of convicted offenders is justified by the necessities of social order, even the highest scientific curiosity would provide no justification for imprisonment of anyone. *Mutatis mutandis*, the same principle applies to the invasion of the private sphere of the individual or of groups. It is true that in the case of the successfully surreptitious invasion of privacy, no physical harm is done, and none might ever be done, and if the persons observed remain permanently ignorant of the process of observation, they are not even, in fact, embarrassed or inconvenienced. (I assume here that the investigators do not use the data thus gathered in a way which brings subsequent publicity to the particular individuals in question.) Nonetheless, quite apart from consequences, it is a contravention of our moral standards.

In the latter part of 1955, a furor arose in the United States over the installation, by sociological investigators, of microphones in a jury room in Wichita, Kansas. The jurors were not informed of the existence of the microphone or the recording apparatus. It was done with the permission of the trial judge and the lawyers of both litigants. The tape on which the record was made was kept away from any situation in which the individual jurors could be identified by any parties involved in the litigation, their associates, or journalists, and in the typewritten transcript their names were changed so that no particular attributions could be made for any assertions made during the proceedings of the jury. The social scientists involved disclosed nothing of the recorded proceedings to anyone on their own initiative, except to members of the team of investigators. The only breach in complete secrecy in custody of the recording and transcription was committed at the request of the bench.

There are several issues involved here. The first is the deception of the individual members of the jury; the second is the infringement on the confidentiality of collective deliberations which are part of the machinery of adjudication; the third is the appropriateness of the scrutiny of major institutions by social scientists.

The first question is, in principle, quite simple. The concealment of microphones that would record discussions that jurors had good reason to believe were not being recorded is contrary to honest dealing, and even if the judge and the two lawyers had a crucial responsibility, the social scientists are not thereby exempted from their share of the blame. It must, however, be pointed out that the subject matter of the deliberations was not in the *personally* private sphere of the jurors. Nonetheless, their proceedings were undertaken with the understanding that, although performing *public* functions, they were performing them with the guarantee of *confidentiality*,[10] like those with which private personal relations are conducted. It was therefore an invasion of the fiduciary sphere in the same way that newspapermen invade it when they interview jurors or when they attempt to get government officials and legislators to say what went on in confidential or secret meetings. It differs from the observation of occurrences within a family or between lovers, if their permission to observe them had not been obtained in advance (which are clearly intrusions on privacy), only with respect to the fact that the jury system, like Cabinet meetings, is a matter of genuine public interest and not merely one of titillating public curiosity.

There are other reasons to be considered for denying the permissibility of such action, even if the jurors had agreed in advance to the observation and recording of their deliberations. The confidential or secret character of jury proceedings is traditionally justified by (1) the desirability of completely free discussion as a means of reaching a collective decision; (2) the necessity of avoiding pressure on jurors by nonjurors, which might occur if the course of deliberations were to become known by nonjurors, e.g., litigants, their lawyers, friends and kinsmen of the litigants. The confidentiality of the jurors' deliberations is not the same as the confidentiality of personal private affairs, and the argument for maintaining it must therefore be different. The invasion is an infringement on a convention which, it is claimed, sustains an important public institution. But no harm would be done to the effectiveness of the jury process, firstly, if the record, once taken without the knowledge and permission of the jurors, remained sealed up under the strictest custody of the trial judge until after any period during which appeals could be made had elapsed, and if the control and custody of the record and the transcript were sufficiently rigorous to protect the jurors from pressures or reprisals from persons who might have suffered from their judgments, and secondly, if members of subsequent juries, knowing that their deliberations could be recorded, were given absolute assurance by the judge either that no improper use whatsoever would ever be made of the record, or that no record whatsoever was being made.

Nonetheless, although the public order might not be

damaged if observations of this sort were made with these safeguards, they would still possess an element of impropriety because they involved subjecting the jurors to deception.

If the jurors had been informed of the arrangements for recording their deliberation and of the secure provision for preventing any breach in confidentiality, and they had agreed to the arrangement, then it would seem to have been permissible.[11] Unfortunately, however, there is no absolute security of such provision. There would be a risk that one or more of the jurors, as jurors sometimes do about the proceedings themselves, would talk to an outsider about the recording, and this might be exploited by one of the lawyers in seeking a reversal of the decision; but as jurors cannot be called as witnesses about deliberations in hearings on appeals from decisions by lower courts, so the records of their discussions could likewise be given the same immunity.

The case of the recorded deliberations of the Wichita juries raises questions not only about the permissibility of deception in social research and the right of privacy in private and public roles but also about the susceptibility of sacred institutions to detached inquiry.

V

The public discussion of the recorded jurors' deliberations in the United States devoted little attention to the problems involved in the invasion of the jurors' privacy and not much more to the possible influence of the recording or the research on the effectiveness of the jury system. The response was largely an emotional and unreflective denunciation of the sociological and legal investigators who had had the effrontery to "tamper" with the jury system. Quite apart from the political motives of the congressional

committee which conducted the hearings and of the officials of the Department of Justice, there was a widespread
feeling of abhorrence for the very notion of a detached
scrutiny of the interior of a "sacred" institution. The abhorrence, although "irrational," is not on that account to
be contemned out of hand.

The nominally secular modern state has no avowedly
"sacred" sphere, and the churches no longer have the
power to prevent anyone outside their jurisdiction from
turning an empirically analytical eye onto their sacred
objects and actions. Nonetheless, there is a sacred area even
of secular societies. The detached and realistic observation
of the actual working of certain institutions arouses feelings
approaching horror and terror in some persons, just as it
exercises the fascination of sacrilege on others. For the
secular state, what goes on in these institutions is sacred,
and no social scientist would be unqualifiedly free to disclose, even if he were to know as a participant, what goes
on in spheres designated as "secret." Those who possess
secret information are not privileged to disclose it in interviews, and the attempts to learn of it without permission
are strictly prohibited under severe penalties, even if the
intention is politically innocent and scientifically reasonable.[12]

It would be misleading to account for this horror of
penetration into the secrets of vital institutions solely to
expediential considerations, such as national security or
the protection from skullduggery or the efficiency and effectiveness of the institutions in question. The secular state
does not confine its exclusiveness solely to matters which
are characterized as necessary for national military security.
The meetings of Cabinets, the President's meetings with his
advisers, the deliberations of the Supreme Court, the
caucuses of party leaders have been closed to scientific in-

quirers, just as they have been closed to journalists; the reason is not entirely that public knowledge of them would harm the state or subvert public order or diminish the prestige or effectiveness of politicians and administrators, but that persons who wield great power feel a deep urge to keep their deliberations from external knowledge.[13] "Official secrets" guard not only knowledge and intentions which ought to be kept from foreign enemies but internally "sacred" things as well.

Even where the society is as populistic as it is in the United States, where the journalists are so inquisitive and where politicians enjoy and are inured to the bright light of publicity, social investigators are denied entry into such spheres. In fact, social scientists usually do not even seek such entry, partly because they believe it would be denied them, and partly, I believe, because they themselves stand in such—seldom acknowledged—awe of the majesty of the powerful, of the sacredness of power, that although their minds are attracted by it, they do not seek direct contact.[14]

Good arguments can be made against continuous publicity about public institutions. It could be claimed that extreme publicity not only breaks the confidentiality which enhances the imaginativeness and reflectiveness necessary for the effective working of institutions but also destroys the respect in which they should, at least tentatively, be held by the citizenry. The former consideration is purely empirical and has a reasonable probability of being right. It stands in contradiction to the liberal-democratic and particularly to the populistic-democratic principles of "the eyes of the public" constituting the "virtue of the statesman." It restricts the freedom of social scientists. The second consideration is genuinely conservative, as it implies that authority must have some aura of the ineffable about it to be effective. It contradicts a postulate of liberalism and of the social science which is a part of liberalism and which has on the whole proceeded on the postulate of unlimited publicity and an easy-going irreverence toward authority.

I think that this latter, more conservative consideration is by no means entirely groundless. But, nonetheless, it should not be carried very far. For one thing, social science, even where it seeks a wide public diffusion of its results, seldom attains it. Most social research reports are works of very restricted circulation.[15] Although it might, under certain conditions, not be desirable that the understanding of man's nature and of the nature of authority, which is forwarded by social science, should be more widely appreciated and shared, that does not happen often enough or intensively enough to endanger any institution or the social system as a whole. Reasonable conservatives have little to fear from the allegedly "disintegrative" consequences of social research, because it cannot affect the views of great numbers of persons. On the more fundamental issue, although I agree that there must be some feeling of the inherent rightfulness of the principles of justice and authority embodied even in a liberal democratic order, I think that the most rigorously scientific social research (assuming that those performing it are not actually seeking fundamentally to discredit the order they are studying) cannot endanger that order. I do not think that all social order rests on cognitive illusions which the results of scientific social research must dissolve.

I myself see no good reason, therefore, other than expediency, why these "sacred" secular subjects should not be studied by social scientists or why they should not be studied by legitimate research techniques. I can see no harm that can come from such inquiries, carried on with judicious detachment and presented with discretion. I can see no moral issue here, such as I can see in the case of manipulation by interviewers and observers or in the case of intrusions on privacy.[16]

VI

As the methods of observation of man's action in society became better controlled and more nearly precise, and the effort to discern correlations in a more nearly exact form emerged, the logic of intellectual development dictated the desirability of experimental studies. The experimental investigation of man as a moral and social being has an old history. It began on a large scale with experimental psychology in Germany in the second half of the nineteenth century. The prototype of the experiment on human action is still the psychological experiment carried out with controlled stimuli, divorced from the world of real experience. The introduction of experimentation into the study of social relations had adhered quite closely to its point of origin. As a result of this background and because of their greater practicability, sociological and social-psychological experimentation has been confined largely to the study of small groups in face-to-face relationships.

There has thus far been very little experimentation with larger collectivities. Social scientists have served as administrative officials or advisers to administrative officials concerned with the organization of communities such as displaced persons camps, prisoner-of-war camps, rehabilitation centers, prisons, settlements of unemployed workers, and impoverished farmers, etc. In these instances, however, experiments of a genuinely scientific nature have seldom been carried out; the social scientists engaged in these activities have been counselors speaking in the light of their general understanding of the situation and not as scientific experimenters. Their scientific procedures have usually not been brought into play. It is rather a precipitate of their scientific knowledge which enters into their judgment and their consequent counsel or decision. Their advice and judgments in these situations are usually formulated with an administrative end in view; the concern of the social scientist in administration has been, like that of all administrators, to achieve or maintain a given condition of order and a certain level of individual satisfaction rather than the enhancement of knowledge as such. In what is called action anthropology, the aim of the anthropologist has been the achievement of certain social conditions in the attainment of which anthropological understanding would be employed. The aim has not been the enhancement of knowledge through controlled manipulative experiments, but rather the utilization of generalized, previously attained, knowledge in conjunction with the power to achieve a practical end.

Such experiments as have been carried on in these circumstances are usually part of the ongoing administrative process. They take a form in which a new measure which is being considered for comprehensive application is tried first in one area, while the previously used measures are retained in another area. These "experiments," insofar as they are conducted by legitimate governments and do not contravene properly enacted laws or general moral standards, are like any other administrative actions carried out in pursuit of the purposes of a legally constituted government. The administrator's authority to command comes from his role as a civil servant charged with particular practical responsibilities.

Sociological or social-psychological experiments of a purely scientific kind cannot lay claim to this same authority. There is nothing in the nature of social science knowledge or in the moral status of the social scientist, or in the tangibility of the benefits which his research can provide, that confers the authority to command or to manipulate.

Most of the experimental work in the social sciences which is aimed at the increase of knowledge does not raise acute moral issues. In the first place, the groups on which experiments are carried on are small. The situations are very often no more than quasi-real at best. They are contrived by the experimenter; they are seldom recurrent, and they are usually of brief duration, falling mainly between a half-hour and two hours. The stimuli or the variables in the situation are rarely of great significance to the experimental subjects and, as far as is known—it has never been followed up—leave no lasting impression on the personality or outlook of the subject. Since, furthermore, the groups which are the objects of the experiment usually have had no anterior life of their own, they disappear from memory with the end of the experiment.

No case comes to mind of an experiment having been conducted on a subject who has not been informed and whose permission has not been obtained for the performance of the experiment. Naturally, the full account of the experiment is not always given, in part because the subject does not seek it and in further and more important part because it does not seem necessary to the experimenter and because occasionally an element of unself-consciousness is thought necessary to the success of the experiment.

There are ethical issues arising from experimentation: (1) the propriety of the manipulation of adult, normal human beings, even for their own good, by other human beings; (2) the propriety of possible injury to a human being on behalf of scientific progress and the progress of human well-being; (3) the depth and permanence of the effects of the experiment on the individual subject.

Experimentation often involves manipulation, although it need not always do so. Manipulative experimentation involves the exercise of influence for an end which is not fully shared between experimenter and the experimental subject. Such experimentation is not a relation between equals; it is a relationship in which power is exercised, at best within a framework of consent and mutual good will.

Now authority is exercised throughout society, and most of us regard it as reasonable to accept within its proper limits. It is exercised by legislators, physicians, priests, teachers, and civil servants. In all these relationships, the end striven for by the person exercising authority is not perceived as clearly or shared equally by the person over whom it is exercised. That is in the nature of authority, and its inevitability renders it acceptable, even though it should be recognized that it often falls very far short of the highest ethical standards of liberal individualism. But apart from its inevitability, we regard it as proper by virtue of the common commitment to membership in the civil community. Even within this commitment, however, which is by no means entirely voluntary, there are limitations. When the exercise of civil authority shades off into manipulation, i.e., when the ends of the instigated action become more and more opaque to the person over whom it is exercised, and the opacity is a deliberate creation of the ruler, the bonds of obligation loosen. The authority of the experimenter has none of the claims of the civil authority; it is more like a contractual relationship, with the limitation on the right to contract away one's will or dignity or to serve unforeseen purposes of the experimenter. The less the experimental subject appreciates or desires the ends sought by the experimenter and the less intelligible to him are the means used for eliciting his obedience, the more problematic it becomes ethically. As consensus becomes attenuated, manipulation increases. This is the kind of power exercised in the operation of a sociological experiment.

The subject of an experiment will practically never know as much about the experiment and its meaning as the designer of the experiment, and if he did, it might prejudice the desired outcome. The problem that remains, therefore, given this irreducible trace of the ethically problematic in social and psychological experimentation, is whether it is kept down to a minimum in its pernicious effects. Here, on the whole, I think the record of social science experimentation is quite unblemished. Its purity, however, can be partly associated with its scientific inconsequentiality. If it studied more important variables which touch more deeply and lastingly on the life, conduct, and outlook of the subjects, it might perhaps have acquired more scientific substance, but it would have done so at a much greater ethical risk.

Recently, a group of Cornell University anthropologists came into control over a Peruvian *hacienda* of two thousand persons on whom they are using their authority to institute large-scale and long-range changes. They are undertaking to rule the lives of men and women without the legitimacy that any government, even a tyranny, possesses, but with the legitimacy of a large landowner. If we assume that they introduce no measures except what they think beneficial for their subjects, then they are a benevolent despotism. If, as seems to be the case, they attempt to establish democracy there, to raise the standard of living, to increase education and civic responsibility, their position is little different from that of the conventional liberal reforming landlord, except that they are also trying to observe precisely the results of their efforts. They have two claims to justification—one, the enhancement of welfare, and the other, the increase in their knowledge of how the changes came about

—but as far as I can gather, no measure is instituted for exclusively cognitive purposes. Although I have not seen any detailed reports on this unprecedented undertaking in which the Peruvian government has rented two thousand of its citizens to a foreign landlord, the dominant impression I receive is that the Cornell group is trying to apply its already available knowledge to the practical task of improving the life of a hitherto impoverished and suppressed group, increasing their self-respect, their desire and capacity for self-government, their productivity, their understanding and skill. It should also be noted that in a formal sense, there is apparently no experimentation.

In trying to arrive at an assessment of sociological experimentation, the Cornell-Peru project is important because it reminds us that, whatever their attitude toward the larger social order and the institutions of authority which play important parts in regulating it, social scientists do not seek the gratifications of aggression in their relations with their experimental subjects. Unlike the experiments of the physicians who worked on Jews, Poles, and other "inferior races" in the German concentration camps, no deprivations are being knowingly inflicted on the Peruvian peasants. Social scientists, whatever their other imperfections, are usually not sadists.

By and large, as the result of an historical accident, the experimental attitude in American social science has been influenced by a liberal, permissive attitude. In great measure, this is attributable to the influence of Kurt Lewin. It has also been deeply influenced by the anti-authoritarian attitude inherent in the culture of American social science, which has concerned itself with the discovery of the consequences of emancipation from authority and particularly from repressive or manipulative authority. The experimental groups are therefore usually relatively indulged as compared with the control groups, who are dealt with in the manner which is conventional in our institutions. In the studies conducted under the inspiration of Kurt Lewin and his students and disciples at Iowa and Michigan Universities and in the work of the Tavistock Institute of Human Relations (London) which has a deep root in the medical-therapeutic tradition, the independent or experimental variable is almost always decentralized authority (as contrasted with the conventional centralization of authority in the control group), discussion and enlightenment as means of instituting changes in the behavior of subordinates (as contrasted with the conventional technique of command in the control group), etc.

This, of course, is not always so. Occasionally, a traumatic stimulus is introduced, and in so doing the experimenter moves toward the ethically objectionable. Moreover, the deeper the level of the system of action which he attempts to influence, the greater is his ethical responsibility and the more objectionable the introduction of a traumatic stimulus. Here the motives of the inquiry enter. To the extent, however, that the investigation is motivated by a genuinely therapeutic desire or is embedded in a genuinely therapeutic culture, then a measure of justification is added. Likewise, when the investigation is embedded in the discipline of a genuinely scientific tradition and is not merely a product of an individual whim, to say nothing of frivolousness or destructiveness, the justification for experimental manipulation is increased. At present, however, much social science experimentation possesses neither the therapeutic nor the genuinely scientific qualification. Even then it might not outweigh the objectionability of manipulation as such. Its ethical acceptability therefore rests on the peripheral nature of the stimuli and the transient character of the effects introduced.

More serious experimentation by social psychologists and sociologists in the present state of the subject must be viewed very cautiously. Many restraints should accompany its recommendation or execution. In medicine, where knowledge is admittedly fragmentary, although undoubtedly less fragmentary than in the social sciences, experimentation is guided by a strongly rooted therapeutic tradition and is almost always a link in a continuing sequence of scientific activity. One of the chief features of social psychological and sociological research today is the absence of both therapeutic intent and a tradition of cumulative scientific growth. This renders more doubtful the scientific value of the results attained by experimentation which would deal with the more vital features of individual or corporate life.

Furthermore, because the therapeutic tradition of medicine is lacking, the probability that sociological and psychological experimentation on more important variables might have harmful consequences is greater. The professional ethos formed by the weight of a powerful tradition and inculcated in medical schools, where ethical responsibility is one of the best precipitates of a course of study which includes much that is not technically necessary for the medical practitioner, is still lacking in the social and psychological sciences. This *ethos* is not by any means just a product of scientific maturity, although the latter does make a positive difference. It flows from a deeper attitude that is still lacking in the scientific study of man.

This problem, which has been rendered more pressing by the advancement of techniques of observation, is brought to a more acute stage by the development of various chemical methods of controlling action, thought, and fantasy. There is no doubt that some social scientists, with their zeal for novelty, will be attracted by the possibilities offered by these means of manipulating the external and internal lives of other persons. It is all the more necessary, therefore, that the leading persons in these fields should declare themselves as strenuously and decisively opposed to such tampering with human autonomy. It would be frivolously and desperately irresponsible for the adepts of fledgling disciplines to take upon themselves powers which, if utilized by politicians, administrators, or priests, would call down their unqualified disapproval. Just as we would be horrified by the private production of nuclear weapons and seek, by every means compatible with the continued existence of our civilization, the cessation of the production of such evils, so sociologists and psychologists without medical qualifications should just as strongly draw back from the employment of the chemical means of controlling the mind and its expressions for purposes which would probably be of very questionable value to the growth of deeper understanding and more fruitful therapy.[17]

VII

Ultimately, the ethical quality of social science research —i.e., the ethical quality of the relationship of the investigator to the person he interviews or observes—is derived from the social scientist's relations, as a person and as a citizen, with his society and with his fellow man. The newly possible techniques of research which would permit the destruction of the spheres of autonomy and privacy, through infra-red films, concealed cameras, microphones and recording apparatus, and chemical and psychological manipulation, will become dangerous only if the more general ethic of the social scientist is hostile toward society and diabolical in its curiosity. Unfortunately, the prospect is not entirely unequivocal.

More than a quarter of a century ago, a German social

scientist said that sociology began as an *"Oppositionswis-senschaft,"* a discipline impelled by the spirit of opposition to contemporary society. In France, the positivist sociology of Comte and St. Simon arose as a scientific criticism of modern bourgeois society; in Germany, the Romantic reaction against the French Revolution and against the spirit of commerce and citizenship of the French bour-geoisie and the *philosophes,* moved in the same direction of hostility toward contemporary society, a hatred of in-dividualism, distrust of the central institutional system, and a deep dissatisfaction with the insufficient integration of the central value-system of the emergent large-scale society. This element in the tradition of sociology has never been lost. In Toennies, in Simmel, and in Durkheim, it occupied a central position, and even in the work of Max Weber, who was less enthusiastic about the desirability or possi-bility of a totally integrated society, it is not entirely absent.

Nor did the alienative European influence fall upon an inhospitable soil when it came into contact with American sociology. The most fertile figures of American sociology before the great upsurge which began just before the Second World War, were William Graham Sumner, Robert E. Park, William I. Thomas, Charles H. Cooley, among the eminent dead, and Professor William F. Ogburn, among the living. With the exception of Sumner, who ex-pected nothing reasonable from any society and demanded only individual freedom and who therefore found himself quite at home in the freebooting capitalistic America of the turn of the century, all of these sociologists were critics of modern society. They regarded modern Western and particularly contemporary American society as in-dividualistic and atomistic in the extreme. They flourished in the traditions of muckraking and populism and shared many of their attitudes toward traditional authoritative institutions. Even Professor Ogburn, who by no means shares the intellectual tradition of the others, was a persistent critic, from a scientistic point of view, of the failure of modern institutions through their incapacity to eliminate the "cultural lag" created by the advances of modern technology.

In the Great Depression of the 1930's, the native American sociological critique of contemporary society received powerful support from the various currents of Marxism which began to flow through the intellectual classes in the United States. Fellow-travelling sociologists, Trotskyite sociologists, and others who were neither but who were attracted by the large perspectives and the humanitarian pretensions of Marxism, began to play an important role among American sociologists. These new influences brought in new subject matters and new approaches to the older subject matters. The new problems of sociological inquiry which came to the foreground in the last part of the thirties and throughout the forties—the psychoanalytical interpretation of ethnic hostility, beginning with Dollard and moving on to the Horkheimer circle, the studies of industrial relations which, leading from Mayo through Warner and Whyte, stressed the anomic character of modern industrial relations, the studies of mass communication which began with public opinion studies and then went on to voting studies, with their stress on the dissensual, and the analysis of popular culture, the study of pressure groups in politics, with similar emphases—these and many other studies have left their imprint on our sense of American reality and deepened our general understanding of society. They have also, it should be recognized, almost all been primarily concerned with the anomic, the irrational, the dissensual, and the vulgar elements in our society. The coherence, stability, and continuity of American society have been left unattended or taken for granted. With all due respect for the devotion to truth of American sociologists and social psychologists and their disciplined detachment, I think that it is not unfair to say that much of their work shows a certain measure of distaste and repugnance for their own society. One often gets the impression in reading their work that they do not feel themselves to be part of their own society and culture, and that if they do acknowledge their "partness," they scarcely affirm it.

Now, although much in this attitude is fruitful of keen insight, it is also blinding to important features of society. More significantly, however, is the moral distance which it expresses. This sense of moral distance is not without dangers for the ethical conduct of social research. Insofar as it expresses a sense of moral disjunction between the investigator and the human beings whom he investigates, it makes it easy for him to disregard their moral scruples. It frees him from obligations to them arising from membership in a common moral community. The objects of his inquiries thereby become mere objects, without valid moral claims. They are accordingly available for the treatment which any scientist can give to his nonhuman objects. Against the background of such a limited sense of affinity, manipulation and deception become perfectly appropriate means of inquiry, and all spheres of life, provided that it is technically possible to obtain access to them, are open to psychological and sociological scrutiny and publication.

This tendency of thought and sentiment is, however, by no means in exclusive possession of the field of contemporary social research. It is in part offset by a genuine pleasure in contact with ordinary human beings, to whom interviewing provides a bridge. It is also offset to some extent by the permissive, equalitarian, anti-authoritarian attitude which flows from many sources in the wider culture and in the culture of the social science professions. It is, nonetheless, a massive and widely permeative influence; and its influence is not least among those with the most lively interests and the greatest intellectual initiative. It is, therefore, in the light of this attitude that we should examine the ethical dangers of social research and the available safeguards within the traditions of the culture of social science, of our academic world, and of our larger society.

VIII

The reserve forces of Western culture which would inhibit social scientists from seeking to establish a tyranny over their fellow men on behalf of their science and on the basis of it are multifarious; they are also, however, by no means free from ambivalence. On the positive side, there is a very real respect and appreciation for individuality, perhaps even more in the United States than in Europe. There is among men of practical experience a distrust, sometimes excessive, sometimes insufficient, for the theorist, for the scientist with his abstract schemes and doctrines. There is also, in the vast majority of the population, a common decency and sense of moral restraint which is common to our Western culture with its tendency toward moral equalitarianism.

On the other side is the *scientific* attitude, and the impatience with imperfection which are also parts of our cultural inheritance from Bacon, Condorcet, Comte, Marx, down to Bernal and Skinner, and which envisage men of science ruling society, bringing it into order, overcoming man's imperfections by the application of scientific knowledge.

Within the intellectual classes, the same ambivalence exists. On the one hand, the great humanistic tradition to which nothing human is alien, the tradition of the British, French, American, and German Enlightenment, of Locke, Hume, Kant, Jefferson, Franklin, Voltaire, Diderot, *et al.,* who, even where they are not read, continue to exercise a great spiritual influence in heightening the appreciation of the genius in every living human being. On the other side is a cranky, embittered alienation, which accentuates the anti-authoritarianism innate to liberalism This alienation cuts the individual off from his society and his fellow man and causes him to despise the irrationality and the triviality of ordinary human beings and the symbols and persons they respect. It is exacerbated by a harebrained belief in the ease with which men can be improved and the unreflective conviction that social science is the right means to that improvement.

Within the social science professions themselves, with the exception of political economy, the situation is also quite indeterminate. Unlike the real sciences, no great tradition has yet established itself, commanding universal assent. Something more like chaos reigns there. Social resentment, and scientific enthusiasm, the desire to legitimize themselves by being useful and influential, the alienation from and the fascination with authority, are all forces which potentially could work in the direction of evil. The public opinion which they create among the incoming generation is not always consistent with the true humanism of liberalism. Yet it must be remembered that they are integral parts of our culture and also share in its values in one form or another. Moreover, even the very curiosity which prompts the investigator's intrusion into privacy is the manifestation of a breadth of empathetic imagination, an openness and attachment to other human beings in their essential individuality, that to some extent provides its own inner curb. It is also just to point out that the theoretical orientation which has come to the fore in the past decade is one which makes ample acknowledgment of man's moral and rational capacities. The theory of action which is increasingly, in diverse ways, influencing sociological and social psychological research sees man as neither beast nor machine. There is room in it for man at his heights, as well as his depths, his lights and his shadows, his creativity and his dreary sameness. Inherent in this scheme of interpretation is a genuine respect for the humanity of human beings. This, too, is a safeguard against the abuse of potential powers which social scientists might exercise.

Finally, and perhaps most important, the social sciences are conducted within and under the auspices of the great universities, which nearly everywhere in the West are the Gibraltars of a genuine humanism. It is on these forces that we rest our aspiration for a self-containing sense of responsibility which will guide intellectual curiosity and imagination amidst the dangerous opportunities which modern technique affords.

NOTES

[1] Social scientists who find the "pseudo-friendliness" of salesmen and radio personalities offensive seem not to mind the beam in their own eye. The following passage is character-

istic: ". . . if the interviewer's task is to obtain information about some aspect of the respondent's habits—marital relations, for example—it would be necessary for him to establish a deeper kind of personal relationship with the respondent. In general, we can say that the more intimate, emotionally charged, or ego-involved the topic of the interview, the more delicate the job of establishing the relationship becomes and the deeper that relationship must be." L. Festinger, and D. Katz, *Research Methods in the Behavioral Sciences* New York 1953, p. 357.

[2] The corporate privacy of voluntary bodies is as much a part of our system of rights as is individual privacy, and deceptive intrusion into their interior affairs is unjustifiable in principle. At the same time, like the events which occur in the private sphere of the individual, it is a legitimate object of sociological inquiry. Such inquiry, however, depends for its conduct on a knowing and voluntary suspension of the barriers which maintain privacy. In its written presentation, particular truths must make many concessions to privacy, as long as these concessions do not make inroads into the general truths discovered by the inquiry.

[3] The jurisprudence of privacy insofar as it exists at all confines its discussion to the protection of privacy from a farflung publicity which permits the individual whose privacy has been infringed upon to be identified. Thus social scientists, when they are cautious to maintain the confidentiality and anonymity of the private information which they obtain, place themselves beyond the reaches of a substantial part of the criticism of the destruction of privacy in contemporary life.

[4] The privilege of entry into the private sphere of an individual by a sociological investigator naturally also entails a strict exclusion of any improper use of the fiduciary and, thus, quasi-personal relationship into which they have entered, e.g., to establish sexual relations with one of the participants, or to derogate or otherwise give publicity to one of the persons into whose private sphere they have been admitted. I men-

tion these infringements on standards of propriety because certain cases are known to me.

[5] The novelty is not, of course, evidence of an irremovable anomaly; it only indicates the need to study the problem carefully and honestly and to be aware of the need to make amends for the infringement by contributing seriously to knowledge rather than just contributing to the literature of the social sciences and the size of the Ph.D.-holding population.

[6] Of course, valuable information can be gained by deception in many situations.

[7] There are situations in which such unadmitted observations are necessary, e.g., in the pursuit of criminals, spies, etc. Their necessity on behalf of social order does not diminish their morally objectionable character; it simply outweighs it.

[8] It is not entirely proper when only one of them does so without the consent of the other or others, but that is always happening in normal life.

[9] I do not mean to imply here that the police should be perfectly free to use these devices to observe the conduct and conversation of any suspected criminal or any person suspected of espionage. On the contrary, in these instances, too, the use of these instruments must be subjected to the strict control of the courts and the highest levels of political officialdom.

[10] A confidentiality which is not, however, always strictly adhered to by jury members and the press, once the deliberations are completed.

[11] Naturally, the knowledge that their tentatively expressed opinions were being recorded might inhibit the free play of imagination and intelligence and thus prevent the final decision from being as good as it might be if such inhibitions were not created. The same holds true for the deliberations of any committee or the action of any person who knows that his conduct is being observed and his statements recorded, even if he has no reason to suspect hostile intentions in connection

with the observation. This is one of the liabilities of properly conducted observation, but it is not inevitably injurious to the research. In fact, it is quite likely that consciousness of being recorded would not play a significant part in the course or content of the deliberations.

[12] The fact that there are so many "leaks" of secret information, utterly unconnected with espionage, is no argument against the interpretation given in the text. The eagerness to penetrate and disclose secrets is not motivated only by professional journalistic pride and democratic concern for the common good, but rather by an urge to be in contact with the sacred zones of authority and to give public evidence of that contact. Likewise, the readiness in the United States of officials and congressmen to "leak" the proceedings of secret meetings is in part a product of political tactical considerations and an act of conciliation toward powerful journalists. Yet it is also the product of a desire simultaneously to give evidence of being in contact with a sacred zone and to degrade it by disclosure to the uninitiated. The populistic ethos is made up of such elements as these.

[13] Such is the ambivalent nature of the human being that the need for secrecy is often accompanied by the equal and concurrent need for publicity about what is secret.

[14] I might in this instance mention the recent work of Professor C. Wright Mills, *The Power Elite,* a work deeply permeated with the sense of the potency of the powerful. The author did not seek even a single interview with those whose deeds so engage his thoughts and sentiments.

[15] Many would be more widely read if they were "classified" as secret or as confidential. Sometimes the best way to assure that something is left unknown is to publish it.

[16] Yet, by and large and for the most part, social scientists hold themselves aloof. They hold themselves aloof partly because they themselves fear the reaction of the public, which might take umbrage at the sacrilegious character of detached direct observation of the seats of power, however much it delights

in reading and retelling gossip about those who sit or have sat in those seats.

[17] This statement does not imply that their use by physicians should be unaccompanied by great and continuous caution and moral discipline. On the contrary, there, too, the application of these new methods of modifying the central core of personality must be attended by the deepest respect for whatever measure of individuality human beings have been able to attain.

INQUIRY AND POLICY: THE RELATION
OF KNOWLEDGE TO ACTION

Max F. Millikan

People do research for two reasons: first, because it is interesting, and second because it may be useful. The relations of researchers with men of action are sometimes complicated by the fact that useful knowledge is not always interesting, or interesting knowledge necessarily useful. Thus, although researchers and decision-makers enjoy flirting with each other, if they are to make a serious and congenial marriage both parties must recognize—more than they usually do—the kinds of circumstances in which usefulness and interest coincide.

In the natural sciences a *modus vivendi* has been evolved over the past few generations which, although it does not avoid occasional domestic conflict, at least permits the necessary degree of cooperation on matters of importance. The engineer knows that he needs the natural scientist and has a pretty good idea of how to use him; the natural scientist in turn has learned something about which of his discoveries have action implications, and how these implications can be elaborated usefully for the operator.

In the social sciences, on the other hand, attempts to effect such a union have too frequently resulted in frustration and disillusion. Recently, and especially since World War II, there has been a growing feeling among both operators and social scientists that the growing body of social science knowledge should be applied to the solution of some of the pressing policy problems of our time. The remaining question is that of how it is to be applied. In certain fields this has been done with some success. Economic theory has proved relevant to the problem of controlling economic fluctuations in the more advanced countries. The work of students of the psychology of learning has influenced educational policy. Business enterprises have improved the productivity and satisfactions of their employees and sharpened the effectiveness of their advertising with the help of social science research. But in other areas the efforts of operators to use social scientists have been much less rewarding.

The contributions of social science to the solution of the great international problems of our time have not been notable. In the United States, at least, this has not been for want of trying. Here, the government has financed a variety of social science research projects designed in one way or another to illuminate foreign policy, and the great American foundations have supported a great deal of work directed to the same end. Yet the results to date have been disappointing to both the operators and the researchers.

The disappointment of those who have commissioned the research shows itself in a number of ways. They feel in the first place that much of what has been done is either useless or irrelevant to the problems they are struggling with. The work is obviously painstaking and thorough, a great deal of material has been surveyed, elaborate classifications have been developed, and a great many facts have been assembled. But there is a frustrated and irritated feeling that, when one has waded through a fat research report, one is no nearer to the answers he is seeking than when he began. When projects are formulated there seems to be agreement as to the problems to be explored; yet, when the results emerge, the problems the social scientist has been grappling with appear to be quite different from those the operator is interested in. The "conclusions" of such projects, in particular, often emerge as conclusions not as to what should be done—and how—but as to ways of describing in technical language a state of affairs with which journalists and diplomats have long felt they were familiar. This leads to a feeling that the social scientist stubbornly rejects the operator's real problems for some relatively unimportant or narrow aspect of a general isue, one which happens to interest him or to which his disciplinary tools happen to apply, leaving the central problem posed but unresolved.

All this is complicated by the operator's impression that the researcher is playing with complex intellectual machinery for its own sake. There seems an unnecessary amount of special language, a wearisome spinning-out of definitions, subtle distinctions, and elaborate classifications, and a ponderous amassing of documentation. Finally, if relevant conclusions do ultimately appear, they turn out to be things one knew in advance. The whole process appears to be a peculiarly complicated way of saying the obvious.

Similarly, and as often, the social science researcher emerges from the experiment angry and resentful at its failure. He probably undertook an applied research assignment with grave misgivings in the first place. There is a tradition in the academic world that to undertake research on behalf of a customer, particularly for pay, is to sell one's soul to the devil. The scientist is apt to have a strong conviction that applied research cannot be "fundamental," that there is something inherently contradictory in the advance of knowledge and the service of practical ends, and that to work for a policy-maker is therefore somehow to prejudice one's professional standing. Allied with this (particularly among social scientists) is a set of moral qualms concerning the ethics of placing scientific analysis in the service of persons who wish, for whatever purposes, to manipulate human beings. It may be recognized that the essence of social action is the manipulation of human behavior; nevertheless, there is a feeling that the scientific objectivity of an observer cannot help but be compromised by his involvement in a manipulative problem.

The recent history of social science is the history of a struggle on the part of social scientists to make their work more positive and less normative, to eliminate from the analysis of human behavior the influence of the value judgments of the researcher. Undoubtedly the clearer separation of social observation from judgments about social goals has been important to scientific advance. The researcher pressed to work on policy problems is plagued by the fear that this will plunge him back into the confusion between norms and observed reality from which he has been struggling so hard for decades to free himself.

These varied initial doubts are often compounded by the researcher's experience as an applied project proceeds. The researcher may face a growing conviction either that the operator has asked the wrong questions, that the questions are too vaguely or too narrowly formulated, or that as formulated they are incapable of being clearly answered. He becomes convinced that the concepts and categories in terms of which the operator has posed his problem are neither meaningful nor useful. If he accepts these categories and tries to frame his research around them, he feels intellectually frustrated. If he devotes himself to an attempt to restate the problem in more meaningful terms, he finds he has lost the operator's attention.

In either case, he submits his report only to find that his customer, though he appeared to be most eager to get it, makes little or no use of it. In many cases there is evidence that his reports have not even been carefully read; in many others they seem to have had little or no effect on the operational decisions subsequently taken. Not uncommonly, the researcher concludes in restrospect that his initial doubts about the wisdom of engaging in applied research were fully confirmed, and he withdraws once more into academic isolation.

In this essay I would like to analyze some of the reasons for this state of affairs. In a sense, they can all be described as failures of communication between researchers and policy-makers. But the roots of these failures do not lie merely in the semantic problems associated with the use of different terminology. Rather, they can be traced to a series of misconceptions on the part of both researchers and operators as to the relation of knowledge to action in the field of human affairs. Action specialists seriously misconstrue the kinds of help they can expect to get from social scientists, and social scientists have a variety of misapprehensions as to what the policy-making process involves. I would like to outline some of these sources of misunderstanding, examine how certain of them are to be explained by the nature and present state of the social sciences, and conclude with a few observations on whether, if some of the gross misunderstandings were eliminated, policy-makers and social scientists might expect to benefit from further collaborative attempts.

The operators, on the one hand, commit their elementary error in an inductive fallacy—the assumption that the solution of any problem will be advanced by the simple collection of fact. This is easiest to observe in governmental circles, where research is considered as identical with "intelligence." The military conception of intelligence as the collection of facts about the disposition of enemy forces (unquestionably an important kind of knowledge for one charged with responsibility for military action) has been uncritically extended to the whole spectrum of governmental policy. Roger Hilsman, in his interesting interview study of the views of the role of research and intelligence held by policy-makers in the U. S. government, has thoroughly documented the pervasiveness of the notion among operators that, if only they were supplied with more raw facts of almost any kind, they could make much wiser decisions on the issues that confront them.[1]

The operator who holds this view of the utility of new facts may find himself disenchanted with research on one of two grounds. In the first case, the social scientist may refuse to pander to this taste for new facts and concern himself instead with restructuring the concepts in terms of which previously known facts are to be interpreted. In this event the operator clearly does not get what he originally expected. Furthermore, what he does get fails to persuade him that he expected the wrong thing. I shall deal further with the reasons for this conviction.

In the second case, the researcher, frequently against his own better judgment, tries to be responsive to this expressed demand for new "factual information" and assembles a handbook containing a large amount of such material. The operator gets what he expected, but finds to his frustration that it gives him very little help in solving his problems. For example, a request for a report on the nature of the leadership of a foreign country may elicit a vast amount of data on the social origins, pattern of incomes, religious beliefs, and past affiliations of all key members of the foreign élite—information that leaves the operator in no better position than before to estimate the probability, for instance, that this élite will be susceptible to Communist blandishments. Indeed, some interesting experimental psychological work has been done by Alex Bavelas and Howard Perlmutter, at the Center for International Studies, which suggests that an individual's capacity for making sound judgment about a complex situation may be seriously impaired by supplying him with a lot of information which he believes should be relevant but whose influence on the situation is not clear to him. The relation between observational data and concept in the natural sciences is so generally understood that no operator would think of expecting an applied research project in the physical sciences merely to come up with a mass of observational data that might conceivably be relevant to the problem at hand, nor would he expect to make much use of such data if indeed it was assembled. Yet precisely this conviction is common among operators with respect to social science research.

A somewhat different misconception, logically incompatible with that just described but frequently held by the same people, is that the usefulness of social science research can be tested by its ability to predict complex social behavior in some detail. Whereas the obsession with the illuminating power of fact expects too little of social science research, the test of prediction expects too much. Here the analogy with physical science research, instead of being imperfect, is carried too far. In the natural sciences it is reasonable to assign a research team of scientists and engineers the task of designing an instrument that will with fair certainty achieve certain specified physical results. One can ask for a weapon of specified weight which will have specified explosive power, or a transmitter of so many kilowatts capable of sending a message a given distance to a known type of receiver, and then test the utility of the results against the requested criteria of performance.

One cannot, however, expect a social science research group to design a diplomatic initiative that can be expected with confidence to produce a desired response or to indicate the content of an information program that will with some certainty produce a specified change in the attitudes of those who hear it. Even abstracting from the philosophical question of whether a completely deterministic explanation of human behavior will ever be possible, it is clear that social science has not yet reached the stage where its formal models can often yield even a statistical prediction of a complex social event.

Our best formal models are still partial; they explicitly exclude consideration of some of the factors at work in any actual situation. The relative weight of the factors explicitly analyzed can seldom be measured, and their combined influence seldom computed. Prediction of a sort is, of course, a necessary component of policy-making. Any decision to act must be based upon a judgment that the net consequences of the preferred course of action will be more favorable than those of some alternative. But in social situations such a judgment can seldom be effectively made by "scientific" procedures. If the policy-maker simply desires advice as to what he should do, he had better rely on the intuition of a man of wide experience and demonstrated understanding rather than on the intellectual skills and techniques of the social scientist. The human brain is an extraordinary instrument, only a small portion of whose analytic powers can be reduced to communicable logic. A net predictive judgment in most human situations can be made more safely by the successful journalist, novelist, diplomat, or businessman than by any social science research team.

If the contribution of the social scientist to policy is neither the collection of facts nor the making of predictions, what is it? First, we must recognize that every practical judgment is based upon a structure of concepts and assumptions that is largely implicit and poorly understood. One of the functions of science is to make these implicit concepts and assumptions explicit, to test their generality, and to set forth more precisely the circumstances in which they are valid. Thus, although social science cannot often predict, it can make very important contributions to effective prediction. Social science cannot replace intuition and experience, but it can greatly enrich them, clarify them, and make them more general. Each of the social sciences concentrates on the relations between certain limited aspects of human behavior. Social science research on a problem can illuminate the variety of forces at work, can place limits on the range of possible outcomes, can force implicit, partial judgments into explicit form in which they can be systematically examined and their applicability tested, and can explore the internal consistency of a variety of intuitive expectations. Most policy judgments involve an implicit appraisal of resources, of motivations, of organizational and administrative possibilities, of political interests, and the like. Economic, psychological, political, and sociological analysis can expose these judgments to systematic scrutiny. Their combination into an estimate of the situation as a whole will almost always require a process that goes beyond the limits of "scientific" analysis, but such analysis can enormously strengthen the validity of the intuitive process.

If this picture of how the policy-maker can use social

science research is correct, the operator must approach social science research with very different expectations from those he normally has. The operator's normal impulse is to ask for the conclusions of a social science research project and to regard the argument as none of his concern. But the payoff for him will usually be precisely in the argument rather than in the conclusions. The purpose of social science research should be to deepen, broaden, and extend the policy-maker's capacity for judgment—not to provide him with answers. Thus, the test of effectiveness will lie not in whether the research leads to a new and unfamiliar conclusion but in whether it clarifies and makes explicit the logical basis for a conclusion already perceived or suspected.

In one respect particularly the intuitive process may be misleading. A great many contradictory things can, by a skillful impressionistic presentation of a case, be made to appear obvious. There is a reasonable, "commonsense" interpretation of almost every form of individual and social behavior. Whatever regularities a study reports, a number of people are likely to feel that no study was required to reach this "obvious" conclusion. This would be equally likely if the findings of the study were precisely the opposite. When Samuel Stouffer's exhaustive study of the attitudes of the American soldier appeared after the war, it was greeted by widespread lay criticism that its findings were apparent before the work was begun and that the whole enterprise was, accordingly, a waste of time and money. To meet this criticism, Paul Lazarsfeld, in a review, began by citing a series of soldier attitudes so described as to leave the reader feeling that these were precisely the attitudes any of us would expect. He then went on to say:

"But why, since they are so obvious, is so much money and energy given to establish such findings? Would it not be wiser to take them for granted and proceed directly to a more sophisticated type of analysis? This might be so except for one interesting *point* about the list. *Every one of these statements* is the direct opposite of what actually was found." [2] It is the task of a social science study to determine which of the contradictory but intuitively obvious conclusions about a situation is in fact true and in what circumstances it may be expected to obtain. The operator can gain from such a study a more sophisticated understanding of the assumptions he implicitly makes and the circumstances he envisions when he states a similar conclusion himself.

An effective marriage of knowledge and action is seriously inhibited in the modern world by an exaggerated emphasis on the virtues of the division of labor. Decision-making and the pursuit of systematic knowledge have come to be regarded as separable activities, and it is supposed to be inefficient for the researcher to concern himself with policy decisions or for the policy-maker to probe too deeply into research techniques. The policy-maker is supposed to recognize what it is he needs to know and to be able to levy a clear requirement on the researcher to supply the missing knowledge. The researcher, using techniques which it is his business and nobody else's to understand, is in turn supposed to answer the questions put to him. In fact, of course, the relations between knowledge and action are infinitely more complex and reciprocal than this image would suggest and cannot be adequately mastered unless each kind of specialist develops an extensive knowledge of the other's mental processes. Indeed, the most important task for both policy-makers and researchers is a better and more communicable definition of the problem to be solved.

To some extent this is true of the relation between knowledge and action in any field. It is much more true, however, of social and political problems than it is of physical and engineering ones. The man who wants a plastic material to do a specified job need not be a chemist to order or to use a research study designed to provide him with it. But a man who wants help on a social or political policy may well benefit more from an understanding of how research bearing on that policy is designed and conducted than from any conclusions such research may reach.

The dominant American theory and practice of administration in both government and industry contributes to this excessive division of labor between specialists in action and specialists in knowledge. In government there is a long-standing tradition of sharp separation of research and intelligence from policy-making and execution. The analyst in a research or intelligence organization is virtually prohibited from speculating about policy alternatives or even from intimate intellectual contact with policy makers. Organizational procedures, based on the false premise that the operator knows what it is that he needs from research, call for the formulation on paper of research "requirements" by operating organizations, the vetting of these requirements by various intermediaries, and their ultimate delivery by courier to the research group. This group, in turn, is supposed to "fill" these requirements by its own occult means and to mail the "answers" back to the operators. These procedures are based on the notion that there are recognized gaps in the factual knowledge of the operator, that he can define these gaps with precision on paper, and that when the gaps are filled by research, as requested, the operator's problem will be clarified. This procedure virtually forecloses any opportunities for a fruitful attack on the really central problem—the joint reformulation of the policy problem by both researcher and operator. In private industry, this gulf between knowledge and action is sometimes bridged more effectively, but usually only over the bitter opposition of the efficiency-minded expert in business administration.

In summary then, the operator's misconceptions of the relationship between social science knowledge and action are of three sorts. First, he frequently has an exaggerated notion of the degree to which the solution of his problems can be effected by the collection of additional factual information. Second, he tends to expect prediction in situations in which this is clearly beyond the capabilities of present-day social science. Third, he too easily assumes that the conclusions of a research project will assist him when the important factor is actually the process of analysis underlying those conclusions. These misconceptions are supported and maintained by a mechanical and inappropriate application to both research and policy of the principle of division of labor.

The researcher's conception of the relation between knowledge and action is likewise plagued by a number of false perspectives. Like the operator, the researcher tends to have an exaggerated faith in the division of labor and, derived from this, an idealized image of the policy maker. If the function of the man of action is, by definition, to act, then what he must want is conclusions, not analysis. Here again is an emphasis—this time from the researcher —on the answer rather than on the process of thinking by which the answer is supported. This leads to a research product consisting either of conclusions regarded as obvious by the operator in advance of research or of recommendations which are not persuasive because they are inadequately supported. The situation reflects a tendency on the part of the researcher to underestimate the intellectual content of the policy-making process. Any policy position is, of course, arrived at in the context of an implicit or explicit appraisal of the nature of the forces at work and of the way they can be influenced by a variety of policy instruments. Because the policy-maker usually does not articulate in social science terminology, his judgments about the variables he is trying to manipulate, the researcher often assumes that the man of action is guided to effective decision-making by some intuitive process beyond the reach of rational argument.

This misconception is frequently associated with another —inconsistent with it—that the operator knows what he wants from research and that his questions are therefore to be taken at face value. Here, the researcher overestimates the capacity of most policy-makers to make explicit the conceptual framework in which they define their operational problems. The researcher who wants to be genuinely useful has an obligation to force his customer to rethink in a fundamental way why he wants research done and the uses to which he will put it if he gets it. Unfortunately, it would seem clear that the policy-maker seldom has a realistic notion of what to expect from research, and that he cannot arrive at a sensible expectation without the help of the social scientist. Yet time and again projects are begun with only the most cursory mutual consideration of just how they are expected to be used. The subsequent result is apt to be bitter disenchantment on both sides, conversely, the most valuable product of many applied research projects considered successful has been a new conception in the mind of the operator of how the problems with which he is confronted are to be defined.

The researcher frequently, although he recognizes the inadequacy of the statement of the problem he has been given, is inhibited by the difficulties of communication from insisting on being provided with a better one. Instead he goes off to his library or his laboratory and makes his independent attempt to describe what he is planning to do in the language of his own discipline.

Here another difficulty arises. His first impulse will be to discard, sometimes without realizing it, those aspects of the problem which do not interest him. He can defend this on the ground that there is no point in his doing research on problems which are inherently not researchable. The higher his standards of scientific research, the narrower will be his selection of problems and the greater the eventual frustration of the customer with the result.

The clash of interest and utility is likely to be most marked in the early stages of a science, which are characterized by a great deal of attention to careful classification, to precise definition, and to the establishment of useful tautologies—that is, to the elaboration of all the logical consequences of a few simple assumptions. Scientific progress at this stage is likely to be gauged not by the number of practically applicable conclusions that emerge but rather by the degree to which a precise language of communication with fellow researchers is established and a set of fundamental categories of phenomena laid down. The early stages are therefore likely to consist of the construction of an elaborate intellectual tool whose cutting edge for shaping practical problems is small and weak.

What the researcher may justifiably regard as a major intellectual achievement in bringing order out of chaos may well strike the operator, who is uninterested in the machinery for its own sake, as a scholastic exercise of little relevance. To establish the proposition that business leaders tend to have a high level of achievement motivation, or that caste inhibits social mobility, or that social overhead capital has a high capital-output ratio may be scientifically significant but of little help to the policy-maker who has asked for an estimate of the "vigor" of the private sector in the Turkish economy or of the probabiity of "class conflict" in India or of whether China's economic development plan "will work."

There is as yet no general science of human behavior. We have only the beginnings of a number of separate social science disciplines, each of which has directed its attention to exploring the relations between certain limited and carefully defined aspects of behavior. Thus the social scientist who values precision and the establishment of repeatable and communicable results must carve the problem he has been given down to researchable size. The policy-maker must pass a judgment on a complex situation as a whole, being careful to take into consideration everything that may importantly affect the actual outcome. These legitimate—but different—responsibilities may produce a genuine conflict between utility and scientific interest as criteria for problem selection. Unless this conflict is clearly recognized, its sources understood, and an explicit effort made to resolve it by both the researcher and his customer, applied research will almost certainly be disappointing to both.

Certain other characteristics of the stage in which the social sciences presently find themselves further limit the utility to the policy-maker of much social science research, especially in the analysis of the relations between states. In many countries there is a vast amount of social science research going forward on the structure and characteristics of foreign societies from which the policy-maker feels he should be able to benefit. He finds, however, when he examines this research, that it has a strong static bias. The questions asked tend to take the form: "What is society X like? What is the character of its institutions? What are the attitudes of various elements of its population? What is the structure of its economy?" rather than the form: "In what directions is the society evolving? How rapidly and in what directions are institutions, attitudes, and structure changing? And where is this process of change likely to lead?"

From the standpoint of scientific development this bias is thoroughly understandable. Dynamics is always more complicated than statics; rates of change are harder to measure and analyze than states of affairs. Beyond this, there is logic in the need to know where we are before we ask where we are going. Also, the empirical study of social change requires a series of observations made according to a consistent plan over a period of years many times the duration of the typical project.

On the other hand, from a policy point of view the most important characteristic of our times is that societies are changing in almost all their fundamental dimensions at a rate unprecedented in history. All our most crucial international policy problems require an appraisal not of states of affairs but of patterns of evolution. Economic development, newly emergent nationalism, trends in the character of Communist society, the political implications of changing weapons technology—these are all questions which cannot even be posed in other than dynamic terms. If the social scientist is to help the policy-maker deal with these situations at all, he must find ways of introducing process explicitly into both his analytic frameworks and his empirical observations. The social sciences are moving toward the formulation of dynamic theories and their empirical testing, but at this stage realistic dynamic analysis can be undertaken only at considerable cost in rigor and precision.

There is the further difficulty of the requirement, in the analysis of most policy alternatives, that a number of factors lying within the focus of interest of a variety of social science disciplines be considered simultaneously. This has led to attempts, particularly in applied research, to tackle problems in an interdisciplinary way, normally by assembling a team of research workers trained in different disciplines. This is not the place to go into all the difficulties and obstacles to effective interdisciplinary team research, but one problem in particular has received inadequate emphasis. The most critical policy issues of our time are those relating to the interaction of complex national states. The international behavior of states, however, is conditioned in important ways by their own internal dynamics. National states, especially the more recently created ones, are not, of course, homogeneous entities possessing a common will but are themselves collections of interacting communities and groups. Thus research on the behavior of larger social units such as nations requires research in turn on the behavior and interactions of smaller units such as provinces, business communities, castes, and even families and individuals. The relation of macro- to micro-studies poses a serious dilemma for applied research. To study intensively all the thousands or millions of micro-units that make up the macro-units is obviously a task beyond the resources of any academic community. On the other hand, the two or three villages or business firms or newspapers or professions that one can afford to look at in detail may be unrepresentative and may tell one very little about how the multitude of micro-forces in a national society aggregate to produce a national or international result.

The different social sciences have developed different capabilities for handling different levels of social aggregation. By and large, psychology and anthropology are most confident and most at home in applying a microscope to individuals or small groups. Political science, on the other hand, has traditionally taken as its province the study of national and international institutions and organization. Economics, similarly, has concentrated a good deal of its attention on national aggregates, though it is the one social science discipline that, more than any other, has mastered the problem of integrating the analysis of the behavior of individuals in small economic units with the study of national and international aggregates. But systematic interdisciplinary research is complicated by the fact that each discipline is most at home in the study of a different kind of social unit. We do not yet have even an embryonic science of social change that offers a framework for integrating the kinds of work carried on by different social scientists. We are moving in the right direction. Political science has been increasingly concerning itself with the intensive study of the political behavior of individuals and small groups. Psychologists and anthropologists are more frequently asking, with the help of sociologists, how representative the phenomena revealed by their micro-studies are in the larger populations with which the political scientist deals. But the bridges between micro- and macro-studies need much more strengthening before they will bear the weight policy analysis places on them.

The final problem relates to the scientific respectability of an explicit analysis of values and goals as a subject for scholarly inquiry. As already mentioned, many social scientists are still powerfully influenced by the conviction that their work cannot be "objective" unless they avoid all analysis of normative propositions. They do not, of course, deny that policy propositions inevitably rest upon value assumptions. But here, too, they exaggerate the possibilities of a division of labor. Let the scientist concern himself only with the world as it is, and let the policy-maker or someone else worry about the directions in which we should be trying to push it. The trouble is, of course, that there is an inherent interdependence between the concepts we use to interpret events and those we use to articulate our values.

Three kinds of elements must be appraised in any policy analysis: goals, environment, and instruments. The policy-maker must sort out carefully the various ends the policy is designed to pursue as well as the costs that are acceptable in terms of other values foregone. He must understand the forces at work in the world which are beyond his control and the directions in which they are likely to carry the environment, whatever he does. Finally, he must appraise the capabilities and limitations of the various policy instruments available to him to influence the environment in what he believes to be desirable directions. The social scientist tends to regard his tools as applicable only to the second of these three elements. But rational analysis of the first and third requires at least as great intellectual subtlety and precision. More important, these three elements cannot be examined in isolation, since each can be defined only in terms of the other two. A study of what is happening in Soviet society will be useful to the policy-maker only if it is written in the light both of what he would like to have happen there and of the instruments he can use to affect what happens. Equally, he cannot even state his goals or enumerate his instruments with clarity except in terms of an implicit or explicit theory of Soviet evolution. The division of labor among different analysts according to the distinction between normative and positive propositions cannot be carried very far without depriving social science of most of its operational utility.

We can summarize this discussion of the relation between utility and scientific interest by conceiving of a spectrum of types of approaches to the understanding of social behavior. At one end lie the net judgments about very complex real situations which the policy-maker confronted with the great issues of our time must make. No scientist can be wholly happy with the necessity to make such judgments, since in the present state of our knowledge they must inevitably rest much more largely on intuition, partially articulated insights, and informed common sense than on precisely defined propositions emerging from a clear theoretical model and supported by documented empirical evidence. At the other end of the spectrum lie rigorous scientific conclusions, unambiguously communicable in a language developed for precise communication and capable of demonstration by repeatable experiment or by reference to incontrovertible evidence. In the present state of social science the propositions at this scientific end of the spectrum necessarily relate to exceedingly simple and hence operationally unimportant phenomena controlled to exclude all but a few variables capable of treatment by the tools of a single discipline. This is, of course, a caricature. There are problems in the analysis of which the scientist can move quite a distance toward the practical end of the spectrum with relatively little loss of rigor and others in which the practitioner can get direct help from investigations conducted according to the strict rules of scientific inquiry. But these are the exceptions. There thus remains in social science considerable conflict between the canons of utility and those of scientific interest.

I have already suggested my reasons for believing that the policy-maker can broaden his insights and deepen his intuition by learning more of what is going on at the scientific end of the spectrum, if the policy-maker learns to share some of the perspectives and motivations of the social scientist. If he has the intellectual curiosity and persistence to learn some of the uses and limitations of social science tools, he can substantially improve the wisdom of his own practical judgments. But he will be continually disappointed if he expects rigorous scientific inquiry to yield conclusions directly and mechanically applicable to the fuzzy problems he confronts.

What of the social scientist? Does he stand to benefit from wrestling with the insoluble problems of the policymaker, inextricably enmeshed as they are in a value context, or will such an activity threaten to compromise his scientific integrity and prevent him from making the fundamental contributions to communicable human knowledge which are his central responsibility? Much depends on how he approaches his task, and how self-consciously aware he is of what he is doing. If he confuses the distinction between a wise judgment and a communicable scientific truth he is likely to make little progress toward either. If, however, he devotes the bulk of his attention to his central scientific objective, uncompromisingly maintaining the highest scholarly criteria in these activities, his work can benefit greatly from an occasional concern with the muddy normative problems of policy. The rules of scientific method do not tell us what it is important to work on. The ultimate objective of social science is a scientific explanation of human behavior in all its complexity. An occasional effort to assist the statesman serves to emphasize not only our ignorance of social forces but also the extent to which our knowledge is intuitive and imprecise. The effort to sort it out, to give it precision, and to make it communicable, even where this effort is largely doomed to failure, can enormously stimulate the selection of promising areas for scientific inquiry. The principle of the division of labor is indeed a powerful one, but only if each of the specialists—in this case specialists in action and specialists in knowledge—devotes some effort to trying to understand both intuitively and logically the total human problem to which his specialty can make a contribution.

NOTES

[1] Roger Hilsman, *Strategic Intelligence and National Decisions* (Glencoe, Illinois: Free Press, 1956). The author's findings are summarized in an article, "Intelligence and Policy Making in Foreign Affairs," *World Politics,* Vol. V., no. 1, October 1952.
[2] Paul F. Lazarsfeld, "The American Soldier—An Expository Review," *Public Opinion Quarterly,* summer 1949, p. 380.

USES

WHAT ECONOMISTS KNOW

Paul A. Samuelson

Economics is fortunate among the social sciences in that many of its findings are directly applicable to public policy. Within the last twenty-five years great advances have been made in our factual knowledge about the financial system and in our understanding of how that system works and can be made to work. So only recently, you might say, has economics earned the right to its ancient name of political economy.

Thus, as I write in early 1958 the American economy is in the midst of a recession. So well charted these days is the pulse of the nation that this is open knowledge. The casual reader of the newspaper has today an awareness of contemporaneous economics events that was just a few decades ago unavailable even to the most energetic scholar. And beyond this knowledge of the facts of the case there is a calculated confidence• in our ability to battle this scourge

• Since this was written events have confirmed the implicit prediction made in early 1958 that the recession would soon come to an end: the upturn came after April.

of depression. A prediction made two decades ago that our mixed capitalistic system would no longer face the same frequency of chronic slumps as in its checkered past would have been borne out by the subsequent record: today's college undergraduate has scarcely known a full year of business contraction! The previous pattern, that each war must be followed by a slump with the same predictability that night follows day, has not thus far reasserted itself. While it would be rash to say that the business cycle has been banished from American life, it would be foolish to overlook the changed betting odds with respect to the likelihood of the *sustained* deflations that occurred in the 1830s, the 1870s, the 1890s, and 1930s.

If one had to associate this changed knowledge and control over national output and employment with but one name, it would certainly be that of Cambridge's Lord Keynes. If one were permitted a second, it would probably be that of Harvard's Alvin Hansen, the so-called "American Keynes" and himself a prolific developer of the tools of fiscal analysis. But the body of knowledge that I am interested in describing is quite independent of its controversial origin: an expert in business cycles as Arthur F. Burns, formerly Economic Adviser to President Eisenhower and now re-associated with the National Bureau of Economic Research, would without doubt reject the notion that he had received inspiration from Keynesian Theory. And so would Sumner Slichter and many other gifted observers of the passing economic scene. Yet, in the mode of analysis used—the emphasis upon the interrelations of consumption and investment spending, upon the past sequences of statistical time series—economists of varied political persuasions can largely agree. Craftsmanship rises above personalities: this is the fact that makes the dream of a science of economics possible.

A prosaic example can often illustrate, better than can thousands of words about abstract methodology, how a science actually proceeds. Therefore, I propose to illustrate, later in this essay, just what things the practicing economist watches and reasons about if he is approaching the important job of understanding the contemporaneous business cycle—understanding it for its own sake, understanding it in order to make predictions about the future, understanding it in order to give policy advice to statesmen or businessmen.

But a brief digression about the nature of economics and its reasoning would be useful at this point.

Uncommon Common Sense

Economists use terribly complicated jargon: long words, fine definitions, cabalistic mathematical symbols and graphs, complicated statistical techniques. Yet, if they have done their job well, they end up with what is simple common sense.

The noneconomist must naturally ask: Was that trip really necessary? The answer is: Apparently yes. Nothing is so rare as common sense—*i.e.*, the *relevant* common sense. Anything and everything can be phrased so as to be plausible. Black is plausible; so is white; and so is grey. Until you have excluded some possibilities, or reduced their probability, you have accomplished nothing as a scientist. So the content of pure common sense—like that of the self-canceling folk aphorisms of a people—tends to be nil.

Economics of War

A subject that is all too important these days provides an excellent illustration—the economics of war. Let any intelligent layman reflect upon what he conceives to be its principles. Then let him consider the relevant sections of any elementary textbook.[1] How much of the subject did he anticipate? And—what is even more interesting—what additions to these doctrines was he able to make?

Lest any one think all this too obvious, let me hasten to point out that until World War I nothing of war economics was at all well understood. Here are a few examples. (1) At the beginning of that war, in both Britain and America, the slogans "business as usual" were not words of reproach; they were being flashed in full-page advertisments urging the consumer to spend his money on civilian goods. (2) In 1914 the young Keynes told his Bloomsbury friends the war was too costly to be able to last long. (3) It was only after 1914 that economists were able to clarify the problem of whether the current wartime generation could, by financing the conflict through loans rather than taxes, succeed thereby in throwing a sizable burden onto the future, rather than on the present, generation. It took the best economists of that day to show that the enemy must be fought with current real resources; and that only to the degree that less of economy's capital (machinery, plants, roads, etc.) is bequeathed to the post-war generations can those generations be made to bear the burden of the war. (4) In 1917 patriotic Americans were urged to borrow from the banks in order to buy government bonds—as if that would release any real re-sources to the war effort or differ in effect from merely selling bonds to the banks directly.

Examples of similar folly could be found in World War II—but not among responsible economists.

Economists in Action

War provided another kind of a test case. Economists in some numbers joined the government to help solve mili-

tary and civilian policy problems. So did numerous businessmen, not all of whom served for a dollar a year. What
were the relative achievements of the two groups? If one
who was not himself directly involved can be permitted to
hazard a guess, I would suggest that the decisions followed
tended usually to be those framed by people primarily from
university life and that these were on the whole the better
decisions.

What were the reasons for this? Certainly not differences
in intrinsic intelligence or articulateness. Aside from the
fact that it is the economists' business to be thinking about
social decision-making, I think there was also the factor
that a considerable advantage attends the exercise of ordinary precautions of "loose" scientific method—a wish to
dig up relevant evidence, and a respect for such factual
data once it had been collected and analysed.

In the realm of decision-making itself, there seemed to
be a military role which persons trained in the discipline of
economics could fulfill. In one agency, units of historians
and economists worked side by side: and I think disinterested third parties would agree that the economists seemed
quickest to make the important policy decisions. It is as if
the repeated study of the imponderables of economic life—
where the data are never complete and where calculated
guesses have to be made—were a valuable preparation for
the wartime problems. I daresay the same type of considerations are relevant to explain why, in the war-created
realm of *operations research*,[2] which involved the use of
scientists to aid in decision-making, statisticians and economists often proved less paralyzed by the need to reach
conclusions on the basis of incomplete evidence than were
those who came from some of the "harder" laboratory
sciences.

It is considerations such as those preceding that fortify

the teacher of graduate economics. As he puts each generation through the paces of advanced economics, he is a rare man if he does not sometimes ask himself what the connection is between these rarified concepts and the concrete realities of economic life. But it seems to be a brute fact of experience that, somehow, going through such a training does alert the trained economist to an important way of looking at things—to a concentration on relevant alternatives and a predisposition to question their relative costs and advantages. Perhaps there ought to be some cheaper way of producing this degree of economic sophistication, but no one seems yet to have found it.

A Demurral

Still I must not give the impression that an economist is to be judged by how much money he can make or by how quick and accurate his decisions are. Economics, after all, is not *home economics*, even though its name derives from the Greek word which means that. The economists I know are, by and large, not demonstrably better at spending or saving their money than other people; nor at outguessing the stockmarket. Some of our most gifted economists would be useless in the tent of the Prince either in war or peace—even though as a result of their researches and theories, political economy is in a better position to render needed advice.

Whether a man makes quick decisions, whether he is good at piercing the veil of uncertainty, is after all a matter of temperament. One would not require the same qualifications in appointing someone to fill a chair in economics as one would in deciding on who is to advise a bank or to invest his widow's money.

There is a sense, however, in which all science does involve decision-making. Some years ago, at a Harvard Law

School Symposium on the role of law in a liberal education, Judge Charles E. Wyzanski, Jr. quoted from Lord Beveridge's biography to the effect that the laboratory scientist is lucky because he never has to make decisions. I bristled at this, for it has long been my conviction that the problems of all sciences can be formulated as the making of intelligent decisions with respect to actual or hypothetical courses of action. Of course, these will often be in the nature of "thought experiments"—hypothetical bets or decisions. They need not be actual decisions, with important financial or human consequences.

After all, why does a scientist make one experiment rather than another? And why do scientists consider the results of certain experiments as so much more interesting and important than those of others? To say that the quantum theory is a better theory than the classical theory of mechanics can be construed to mean: If my life was wagered on the probable outcome of as-yet-unperformed experiments, would I—or would I not—base my forecast upon the quantum theory? And my degree of confidence in that theory might be revealed, or at least illuminated, by the odds that I could be forced to give if necessary.

An Interpretation of History: A Digression

With respect to the natural sciences the above reformulation, even if admissible, is not needed. A physicist or chemist need not be much of a methodologist: his disciplines have a logic of their own which often will unobtrusively point the way. It is otherwise with the "softer" social sciences. So little spontaneous guidance is provided by the subject matter, that in some of these disciplines substantive research is displaced by repetitious and inconclusive discussion of methodology.

History is a discipline now passing through some kind of a crisis, as historians are themselves the first to testify. Few still regard it as an exact science. Yet not all historians are willing to have it become mere antiquarianism, sequestered behind the walls of the Humanities and separated from the Social Sciences. Because history borders on economics, the views of the latter may throw some light on the interpretation of history as a discipline.

"We pass this way only once," is the essence of the problem for the historian. If Nature were to provide its own controlled experiments; or if, in the absence of controlled experiments, she were to supply us with repeated experience from which we could infer regularities—in either event the peculiar differences between history and any science would disappear.[3] But things happen as they happen. To say that things might just as well have gone another way than the way they did go cannot be judged.

Yet we do distinguish between good and bad historians. Two writers may both tell the truth, but neither can tell the whole truth. Nevertheless, we find one profound and interesting, the other trivial. For example, if we are interested in the view of a man who has weighed all the available evidence bearing on the historical question of whether the *Odyssey* was written by a woman, it is not because we can ever perform an experiment that will answer the question. Either Homer was or was not a woman, and the concept of probability and forecasting cannot directly apply to that dead fact. But we can ask ourselves the hypothetical question: Suppose new documentary finds should become available in the future. What would a jury of responsible historians or scientists be willing to guess would be the bearing of such documents[4] upon the question?

Some such scientific method as that just described is used

by the historian all the time, and it is by exercise of such methods that we decide that one writer produces foolish and far-fetched history whereas another's is cogent and interesting.

Within the discipline of economics itself, consider the scientist who studies the business cycle. As the 1957-58 recession developed, he pored over the facts that emerged concerning it and tried to discern a pattern from these facts, in order to narrow down the field of open possibilities that were relevant to the immediate future. He was aware that the present recession is exactly like no previous one, but he knew also that, by careful marshaling of the relevant analogous events of past experience, he could gain insight into this unique event.

Let any one who thinks the world was born anew this morning—possessing no tendency to favor certain uniformities with yester-morning—beware of making bets about the future. Such an agnostic will lose his money—I assert this as a fact of experience!

But this is not to say that it is fruitful to regard the whole of past economic history as a homogeneous sample from what the statistician calls a "stationary time series." On the contrary, one feels that new data about 1836 will contribute something—but relatively little—to the dynamics of contemporary capitalism. The system has evolved; and to have a feeling for the rate of its evolution one must apply the canons of ordinary scientific method to study its "stationary part."

The depression of 1893 would certainly be called "history"—if only because the statute of limitations has run out. But you would, in principle and with due respect to gaps in the data, study it by the same methods to be applied to such recent history as the depression of 1932—or, for that matter, the recession of 1958.

We shall return now from the digression on history to the peculiar problems of economics itself.

A Babel of Voices?

According to legend, economists are supposed never to agree among themselves. If Parliament were to ask six economists for an opinion, seven answers would come back—two, no doubt, from the volatile Mr. Keynes! If economists cannot agree among themselves, how can the rest of the world be expected to agree with them and to respect their recommendations?

This is a fair question. It is a matter of record that, on any broad issue requiring decision, you often find economists giving quite different recommendations. The reasons for this are at least twofold:

First, most decisions involve questions of future fact. No one has yet found a crystal ball that will make the future transparent.

Second, most decisions involve *ethical ends* that transcend positive science. Thus, one economist may seem to favor repeal of the oil industry's privilege to go untaxed on its 27½ percentage depletion; another may argue for retention of this tax privilege. Both may, nevertheless, be in agreement that such a change will (1) slow down the search for oil and (2) speed up the equalization of incomes that has been going on for some decades. Their differences may lie in the ethical weights each gives to égalitarianism and to material progress. And such differences of opinion can never be finally arbitrated within the halls of economic science itself, but must be decided in the political arena.

Some other reasons for disagreement among economists can be expected to disappear as our knowledge of the facts and our analytical abilities increase. What needs emphasis to the layman, perhaps, is this truth: when two good economists are arguing with each other, they can quickly narrow down their differences and identify them—in a way that a good economist cannot always do when carrying on economic arguments with noneconomists.

The New Uniformity

It is possible to argue that American economists—and Western economists generally—far from being too divided among a number of competing schools, today present a united front that reflects *too little* basic disagreement on fundamentals.

It was not always so. In the past, particularly in nineteenth-century Germany, there was great methodological conflict between the Historical School and the Classical School. In the first quarter of the twentieth century this same quarrel came to a head in America. The so-called Institutionalist School—associated with such names as Thorstein Veblen, John R. Commons, Wesley Mitchell—rose to challenge traditional economics. But, with the passing of the years, the Institutionalists have not perpetuated themselves. Today, surveying leading graduate schools, one finds them competing for the same men, teaching the same basic economic doctrines and methods. Although there are one, two, or three exceptions to this, even they are moving toward the common pattern—and one might have expected, in a great nation, countless exceptions to any one pattern.

It is impossible to discuss here the detailed reasons for the decline of historicism and the ascendancy of neoclassical economics. Briefly, one reason lies in the fact that the former became stale and sterile and did not produce the results it had promised. A second factor lies in the roots of the Keynesian Revolution, which was developed by economists working within the older Anglo-

Saxon tradition; it provided an outlet and a program for those with strong reform aspirations who had previously provided the best recruits for the anticlassical movements. Finally, the existence in America of numerous business schools and of flourishing areas of applied economics—such as labor economics and industrial relations, market organization and price policy, public finance, etc.—meant that economists with an empirical bent could follow their inclination without necessarily cutting themselves off from the body of economic theory.

Marxian Economics

Obviously, there has been so far no mention of the economic doctrines that are considered official for half the people in the world—for the hundreds of millions in Soviet Russia and China. But there is in fact little contact between the tenets of the economics studied in the Western World and that of the Iron Curtain nations.

For a dramatic indication of the differences between these two traditions, one might consider the elementary textbooks on economics that have been published in both societies (for it may indeed be more important to write a people's songs and textbooks than to write her laws). One of the most widely used American introductory textbooks—one that has been translated into many languages—has outsold in number such past books as those of John Stuart Mill, Adam Smith, and Alfred Marshall. One might assume, from sheer number of sales alone, that it might be taken as representative of Western economics. However, any illusion that it represents the best-seller in the field of economics would be decisively shattered by the information—and reliable information—that the official economics textbook of the Soviet Union, *Political Economy*, sold four or five million copies in its first printing.

It is instructive to compare the two texts. The Soviet book was written by a committee, and within a year after 1954 it had to be revised for deviations from official Soviet ideology. It is required reading for all college students; and units of the Communist Party—be it a cell of engineers or scientists, or a philosophical discussion group—must master its catechism. Of its 800 pages, scarcely 200 are devoted to the economics of the Soviet Union or of a socialist society. (The absence of consecutive statistics and detailed facts is noteworthy.) The rest is devoted to the shortcomings of capitalism. The quotations from economists and other writers are few and extremely selective: Marx and Engels, Lenin, and (to a diminishing degree) Stalin[5] are predominant.

Is it a good book? If it provided a good framework of analysis for the development of capitalistic society, then—however distasteful its dogmatism, however uneven its contents—we of the Western World would mine it for its insights and shamelessly plagiarize it for its conclusions. But, alas, for reasons that would have to be substantiated elsewhere this Marxist economics is not well adapted to predicting the next five months of capitalistic society much less the next fifty years! When the Soviet economists, in actuality, find themselves having to adapt the price analysis of traditional economics to the problems of collectivist planning, and to explain the 1958 decline in American business activity, they will have to go through the same routines of national income calculation as do their Western counterparts.

How To Be Your Own Economic Forecaster

For the remainder of this discussion, I should like then to turn to the area of business cycle control. Here, after all, is the area which signifies to most people the progress made by economic analysis.

There is no easy way to become a sophisticated economic forecaster. But no better introduction to the problems faced by the modern student of business cycles can be had than to go through the prosaic steps followed by the actual forecaster in his day-to-day activities as he advises the government or his business firm. Obviously, the judgment that he brings at each stage to the analysis cannot be learned overnight, and can scarcely be learned at all without a prolonged apprenticeship of economic study.

Can Forecasters Forecast at All?

Anyone who reads the daily paper will have some impression of what is happening to business. But, unless he disciplines his observations, his impression will be a rather chaotic one, and he will not be very prompt in recognizing the turning points in the economic climate.

On the one hand, trained economists are not impressively accurate in forecasting the near-term future, as is attested by the fact that in 1945 most members of the profession wrongly predicted a sizable postwar depression. On the other hand, the month-to-month forecasting that takes place in the financial and industrial community, in government, and in universities will provide a general estimate of the "batting averages" of the different groups. And significantly, in forecasting the economy, economists, poor as they are, do better than noneconomists. A personal impression, drawn from filed records of past behavior, is that the forecasting departments of large corporations do slightly better than their more impressionistic, less systematic, brethren. On the whole, the forecasting done within the government, although far from perfect, is among the best there is; and it is impressive how well informed federal departments are on the changing state of the economy.

Weekly Statistics

Which statistics will the prudent forecaster watch most closely? The layman, probably because he remembers the great stock market crash of 1929, is prone to think that the daily reports of common stock prices is the primary index for the forecaster. True, the day-to-day and minute-to-minute speculator is concerned most with these reports. However, a speculator in onions, studying nothing but onion statistics, is not likely to imagine that such information is pivotal for the economy as a whole.

The stock market, too, is more effect than cause of what is developing in the economy. Its testimony, although of some interest, is hardly of prime importance. The forecaster interested in economic policy' will dismiss the daily Wall Street returns in favor of the indexes of stock prices, released later by the Securities Exchange Commission on a weekly or a monthly basis.

The significant weekly reports for the analyst are the Federal Reserve Board figures on department store sales. These are already several days out of date, but any significant changes in them may herald an important change in the consumption spending of the nation. Since consumption is the greatest single component of national income spending, any change in its trend would be of highest interest to the analyst; he would like to know about it early.

There are obvious pitfalls in interpreting the movements of this current series. Have store sales gone up simply because the arrival of Easter has stimulated sales? The experienced economist will invariably make some kind of correction for the season. Thus, he will want to study how this week's sales compares with the similar week one year ago. For seasonal events such as Christmas, which always falls on the same date, such a simple year-to-year comparison may be enough. But he knows that the complicated nineteen-year cycle of Easter makes it harder to judge whether the current sales are ahead of, or behind, the previous year's. Even when he has allowed for the month and day of the year, he knows that a fortuitous event, such as a heavy snow storm on the Eastern seaboard, may contaminate his comparisons. An unusually warm and late winter may reduce apparel spending in a way that is never made up in later months. The analyst must take all these factors into account. If he is experienced, he realizes that, whenever retail spending is weak, a host of apologists will arise who will attribute this weakness to some vagary of the weather. The analyst must be able to give the weather no more than its due—not an easy task.

There are other important weekly indicators, such as railroad freight-car loadings or electric-power production. As the railroads lose ground to the trucking industry, railroad carloadings are subject to a long-term declining trend. The analyst must allow for this—and, likewise, for the strong growth trend characterizing electric-power production. Thus, as the nation goes into a recession, he must not be taken in by reassuring utterances that this week's power production is 1 or 2 per cent above last year's. Such a report is far from cheerful. Ordinarily, in our growing economy, in which electricity becomes ever more important, we expect each year to use 5, 7, or 10 per cent more electricity than did the previous year. It is a severe recession indeed that makes electric-power production go down absolutely. Thus, the ups and downs of business activity in the electric-power production figures are not merely ups and downs in the rate of growth of that series. And this the experienced observer will have learned.

A number of financial services average together several of these weekly indicators of business activity into what they call a comprehensive index, or barometer, of business activity. Thus, there is the New York Times index of business activity, which takes into account electric-power production, carloadings, steel production, paper, and still other indicators of current activity. When corrected for long-term trend, seasonal factors, and fortuitous events such as strikes, these barometers can serve a useful purpose.

Another important weekly source of information is the Federal Reserve report on its balance sheet and the changes in position of its member banks. Ordinarily, the day-to-day operations of the Federal Reserve open market committee, as it buys and sells government bonds, are shrouded in secrecy. Those very close to the money market may suspect on Monday that the Federal Reserve is buying government bills in order to make credit a little easier, but even they cannot be sure. Only at the end of the week, when the new balance sheet of the Federal Reserve Banks is published, do we get a concrete clue as to what has been happening.

Seasonal and irregular factors will becloud the testimony of any one week's report. Certainly a neophyte can be thrown off by changes in such mysterious entities as the "float" and be led into thinking that the Federal Reserve has reversed its policy when in fact nothing significant has been happening. However, one learns to allow for such factors, and in the fall of 1957 careful analysts could anticipate a change in Federal Reserve policy some weeks before the Federal Reserve Board, on November 14, dramatically lowered its discount rate to 3 per cent from 3½ per cent.

The information provided by the reporting member banks may be even more significant than that of the

Federal Reserve itself. For example, 1957 bank loans were languishing for months before the Federal Reserve decided to abandon its policy of credit restriction in favor of a policy of credit ease. Because the movement of business inventories is one of the most important bellwethers of the current situation, and because of the unfortunate fact that estimates of inventory changes are always late in coming out each month and that the corrected rate of inventory change needed for national income information is available only quarterly, it is all the more important for us to watch the behavior of bank loans as a possible quick indicator of what the more complete inventory figures will later show.

Monthly Statistics

Additional important economic statistics become available on a monthly basis. Not long after the end of each month department store and mail order sales data, and also sales data of grocery, variety, apparel, and drug chains are published. These significantly re-inforce the testimony of the weekly department store sales. Indeed, since department stores in many urban areas are losing ground to the suburbs and also to so-called discount houses, they are an imperfect reflector of retail trends. The great department and mail order houses, such as Sears Roebuck and Montgomery Ward, give a surprisingly accurate portrayal of what is happening in the economy at large. They, with the sales data of other chain stores, enable us to guess what the Department of Commerce will later report for retail sales. Early in each month there is a census of unemployment, employment, and size of labor force. Taken together with the reports on employment provided by a sample of business firms, this is a valuable indicator of what is going on in the economy. It can be supplemented by information on hours worked per week and on how many workers are making new claims for unemployment compensation. Moreover, by breaking down the unemployment figures into those relevant to partially and fully unemployed and into those unemployed for a long or short time adds to our ability to guess whether a given upswing or contraction is likely to be especially significant.

Perhaps the most important of all indicators of current business activity is the monthly Federal Reserve Board index of production. This is available some weeks after the month's end and provides a comprehensive measure of physical production in manufacturing and mining. Because it does not include the less volatile item of services, it tends to exaggerate the amplitude of short-term fluctuations— which is really an advantage to the forecaster interested in picking up on his seismograph the slightest rumblings of trouble ahead.

It is interesting that the Federal Reserve Board production index reached its (seasonally corrected) peak in December 1956, some seven months before the majority of the various economic time series turned downward and a good ten months before the Federal Reserve authorities recognized that we were indeed in a recession. Similarly, its turn down in the middle of 1953 served to announce the 1953-1954 recession. A producer of steel, copper, or oil could find it enormously useful to know, in advance, the Federal Reserve Board index of production for twelve months, in order to gauge his output accordingly.

Another important monthly bit of information is given by personal income. This is a seasonally corrected estimate of how much people have received in the form of wages, interest, dividends, government relief and transfer payments, and earnings from unincorporated enterprise. After they pay their direct taxes out of this total, people are left with disposable income, to be spent on consumption goods or saved. If at any period the reports on personal income were down for three or four months in a row—as in the period following August 1957—one would be forced to conclude nervously that some kind of recession was taking place. For it is the usual case that personal income rises from decade to decade, from year to year, and from month to month. The short-term changes in reported personal income give the economist the basis for guessing what the not-yet-reported quarterly figures for national income will later show.

There are a number of other miscellaneous statistical reports that the careful forecaster will take careful note of. If he reads *The New York Times* or *Herald Tribune*—or his *Wall Street Journal* or *Journal of Commerce*—he will watch for the latest reports of sales, new orders, and inventories in the retail, wholesale, and manufacturing sectors, and for data on housing starts and construction awards.

Most of these important magnitudes will be summarized for him in the convenient Congressional publication *Economic Indicators,* which is published late in each month by the Joint Economic Committee for the Council of Economic Advisers. This merely presents the figures without analysis. For a deeper understanding of what is going on, the forecaster will be sure to read the Department of Commerce's *Survey of Current Business* and the monthly *Federal Reserve Bulletin.*

Most monthly newsletters put out by banks are dispensable, although an exception should perhaps be made for the influential First National City Bank monthly letter and for the monthly review of the New York Federal Reserve Bank. These various letters will comment on, and attempt to interpret, the striking events of the passing parade.

Quarterly and General Statistics

Soon after each quarter of the year the economic analyst will receive the first reports on national income statistics. Strictly speaking, the gross national product, the GNP, attracts the most publicity and attention; the particular magnitude that the U. S. Department of Commerce chooses to call "national income" does not become available for some time and does not in any case represent so inclusive and important a magnitude as GNP.

The significant points in these reports are changes in consumption or government spending and changes in the various components of domestic or foreign investment. Among the investment components, the net change in inventories is the one most likely to fluctuate in the short run. And any change in the percentage of disposable income that people save will be examined with great interest.

The quarterly statistics of GNP will be averaged for the year in the new January Economic Report of the President. Still further revised estimates will become available in the February *Survey of Current Business;* but not until the July national income number of that *Survey* will reasonably definitive annual estimates be available ("reasonably definitive" because the time will never come when all such estimates become final: the Department of Commerce is constantly revising its historical estimates as new ways of improving them become available).

Surveys of Future Intentions and Hopes

The statistical observations described so far refer to past facts. Today we have a new and exciting supplement to such timely observation on past facts—the periodic surveys that bear on intentions of businessmen to invest and of families to consume.

Thus, the McGraw-Hill Publishing Company puts out periodically a valuable poll of businessmen's intentions to invest, broken down by industry. The National Industrial Conference Board and *Newsweek* give estimates of the "capital appropriations" of business. The official SEC-Commerce surveys of business investment give estimates for two quarters ahead on such spending, broken down by industrial classification.

The credit rating organization, Dun & Bradstreet, takes periodic polls of businessmen's expectations with respect to their own sales and those of the over-all economy. Purchasing agents of industry draw up reports monthly concerning their own expectations and current experience. There are even continuous observations available upon the opinions of a fixed panel of academic and business economists.

Especially around New Year, there is no shortage of utterances about what can be expected in the coming year. To be sure, the number of independent bits of information in these communications is not great: typically, the year-end forecaster predicts no change in the economic winds for the next six months—followed thereafter by a reversal. However, you will probably be wrong to agree with the old aphorism: "When all the experts agree, watch out, for that's when they are most likely to be wrong." Historical observation does not suggest that such a hypothesis can be validated.

Historical observation suggests that, indeed, "One peek is worth a thousand finesses." It is better to have a man tell you of his plans than to have to guess at them. Consider, as a concrete example, the fall-off in fixed investment spending by business that began in the last quarter of 1957. As early as the summer of 1957, the Conference Board survey of capital appropriations alerted the analyst to this possibility. And by fall both the McGraw-Hill and SEC-Commerce Surveys confirmed the prognosis. Then, in the Spring of 1958, we learned how terribly accurate these surveys had been.

To get a notion of the mood and intention of consumers, the Group Survey Center of the University of Michigan conducts a scientifically random poll of consumers all over the nation. The results of this are published and analyzed in the Federal Reserve Bulletin and give a clue as to whether the typical consumer is feeling more optimistic than before, more thrift-minded, or more disposed to buy durable goods such as homes, cars, and appliances.

It is too soon to make sweeping claims for the validity of usefulness of such information, but experience of the last decade has suggested that this is a promising source of information about the current economic situation. Certainly, in early 1958, the reported pessimism of consumers was worth worrying about.

Three Methods of Forecasting

Economists differ in methodology—specifically, in their techniques of analyzing accumulated data—but the following three categories are roughly representative. First, there are the crude empiricists, who simply form an impression from the variety of pertinent data as to whether things are going to remain the same, go up, or go down. Second, there are the refined empiricists, who look for certain early indicators to alert them to what is later going to happen to the economy at large, or who take careful numerical count of the number of economic time series that are going up in comparison with those that are going down and compute a "diffusion index" in which every statistical time series is given the same weight, although one may be GNP and another pig-iron production. Third, there are the national-income model builders, who try to make estimates of the different components of GNP and who, in order to do this, find it necessary to make consistent estimates of the inter-relations among the different magnitudes.

How do followers of these three different general methods fare? No final answer can be given with confidence, but it would be a personal guess that the crude empiricist does worst of all. Indeed, the human mind being what it is, the crude empiricist rarely remains a nonselective averager of the information fed him but becomes instead the prey of each passing theory and fad.

The refined empiricist who searches for early indicators puts great weight on the following series: stock market prices, sensitive commodity prices, residential and other building contracts, new orders, average hours worked per week, number of new incorporations, and absence of business failures. When any or all of these turn up, he considers this an indication that within a few months general business activity may turn up. And a turn down in any or all of these would indicate to him that business is the more likely to turn down in a few months.

More eclectic economists of this persuasion keep track of the relative number of different economic time series that are currently going up. If the diffusion index shows that only 25 per cent of all series are going up, they reserve judgment as to when the upturn will come. As the diffusion index rises toward 50 per cent, they become more confident that the upturn is imminent. The really cautious ones will not actually call a turn until the 50 per cent level has been passed.

A careful person who follows these methods can hardly fail to detect any sizable movement in the modern economy. Unfortunately, his seismograph is also likely to record many small fluctuations, some of which have to be regarded as false alarms. Watching the more sensitive of the early indicators is calculated to keep the analyst in a constant state of agitation and alarm. Thus, in 1952 the method called for a recession which never came. And in August 1957 a temporary firming of many of the early indicators gave the false signal to some analysts that there was not to be the impending recession. The next month's information decisively corrected this misinformation.

This is not the place to attempt a definitive appraisal of such methods. But a few cautionary remarks are in order. Take the case of a typical early indicator—the behavior of stock market prices. Although business turned down in the middle of 1929, the stock market was some months late in taking account of this fact. So this particular omen did not work well at the outset of the biggest depression in our recent history. Or take the case of the 1937-38 recession, where in hindsight it is given a better score. Here the market did fall in the first part of 1937, but unaccountably then proceeded to recover. Its subsequent decline did agree with the decline in general business activity. But think of the nervous agitation of the analyst who was contemporaneously following this barometer and who didn't have the benefit of our generous hindsight. Still another case is that of 1946 when the market fell in anticipation of a recession that never came. Nor can the behavior of the market in 1953 be considered a triumph for the method. In the first part of 1953 when business was strong the market was weak. Then in September, just as the Eisenhower administration, along with everyone else, began to recognize that we were in for a recession the stock market proceeded to take off on a rise that was to persist throughout and beyond the 1954 recession, ending only at the peak levels reached in the middle of 1956 and again in the middle of 1957.

There seems to be an inherent bias in the way that economists use hindsight to claim validation for the prophetic powers of a volatile series like the stockmarket. The truth is that such economic time series fluctuate a good deal. If every time they go down and the economy does not subsequently go down, you ignore such a movement and only record those cases where you know by hindsight the economy did validate the move, you will get an exaggerated notion of the prophetic powers of the volatile series. (In some experiments at the Massachusetts Institute of Technology we found that experimental subjects, who didn't know the future and who were shown the chart of stockmarket prices with successively larger sections exposed to view, tended to call three times as many turns in the stockmarket as are recognized to have taken place in general business activity!)

It appears that most serious minded forecasters take account of the mehod of economic indicators and diffusion indexes but combine them with some kind of a rough gross national product model. Few such forecasters go to the extremes represented by Lawrence R. Klein of America, Colin Clark of Australia and Britain, and Jan Tinbergen of Holland. These latter have complicated sets of mathematical equations, fitted to the past facts to determine their best numerical parameters; certain recent information is then incorporated into the equations and, with the aid of modern calculating machines, the results state definite forecasts of the future values of gross national product components, employment, production, and prices.

Although few analysts use such elaborate and inflexible models, most of them, in using a process of successive approximation—*e.g.*, in making first rough estimates of an interconnected table of all the variables and then adjusting them for apparent inconsistencies—are trying to accomplish much the same thing.

The process can be only vaguely sketched here. Typically, a relation based on past experience is used to connect consumption spending and disposable income. (If there is reason to think that the past relationship will in this period be a little high or low, this can be built into the model.) Past relations connecting dividends and corporate earnings, taxes and income, welfare expenditure and income, etc., are also utilized. Then, estimates from surveys or recent history are used to introduce investment figures into the model. Finally, the trends in government expenditure and foreign trade are introduced. When all these different figures are made to confront each other systematically, various corrections take place; you will emerge with either a single set of predictions of the various economic magnitudes or a range of predicted values within high and low limits. Depending upon temperament, the analyst may never structure this into a systematic model but may, nonetheless in effect, be solving simultaneous equations in an approximate way by intuition. Some analysts, although they have learned that they speak prose all their lives, have yet to learn that they may be solving complicated simultaneous equations when they exercise judgment about economic compatibility of various estimates.

Hitting the Target

As a result of watching carefully all past and present events and scanning the portents of future events, the analyst usually finds it easy enough to decide whether total dollar spending is too little or too much. If total spending is too much, employment tends to be overfull—the number of job vacancies tends to outstrip the number of unemployed workers, and there is an upward pressure both on money wages and on prices generally. If total spending is too little, there is a residue of unemployed workers and an inadequate level of production and consumption.

When the economy is diagnosed as clearly needing less or more total dollar spending, the government knows what fiscal and monetary programs ought to be followed. Thus, to help increase total spending, the Federal Reserve Authorities will buy government securities in the open money market: this will raise bond prices and lower interest rates; at the same time, it will tend to increase the reserve balances of the commercial banks, which they, in turn, will hasten to offer for loans or investment. The net effect is to make credit more available and also cheaper to investment spenders. In addition to these day-to-day open market operations, the Central Bank can also lower the discount rate at which it lends to banks and can periodically lower the legal reserve ratios that it requires the commercial banks to keep uninvested and on deposit with itself. These measures will also ease credit and tend to add to total investment spending.

What must Congress and the President do to help add to the total of spending and job opportunities? The fiscal authorities must reduce tax collections and/or increase government expenditure in order to add to the total of spending. Because of well-known "built-in stabilizers" the modern economy automatically drops its tax collections and steps up its spending when income falls *even without* any authorities being aware of it or taking any explicit, discretionary acts; but over and beyond these first-line-of-defense automatic attenuators of instability, there are explicit fiscal programs of expansion to be followed.

If economists' diagnosis declares the economy to be suffering from an excess of demand, the needed therapy calls for a reduction in total spending. Then all the above monetary and fiscal programs have to be operated in reverse. For example, taxes must be raised and expenditures cut; credit must be made tight and expensive, by openmarket sales of bonds, by discount rate hikes, and legal reserve ratio increases.

Nor is any of the above academic. In the late 1950's we are getting samples of all these fiscal and credit measures. It is wrong to think that all these decisions must be made with a surgeon's precision, that there must be split-second timing without any delays, and that there must be instantaneous reversal of policy when conditions change. The modern economy is a great sluggish thing. It changes but it changes slowly. Remember that our goal is not the abolition of all business cycles—even if that were feasible, it might not be desirable. Instead we aim to wipe out persistent slump or unsought inflation. If only capitalism had succeeded in the past in this more modest goal, how different would have been the course of human history!

A Final Dilemma

Lest this end on too complacent a note, it must be pointed out that, although economics has solved many problems, the solutions have given rise to new problems. Not the least of these is the fact that many economists feel technologically unemployed: having helped banish the worst economic diseases of capitalism, they feel like the ear surgeons whose function modern antibiotics has reduced to a low level of priority.

From the standpoint of society at large, perhaps the greatest problem still facing the student of political economy is the threat of long-term inflation. In the past, the periodic bouts of economic depression tended to bring prices down. History witnessed the averaging of price drops against price rises, with the long drift being one of caprice and accident. But the contemporary social conscience is very sensitive to what would have been regarded years ago as quite modest levels of temporary unemployment. We seem no longer willing to tolerate distress that is persistent enough to have a downward influence on prices and wages. All our adjustments tend then to be made in the upward direction. This not only shifts the betting odds toward long-term rising prices but also breeds an understandable concern over inflation. The problem of continuous inflation tends to weaken society's motivations to seek perfectionist standards of full employment. And a candid appraisal of some recent attitudes would indicate that, in its effects upon future policy formation, the fear of inflation should awaken some other fears.

But this danger need not strike too dismal a note. As old problems are conquered, we expect to turn up new problems. A discipline lives on its unsolved problems; and so, for better or worse, economics is likely to be a lively subject for as many years ahead as man can see.

NOTES

[1] A typical textbook treatment would be P. A. Samuelson, *Economics* (4th ed.; New York: McGraw-Hill, 1958), Chap. 36.

[2] See Philip M. Morse and George E. Kimball, Cambridge, Technology Press of M.I.T. and Wiley, New York, 1951, for

a first discussion of what has since blossomed out into a vast discipline.

[3] As John Dewey said, "We never step in the same river twice." The river is different and so are we.

[4] Only occasionally are new documents found that enable us to test alternative views or forecasts—which make the problem of validation all the more difficult for the historian.

[5] This book replaced Stalin's *Short Course* as the official textbook of Marxian economics.

PSYCHOLOGY AND SOCIAL ORDER

Lawrence K. Frank

Only within recent generations has man begun to look
beyond familiar beliefs about human nature for more dependable knowledge based on systematic observations of
human behavior. As many orderly and regular designs were
recognized behind accounts of seemingly fantastic lifeways, culture became a focus for investigation.

The perplexities of contemporary society have evoked
efforts by relatively recent researchers, the social scientists
—economists, anthropologists, sociologists, political scientists, psychologists, etc.—to understand how disorders occur
in familiar practices and institutions. Of all the social
sciences, psychology—because of the grave personal consequences that the application of its findings may involve—
bears a special responsibility. Its theories are often eagerly
applied by non-psychologists—notably in advertising, business, and politics—and attempts are made to direct human
relations according to some theoretical model. Such application can be dangerous, for psychology today is still only

an aspiration toward a science. Its different and often con-
flicting schools can be cited to support a variety of different
economic, political, and social policies.

This point gains significance if we remember that human
behavior occurs in a symbolic cultural world, patterned by
beliefs, laws, and customs. A culture—a social order—is
not the simple product of physical, chemical, and biological
processes. It is a human creation, man's own attempt to
maintain an essentially human way of life as contrasted
with the biological existence of other organisms. Everywhere man has attempted to transform nature and human
nature into that which he believes to be true, desirable, and
worth striving for. His social order in the Western world,
therefore, is continually being altered; and his design for
living is rarely, if ever, static.

A society becomes aware of its traditional assumptions
only when they are no longer adequate. This raises "social
problems"—indications that the established belief, practices, rituals, and symbols are no longer acceptable. As
some individuals begin to question tradition and try new
patterns of behavior, they provoke resistance and generate
conflicts in their social order.

If we think of a social order as continually seeking to
escape its own limitations and to find new, less onerous or
less costly ways of living, we will recognize one aspect of
a rapidly changing society such as our own. But we must
also recognize that some persons, for a variety of reasons,
oppose change and use every means to retain accepted
patterns, even though they may realize that the cake of
custom has been cracked and that, sooner or later, they
will be overwhelmed.

A science that attempts to understand the operation of
this complicated web of relationships has a more difficult
task than that posed by attempting to understand the

activities of molecules, atoms, and electrons. These, however complicated, do not alter their behavior unless the scientist, through the application of enormous energies, deliberately changes them. By contrast, the social scientist, *in* the system he is studying, is not like the chemist or biologist, outside it. Thus, social scientists, by entering into the very operations being studied, often accelerate changes in a social order.

Another peculiarity of major significance for psychology, is that interpersonal relations are conducted primarily through symbols, verbal or written. Symbols, being man-made artifacts, are probably the most elusive and confusing of all phenomena. Each person using the symbolic process imposes upon his words a specific, individualized meaning. The hearer, however, decodes and interprets them according to the meaning those words have for him, which is often quite different. Even the most rigorous semantic practice cannot abolish, but only reduce, this essential ambiguity of language; hence a scientist relying upon verbal reports is compelled to interpret them with inadequate means for validation. Lawyers over the centuries have recognized this and have developed an array of tests of credibility, through techniques of cross-examination, which show what a witness may be trying to say or not to say.

Like lawyers, psychologists rely upon a prolonged series of verbal disclosures spontaneously made (not just replies to questions or to directions), to help them discover what verbal symbols mean to a person who uses them. Especial care must be taken to detect deliberate falsehoods and attempts to deceive. But such detailed testing may not always be possible, leaving the investigator at the mercy of this idiosyncratic use of language. This danger is especially marked with written questionnaires in which the investigator cannot observe various behavioral signs that could alert him.

Thus, when a psychologist reports to his colleagues, he usually indicates the limitations, and bespeaks caution in the interpretation, of his findings. The non-psychologist, however, often takes the reports of psychologists, which today are widely publicized, as scientific findings and therefore valid. As a consequence, psychological studies are often translated into practice by those lacking professional training. Accordingly, before describing the social consequences of psychological studies, we should recognize the frequent diversity between a particular research result and its attempted application by others. We shall focus, therefore, rather upon the cumulative impact of psychology upon our ways of living, more especially its incorporation into the agencies and institutions through which a social order simultaneously maintains itself and changes.

1. *New Social Inventions Arising from Psychology*

Many of the psychological organizations and services that we now consider indispensable did not exist fifty or sixty years ago. They have arisen in response to two main needs: first, the elaboration of clinical services for diagnosis and treatment of disturbed personalities; second, the development of psychological testing and measurement, and the application of these procedures in the administration of organizations and provision of public services. These underlie the present prestige of the psychological professions, which owe their remarkable rise in public esteem to their responsiveness to the need for psychological services, public and private.

Concern for the so-called insane person (a legal, not a psychological, term) goes back a long time. By 1900 "insane asylums" (the term "mental hospital" was not yet in use) were established throughout the nation, primarily as custodial institutions to house and to restrain "lunatics." Little was done to treat them, because there was little understanding of "mental illness"—another term not then in use.

Mental illness, the so-called psychoses, are still not clearly understood. Nor have any dependable specific methods of treatment yet been developed. Special treatments, such as insulin- or electro-shock therapies, seek to produce such severe physiological-neurological disturbance as to interrupt the long-established psychotic patterns. More recently, tranquilizer drugs have been used to induce temporary calm, so that the patient will be accessible to psychotherapy. In some mental hospitals considerable improvement has been achieved by group therapy, where several patients meet with a leader and, by the sharing of experiences, are often helped to understand themselves and to release their repressed feelings.

But to date, mental illness is still a baffling problem. The number admitted to mental hospitals is large, and probably increasing, since the availability of hospitals seems to encourage more admissions, especially for the aged. But the number being released, as apparently cured by the new forms of treatment, is also increasing. Some will not be able to resume their place in society and will have to be returned to the hospital. In these cases, "cures" have not solved the problem of mental illness. This is bound to happen as long as no one knows how such illnesses begin, how they function in the individual personality, or what happens when treated by the various methods. There are many theories, but these are still being debated and await conclusive testing.

For the first time, in 1918-1919, we began to recognize

that there was a serious, nationwide psychiatric problem, which had been revealed by the large number of nero-psychiatric cases in the armed forces. Following the war we saw bootlegging and racketeering, increased juvenile delinquency, and growing instability of family life. Led by the National Committee on Mental Hygiene, new agencies and institutions were started, notably child guidance clinics designed to diagnose and treat so-called problem children and, as far as possible, to guide their parents. These clinics —often associated with juvenile courts, social agencies, school systems—were modeled after the Institute of Juvenile Research in Chicago, started by Dr. William Healy in 1909.

The child guidance clinic was organized as a team, with a psychiatrist who was then responsible for all the treatment work, a psychologist who tested the patient, and a social worker who interviewed the parents and reported on the family and neighborhood conditions surrounding the patient. Thus began the effort to pool the skills and techniques among psychological workers. Each sought to understand the personality of the patient, his relations to parents, brothers and sisters, teachers, peers in order to gain a composite picture of the patient and his major problems in living with himself and with others.

The establishment of child guidance clinics all over the country, aided by Commonwealth Fund grants, increased the need for psychologists, psychiatrists, and social workers. It also required an enlarged conception of their roles and responsibilities. Psychiatrists had previously been concerned with patients only in mental hospitals; now they had to work in homes and schools and social agencies, with patients who were not under twenty-four hour control and who continued their activities while being treated. This was the beginning of social psychiatry, probably the major development after the introduction of psychoanalytic principles and practices.

More or less parallel with the development of child guidance clinics was the development of psychological testing, known as psychometrics. Started in France, these mental tests were designed to discover the intelligence of a child by evoking his response to a series of questions that involved reason, judgment, understanding, perception of relations. The military draft of 1917-19 made it possible to apply various psychological tests—especially the Army Alpha, as it was called—to large numbers of young men. The results provided the first large-scale findings on the intelligence of our youth and occasioned considerable surprise among those who had assumed that, although people were different, they were all more or less intelligent and competent to face life. The findings that different regions of the country, and different ethnic-cultural groups, had different levels of intelligence gave rise to many disputes over the meaning of such differences.

In the 1920's the whole country witnessed a prolonged controversy over the question of "nature versus nurture." Was intelligence inborn, due to inherited genes, or was it a product of such life experience as education and training? Although this controversy has subsided with the recognition that both nature and nurture are involved, it made the public aware as never before of what some psychologists were doing, what their work meant, and the large social impact of its applications. Since World War I, the application of standardized tests has become almost universal in clinics and mental hospitals, custodial institutions; in the army, navy, air force, and marines; in examinations for jobs and admission to schools and colleges; in business and industry.

In addition to intelligence tests, achievement tests have been devised to rate performance in schools, especially in reading, writing, arithmetic. Such tests also rate comprehension of subject matter, comparing what a child actually does and what, according to his age and I.Q., he should be doing. A number of standardized tests have been devised to rate special abilities and vocational and other aptitudes; others assess personality make-up and emotional stability. The testing movement has, by now, pervaded our social institutions.

Psychoanalysis met a cooler reception in this country. In 1912 Freud visited the United States and lectured at Clark University at the invitation of the pioneer psychologist, G. Stanley Hall. For many years thereafter, only a few were prepared to accept Freud's revolutionary concepts of human personality. Some went to Vienna, where they received a personal analysis while studying psychoanalytic theory and practice with Freud and his associates. They returned with the Freudian orientation that has progressively transformed psychiatry. In the 1930's, when the Nazis outlawed psychoanalysis in Germany and then in Vienna, many practitioners came as refugees to the United States, thereby enlarging the corps of trained analysts.

Although psychoanalysis is still controversial in some circles, it has become the major orientation in psychiatry and has been increasingly accepted by many psychologists. As a form of psychotherapy, it is practiced by psychiatrists (M.D.'s who have had postgraduate training in psychiatry and have received a diploma from the National Board of Neurology and Psychiatry); by psychoanalysts (usually, but not always, M.D.'s); by clinical psychologists (who hold a qualifying diploma from the American Psychological Association); and by a number of lay analysts, persons who, like the others above, have been personally analyzed and take private patients under analysis.

Freud considered his investigations as essentially psychological studies, not as an extension of medical practice. And Viennese medicine was in fact highly antagonistic to psychoanalysis and to Freud personally. In Vienna and elsewhere, nonmedical personnel were accepted as candidates for analytic training (many teachers, pastors, social workers became practicing lay analysts), a development that spurred heated attacks by the medical profession. And, even today, lay analysts are not considered quite respectable by the medical profession, although Freud years ago wrote that medical training—certainly not a prerequisite—might be a handicap. His own daughter, Anna Freud, who is recognized as an outstanding leader in psychoanalysis, especially analysis of children, is not a physician but a former teacher. Other lay analysts have made important contributions to analytic theory and practice, as have psychologists who became analysts.

These details become significant when we recognize how widespread and rapidly enlarging is the use of psychiatry and psychoanalysis—in private practice and in clinics operated by hospitals, schools, welfare organizations, and local and state governments. Some groups of psychiatrists, psychologists, analysts, provide low-cost treatment, under the supervision of experienced teacher-analysts, as a required part of the training of new analysts. So numerous and widely dispersed over the United States are these psychoanalytic services that we may regard their establishment as the emergence of a new social institution.

Society has come to recognize that many delinquents and criminals, alcoholics, drug addicts, homosexuals, and other deviants are suffering from acute personality problems or severe neuroses; psychiatric and psychoanalytic treatment in institutions or as out-patient services is being provided for them. Likewise, because research confirms that the problem of the adult starts, usually, in childhood, more and more children are being treated. If they can be treated early, there is a possibility of saving these children from lifelong difficulties and of protecting society from the harm they may wreak.

In this situation psychiatric services offer some equivalents for the traditional relationships and rituals that have disappeared or have lost their efficacy for many persons. Here we observe the familiar process of social change, in which a traditional pattern, a ritual or an institution, having become obsolescent and ineffective, is replaced by a new institution that serves equivalent functions in human living. But this new psychological function is bringing far-reaching changes in our traditional ideas about human nature and is provoking many alterations in all our human relations. The consequences are plain in all the professions, agencies, and institutions that deal with people, providing services and help. We have gone so far in this direction that today we are discussing a more comprehensive approach—the idea of fostering mental health as a positive goal through the rearing and maintaining of healthy personalities.

Although it is difficult to define what a healthy personality is, or should be, we can at least tentatively establish some limitations for the term. A healthy personality does not mean a "perfect" person, one who has no problems and is never disturbed by any emotions. It is not a person who is "well adjusted," as we often say, meaning someone who accepts whatever exists and has no dislikes or criticisms of our contemporary society. The healthy personality, as we conceive it today, recognizes and faces the life tasks and problems that confront him. He copes with these tasks with self-confidence and courage, and with generosity and respect for others; he responds with feelings that are appropriate to his stage of development, he carries into the future a minimum of "unfinished business" and "dated emotions" from adolescence and childhood.

The conception of "society as the patient" has grown with the recognition that we cannot cultivate healthy personalities within an unhealthy society, and that a healthy society requires healthy personalities. This is not a vicious circle but expresses rather the reciprocal relations between the individual and his society. This two-way relationship seems obvious today. What the individual does—and refrains from doing—impinges on his social order; what that social order does to and for the individual, especially through its care, protection, services, is crucial to his health as an organism and as a personality.

This approach calls for a critical scrutiny of all our laws and institutions, our traditional beliefs and assumptions, our prescribed codes of conduct and relations, indeed, it must embrace the whole of our culture and of our social order. We need to see where and how we are unnecessarily stunting, warping, distorting the emerging personality of infants, children, and adolescents; how we are frustrating, depriving, coercing and otherwise humiliating, degrading, or dishonoring adults who exhibit their distress and their dismay in so many forms of self-defeat and antisocial behavior. We are learning to interpret such behavioral patterns as cries for help from persons who are in need of professional care or guidance.

This is no short-term goal to be achieved, like a commercial promotion campaign, by catchy slogans and tricky devices. It is a long-term effort, a goal to which we must strive; and we must pass on the aspiration to our children. We can take only a few, but crucial steps in that direction. Some of these steps have been initiated through the application of psychological methods, especially in our schools, through which virtually all of American youth passes from childhood into adolescence. Within the past three decades there has been a cumulative development of counseling and guidance services for pupils—from nursery schools through higher education. Much of this guidance concerns problems arising from the academic program or school life, but counseling of a student may give him much needed support on deeper perplexities which, at that moment, are manifest in his ability to cope with academic demands and expectations.

Counseling and guidance are closely associated and are often used as synonyms. Counseling, which involves face to face discussions over personal problems, has frequently been developed into a non-directive therapy. Guidance may be accompanied by counseling, but relies more on tests to help the individual find a solution to his problems. Since guidance is often oriented to jobs and vocations, it usually involves the use of vocational and aptitude tests designed to reveal the subject's potentialities for a job or for a family of jobs involving similar or related skills.

Counseling and guidance in our schools form a new social institution that has arisen to supplement, and in some cases to replace, the advice which traditionally was given by the church and the family. In our complex industrial society, with its new jobs and skill requirements, few families are able to provide adequate guidance, even if they could impartially and objectively assess their children's capacities. Moreover, boys and girls today rarely follow in their parents' footsteps; no longer does the boy automatically enter his father's calling or the girl follow her mother's pattern. Increasingly, new youth-serving agencies sponsored by civic or religious organizations are providing counseling and guidance services.

The social utility of such services will grow, since an advanced industrial civilization cannot operate at the mercy of unguided individual choices and uninformed decisions. Selective recruitment for the growing professions will be required, so that their needs will be met by the professional schools. Psychology faces a large responsibility in providing the personnel and techniques for such a task. It also is confronted with the ethical challenge of how to provide guidance without regimenting individuals, in the name of science, by psychological techniques.

Like all professions that have attained a large measure of authority and control over human affairs, psychology will increasingly face problems that cannot be answered by psychological techniques, no matter how scientific they are considered to be. One of these problems is how to ensure that the psychological practitioner possesses personal integrity—which may or may not accompany scientific skill and professional competence, as medicine and law have long recognized. Here arises the problem of how to protect society from those members of a profession who are power seekers or malevolent personalities? These issues may be more acute for psychology than the other social sciences, because of the strategic position psychologists are assuming in our society.

Psychologists are today providing a wide range of organizational services in government, business, and industry. They participate in a series of operations for recruiting and selecting personnel for all ranks, from executives to the lower manual occupations. The old casual employment practices have become too uncertain and even hazardous, when job specialization requires selective recruitment and on-the-job training. Moreover, union regulations about hiring, promotion, discharge, or lay-off likewise require a more systematic and reliable personnel administration. This includes, in many plants, facilities for counseling and guidance, discussion of grievances, selection of individuals for further training.

These psychological services have developed parallel to the expansion of personnel departments of large establishments. The employing organization has, within recent decades, become a locus for the individual belongingness and loyalties and also a source of help for individual and family difficulties. This has been fostered by the shift from *making* a living—when we exerted our strength, skill, endurance, and foresight against nature to wrest a living from the soil —to life in a money economy, where we *earn* a living and purchase what the family once provided for itself. The relative helplessness of the urban worker and his family, especially with wives increasingly engaged in out-of-home gainful work, has evoked many new services, some of which are supplied by psychologists. Beyond these direct services, psychologists are also becoming active participants in industrial research, where it is recognized that a machine, a vehicle, an aircraft, a weapon, must be operated by a person whose behavior is as crucial as the behavior of the metals or the engine.

Psychological counselors are now active also in family life, marriage and divorce, parent-child relations. Until recently, these questions were almost exclusively the province of ministers, priests, rabbis, lawyers, and physicians (especially when there was an old family doctor). Although people still go to these long-established sources of advice, many are turning to psychologically-oriented counselors, some of whom may be social workers, and to professional psychiatrists. Within the past decade or so, theologically trained ministers have been seeking further training in what is called pastoral psychology so that they will be better prepared to counsel members of their congregations or of those organizations—the army and navy, prisons, mental and other hospitals—where they serve as chaplains.

Psychologists are also providing guidance in another capacity to various organizations, through opinion polling and interviewing of large samples of the population. Polls seek to discover what people believe and expect on a variety of questions, and their findings are reported to the public by university, public service, and commercial agencies. The spread of political polling is now nation-wide. Increasingly the sale of goods, equipment, and services is being based on the findings of market research, often organized and conducted by psychologists or a psychologically-oriented staff. We are aware of dangerous innovation when professional knowledge of how persons think and feel, and especially of their susceptibilities and frustrations, is used to persuade and cajole them into buying. The so-called motivation research, based on psychologic and psychoanalytic concepts, indicates how the growing knowledge of the human personality may be exploited for commercial purposes, as it has been used for political propaganda and electioneering.

Psychological concepts and findings thus have entered into a number of new and unprecedented organizations, service agencies, and social institutions. These new agencies, replacing older organizations which are no longer adequate, reflect the fruits of psychological thinking and investigation. The full impact of psychology upon our contemporary living, however, is shown in the ways it has altered, and even radically transformed, our long-established institutions and familiar practices. These changes sharpen the intangible but pervasive alterations taking place in our climate of opinion and in our traditional culture. They lead us to consider what may lie ahead, as we continue to study ourselves and to work for the future that is illuminated by our new psychological insight.

2. *Transformations in Social Institutions*

Every society, however simple and crude it may appear, has developed more or less formal procedures for ordering and regulating its basic functions. Thus every society must produce goods and services, involving some kind of organization with superordination and subordination—those who manage and those who work under them. Likewise every society, to ensure the perpetuation of its social order, must educate its youth not only in the skills required for their work, but also in the prescribed ways of thinking, speaking, acting, feeling. Every society must also cope with illness and accidents, providing some kind of care which we call medicine. In many cultures the healing function is not secular but religious—hence closely associated with the group's basic beliefs and values, which prescribe how the individual relates himself to the universe and to its deity. We here look at the transformations worked in these four basic institutions—industry, education, medicine, religion—by the spread of psychology.

a. *Industrial Relations:* For generations the Common Law provided clear rules governing the relation of master and servant. In the guild society, servants and indentured apprentices had worked under the unchallenged authority of the omnipotent master craftsman. With the coming of factories, there was some attempt to modify the master-servant relation and to protect employees by the early factory acts. Efforts at concerted action by employees were usually defeated, since the employer had the law and the influential citizenry on his side. In the United States there have been many bloody strikes, with the law supported by military forces aiding the employer to break the strike. This background highlights the recent transformation of industrial relations by governmental action, labor organization, and employment practices guided by psychological concepts. The idea has spread that employers were wasting human energy by the traditional authoritarian ways of imposing their decisions on their employees.

Psychologists—collaborating with engineers and economists and, more recently, anthropologists—have made many studies concerned with the impact of physical aspects of the workplace, such as lighting, color of walls and machines, temperature and humidity; with working conditions, such as hours, shifts, rest periods, piece rates, and especially relations of foreman and supervisors to their groups. Such studies helped to articulate a new view of corporate life.

Executives being trained for administrative positions frequently participate in courses dealing with industrial relations and personality problems. In many large industries a full-time psychiatrist is on the staff for consultations on a variety of problems and sometimes for group therapy for the executives.

As technology advances and automation embraces more processes, large organizations must have a stable working force of persons who are emotionally balanced and reasonably content with their working conditions. Otherwise these complicated processes may be liable to all manner of breakdowns. However much the future of industry depends on the competence of engineers who design the equipment and plan operations, the future is almost equally dependent upon the quality of industrial relations that are maintained. Hence this cumulative improvement in employer-employee relations—to which psychology, along with other social sciences, is contributing so much—may be regarded as one of the major transformations in our social institutions.

b. *Education:* Educational psychology has focused on teaching, learning, school practices, pupil-teacher relations, and the social implications of education. Its findings stimulated a transformation of American schools which is still in progress. The current concern for science education will probably bring further changes based on studies of learning and growth.

The development of nursery schools, largely under the direction of child psychologists, has been guided by systematic study of child growth and development. It has aimed at providing education that is relevant to the child's individual developing needs and capacities. Experimental elementary schools have pioneered in establishing new programs that are responsive to children's evolving interests and abilities. A major contribution of such work in educational psychology has been the articulation of individual differences. We have learned much about how each child differs from others and how the many handicapped and atypical children can be helped to learn within their capacities. Thus our schools today provide for many groups of children with special needs and limitations—such as crippled, heart cases, high I.Q. and low I.Q., intellectually inclined and motor inclined, and emotionally disturbed children.

The schools are being increasingly transformed into agencies for fostering the development of children who must live in a changing society, not by passive adaptation but by actively incorporating those changes in their own lives. This is a new task for education, which for ages had only the responsibility of teaching the wisdom of the past, preparing students to carry on what had long existed and was expected to endure. With universal free public education, all children go to school—a truly remarkable change. They then go from school into an adult life in which there are few stable and dependable guides—another remarkable change. Thus education must, for the sake of the child and for the future of society, be ever more concerned with the kind of personalities it is helping to develop. Our world requires not submissive acceptance, but rather an ability to make changes. To make rational decisions, a person must understand the rapidly changing technology he must work with and the science upon which that technology is based. Education has, apparently for the first time, to undertake the difficult task of aiding students in un-learning— that is, freeing them from folklore, traditional beliefs and assumptions that have become obsolete.

This is a delicate task because to give up what one has learned, often painfully, to accept new concepts and to use new assumptions, can be threatening to the stability of the personality. This is not unlike what the psychoanalyst tries to do with a patient whose life is blocked by persistence of childish ideas and feelings that are no longer appropriate to, nor compatible with, his adult status, responsibilities, and privileges. But this is the long-term transformation that psychology must help to bring about in education, a task made even more hazardous by the often strong resistance of parents who want their children to have the same education they experienced and who resent having their children learn to think in ways that are alien to their older patterns. Thus, this large task can be achieved only as rapidly as the public will permit. If the progress seems slow and halting, it is well to remember that transforming our schools is the institutional fulcrum transforming our social order. In a democratic society this can be done only by education and persuasion.

c. *Medicine:* Like industry and education, medicine has also been undergoing a profound transformation, the full implications and expression of which will become apparent only in years to come. Whereas early medicine was concerned with the whole individual and his relations to the world, as Hippocrates taught in Greece long ago, modern medicine became increasingly focused on the body segments and their functions. This focus became dominant when the old humoral doctrine of disease was displaced by the work of Pasteur and Virchow, which showed that invading germs, bacilli, or bacteria started the pathological process of disease in cells and tissues. Attention was therefore directed toward the discovery of what kind of infections were involved in each disease and how these could be combatted by various drugs. For many physicians the patient became a focus of infection, of little significance as a person but treated primarily in terms of his disease. This contrasted with the practice of the old family doctor who—knowing his patients, often from childhood, and familiar with their physical characteristics and habitual patterns of reaction—intuitively mixed understanding with his drugs and provded what the sick patient needed as a personality.

In the late 1920's and early 1930's psychiatric attention was focused upon patients suffering from chronic illness and repeated accidents—the "accident-prone" group. Careful study showed that many patients with high blood pressure or peptic ulcers had chronic anxiety or strong but repressed hostility against the world. Others, who showed excess of endocrine functions, such as hyperthyroidism, were also found to be carrying a heavy load of anxiety or resentment. Clearly, the different organ systems, sensory processes, and bodily functions can be disturbed by the chronic inner "feelings." In the past generation psychoso-

matic medicine has emerged as a major conception of healing, which not only seeks the sources of many illnesses and
dysfunctions in the patient's personality but also provides
psychotherapy for such disorders.

Today medicine is being increasingly taught and practiced in terms of the psychosomatic unity of the patient.
Future physicians will be familiar with the concept of the
organism-personality which holds what the patient thinks
and feels to be of necessity, expressed in his bodily functioning. Conversely, his bodily functioning participates in
his thinking, acting and feelings toward the world and
himself. Thus emotions are to be seen as physiological up-
heavals, persisting in such chronic affects as anxiety, guilt
or hositility and becoming localized in an organ system or
functional process which thereby becomes disturbed, gradually breaks down, and becomes pathological. While these
questions of etiology are still in dispute, a new concept of
the human organism-personality is emerging, one that is
more consonant with the full range of observations—
anatomical, physiological, biochemical, and especially psychological.

We can look forward to the invention of new instruments and techniques for recording precisely what the human body does, especially under stress and strain as well
as in normal functioning. Brain waves, for example, are
being recorded to yield much new knowledge for both psychology and physiology. Such collaboration will increase as
psychologists participate in the research teams now needed
for adequate investigation of such organized complexities
as man, his machines, and his institutions.

d. *Religion:* Religious leaders and prophets have long
been concerned with man's behavior, especially his misbehavior. They have conceived of human nature in various
ways, but our Western culture has, since the time of Augus-

tine, accepted a belief that man is evil—either innately wicked and sinful, or fallen from grace—but in either case prone to evil ways and errors. These theological views have long dominated our thinking about human nature and conduct, as we see in our traditional patterns of child rearing and regulating of human activities. As a corollary of these views, man's behavior has been interpreted as the product of his will, as his own choice between good and evil, or, in the law, as an expression of definite motives and intent, voluntarily expressed by all except infants and the so-called insane.

These long-accepted ways of treating individuals who exhibit antisocial or self-defeating behavior have been slowly modified by the impact of psychological studies. More and more theological students today are given courses designed to orient them to contemporary theory about human behavior as it appears in a cultural-social field; they are also learning to look at human behavior in the light of psychological and psychoanalytic findings and interpretations. They are reading and discussing Freud's formulations and current thinking by analysts. They are spending time in mental hospitals and clinics, where they sit in with the staff and hear individual cases being discussed in terms that differ markedly from the traditional theological conceptions.

Perhaps the most striking departure from the older views is the growing acceptance of the idea that an individual's behavior should be seen and interpreted in the light of his past experience, going back to his forgotten childhood when he developed his characteristic patterns of behavior and especially his persistent ways of feeling toward the world and himself. Guilt, which has been a central theme in theology, to be atoned by seeking grace and forgiveness, is now recognized as a product not so much of current misdeeds as of early experiences. Indeed, it is now recognized that a person often will commit a crime in order to get punished for the burden of guilt he carries from childhood. Likewise, many other forms of misconduct which the church has for ages denounced and castigated are being understood in new terms.

Instead, therefore, of the familiar approach to a wrong-doer—of heaping opprobrium on him, intensifying his feelings of guilt—the more recent approach is to help the individual gain some insight into his own personality, to recognize how much of what he does arises from the long-forgotten, repressed experience of childhood of which he has no awareness. Moreover, every effort is being made by these newly-oriented pastors to reveal to the individual how his behavior is directed by anxiety and hostility which he does not recognize or consciously feel. This viewpoint was presented by the late Rabbi Joshua Liebman in his book *Peace of Mind*.

Thus, in current discussions, the emphasis is upon anxiety, the persistent feeling of apprehension, of expecting the awful that keeps the individual tense, ever alert, as if he were continually threatened. The emphasis is also upon unconscious aggressive hostility which operates to poison human relations by making others seem potential enemies that a person must counter with defense or retaliation. As Seward Hiltner has aptly remarked, we are aware as never before how much our lives are governed by "dated emotions." Feelings that were once aroused by a real experience continue to reverberate in our lives, so that, like a shell with a proximity fuse, we explode at every random target. We now see that the most aberrant and shocking misbehavior may be understood as fulfilling a person's repressed needs and releasing his pent-up feelings. This viewpoint conflicts sharply with the older concepts of deliberate, wilful, or intentional activity that theology and the law have long maintained. It shifts the focus from the action, however deplorable, to the actor. We see the person as often the victim of his own past experience, the unwilling possessor of ideas, beliefs, strong feelings that were inculcated in early life—and from which he has not been able to escape.

The full consequences of these recent alterations are still to be realized in theology and in the church. But already there is a marked change in the Protestant churches, as pastors learn to think in these new ways and to deal with individuals as personalities in need not of exhortation but of help. Pastoral psychology (with a journal of that name) has emerged as a religiously-oriented form of counseling or psychotherapy, offered by pastors and by chaplains in hospitals, mental hospitals, jails, and other custodial institutions. (That this new approach is not however acceptable to all religious leaders is shown by Bishop Sheen's *Peace of Soul*.)

As this reorientation proceeds, it will undoubtedly permeate many phases of the church and bring a progressive alteration in theological teaching and preaching. Some seminaries, such as Union Theological Seminary in New York, have a psychiatrist on the faculty and devote considerable time in their curriculum to psychological problems and techniques. The church may become one of the major agencies for fostering the ancient precept "Know Thyself," recognizing that people are at the mercy of their forgotten childhood only so long as it is forgotten and that self-understanding comes with the ability to accept and live with oneself. Religion in our Western culture may undergo its most profound reorientation, if not reformulation, as these psychological ideas and practices are increasingly accepted by the churches. They offer a new conception of the doctrine of love and a more insightful understanding into the "cure of souls."

3. *Society as the Patient*

The many attempts to explain society—its nature and origin as well as its operations—have, for the most part, viewed society as something imposed upon man by superhuman authority, arising from Nature and subject to what has been called Natural Law. The emergence of social science has come with the gradual emancipation from these *a priori* concepts and orientation toward an increasingly secular concept of social order, viewed as an essentially human creation.

Studies by social anthropologists have shown that each of the many kinds of social order developed as a design for living, for ordering human affairs according to the basic beliefs of a cultural group. Every social order, then, depends upon the way members of the group attempt to meet their persistent problems of living and attain their enduring goal values. Accordingly, a social order changes when the behavior of its members changes.

The concept of a man-made social order is essentially a psychological concept, which embraces the full range of man's behavior, be it labeled economic, political, social, sexual, religious, legal, or criminal. True, in some isolated cultures not exposed to the outside world, people converge around their modal patterns or norms. But in the large societies which form a complex civilization such as the United States, embracing people who have come from a variety of ethnic stocks, we observe the emergence of a multi-modal culture with a variety of norms in different regions and in different socio-economic, educational, and religious groups.

A social order which tolerates such wide-ranging pluralism of norms must seek unity through diversity. This means recognizing and cultivating differences while simultaneously enlisting people's loyalty and allegiance to a core of conduct and relationships. Only education and persuasion, not force, can build a social consensus out of these massive and varied elements. This is the difficult problem facing free society today, when it is already staggering under the demands for rapid change imposed by the accelerating development of industry and technology. Such a view of consensus assumes that social change and improvement must come through the concert of a population composed of individual personalities. These personalities can and probably will collaborate in this great undertaking when they realize that they are what we call society and that they can achieve these difficult tasks. Thus instead of relying chiefly upon legislation, as in the past, we begin to think how each person may become self-consciously aware of his role as a participant in his social order.

This is the problem studied by Group Dynamics, pioneered by the psychologist Kurt Lewin, wherein persons see themselves not as passive anonymous units but as active participants in group decisions, seeking improvements in their community, their state, their nation. Wholly unsuspected, and previously unavailable, human energy may be released in such groups by the common effort to attain self-selected goals. We know how a mob can release individuals from all their normal inhibitions and lead them collectively to destructive violence which no one would probably ever exhibit alone. But we have just begun to tap the capacity for spontaneous group activity directed to common goals that multiplies genuine constructive effort at social improvement. This, it should be emphasized, is not produced solely by group decision; it involves a changing image of the self, a new awareness of one's place, role, and participation in living that has been overlooked in our traditional social theories and largely neglected in our community programs.

Out of this re-orientation of the individual as an active participant in his social order is coming a recognition of the crucial significance of the personality make-up of individuals. Those who are neurotic—warped and dis-. torted with chronic feelings of anxiety, hostility or corrosive guilt—are not capable of this kind of participation. They will either refuse to join or will try to dominate and exploit the group for their own ends, resorting to sabotage when thwarted in these attempts. A mentally healthy society requires mentally healthy personalities.

A conception of a social order as self-regulating and self-repairing therefore re-inforces the idea of individuals as the dynamic agents of change. It also calls for systematic social research on every aspect of society to see how well it is serving the common purposes, recognizing that historic social institutions may frustrate human efforts at improved living. This calls for comprehensive planning on the local, state, and national or supranational basis. Such planning is not designed to impose bureaucratic blueprints on people and to regiment them to an authoritarian program. Rather, planning may be seen as the art of the potential, as politics is called the art of the possible, since its function is to discover how we can use the marvellous resources of science and technology now becoming available to create designs for living that are humanly desirable and fulfilling of our aspirations. This function is essential in a free society because, without social research and planning, people cannot assess the risks and costs, or realize the gain, financial and human, of the policies and programs they are asked to approve.

If, however, we expect people generally to undertake active participation in their social order, to function as citizens not just on election day but in their daily living, then they must gain a new image of themselves and their own behavior in relation to their society. We must realize that no one, no matter how insignificant he may seem, may be unnecessarily deprived, frustrated, humiliated, injured or otherwise impaired. It is clear from the cumulative evidence that anyone ill-treated, neglected or subject to indignity will in such measure be incapable of doing his share in the advancement of his social order.

The old saying emphasized that man is the measure of all things; we are today just becoming aware of its full significance. Psychological concepts are giving man a new conception of human nature—a confident new image of himself as an essential participant in his society.

PROSPECTS

COMMON HUMANITY
AND DIVERSE CULTURES

Clyde Kluckhohn

Anthropology is the study of the similarities and the differences, both biological and behavioral, among the past and present, primitive and sophisticated peoples of the world. Nature having carried out many "experiments" in biological and cultural variation, the task of the anthropologist is to read off, analyze, and compare the results of these "experiments." Thus, the investigation of "primitive" groups is not an end in itself, but rather the equivalent of a laboratory. In principle, the anthropologist is as much concerned with Americans, Belgians, Chinese, and Russians as with the Ashanti, the Arunta, the Chukchee, and the Tupinamba. But "primitives" must be included to get the full range of variability of human nature.

Methodologically and conceptually, anthropology has borrowed from the humanities, the natural sciences, and the social sciences. Intellectually, the discipline has only four unifying factors:

1. A focus on man in all his variation and similarity.

2. A consistently comparative point of view.

3. A stubborn conviction that history, physique, environmental situation, way of life, and language are all related in discoverable patterns.

4. A premise that the nonrational and irrational aspects of human behavior must be investigated along with the rational.

These points of departure largely determine the specific characteristics of anthropology as opposed to the other disciplines concerned with man and his works. The unique and the general are equal concerns of anthropology. Its data (whether handaxes or blood pressure or values) are eventually seen in the perspective of similar data from various populations. In other words, the comparative perspective is as constantly dominant as is that of "holism." Anthropology, rather than restricting its attention to the purely biological, geographical, political, or whatever, considers phenomena in the widest feasible context. In contrast to economics, for example, anthropology emphasizes the nonrational and irrational factors as much as the rational. Indeed, it may be said that the primary specialty of cultural anthropology is the nonrational (i.e., customary) aspect of human conduct, whereas psychiatry and areas of psychology have taken the irrational factors as their specialty.

Anthropology, psychology, and sociology all deal with the same data or, at any rate, with data of the same order, though only the first two have an explicit and sustained concern with the biological dimensions. But the questions asked of the data, though overlapping, have characteristic stresses. Psychology devotes itself mainly to the individual as a unique organism: his maturation, learning, perception, and motivation. Anthropology and sociology take, as their primary point of reference the individual as a member of a particular group. To differentiate further, the sociologist is most interested in interaction processes and in such topics as stratification, delinquency, and demography which have been abstracted from their total social and cultural contexts.

On the other hand, cultural anthropology—to which the remainder of this essay will be devoted—takes as its focus those forms and modes of behavior that are the resultants of universal human nature as affected by the accidents of history, precipitated in so many distinct cultures. The most specific quality of anthropological research arises from its preoccupation with culture. This concept (in the technical, anthropological sense) refers to those *selective* ways of feeling, thinking, and reacting that distinguish one group from another—ways that are socially transmitted and learned (with, of course, some change through time) by each new generation. In the strict sense, we can speak of culture only when there are two or more objectively possible and functionally effective means or modes of meeting the same need (for example, shelter, choice and preparation of food, weaning of children), and a given group exhibits a consistent and stylized preference for one path to the goal among a number of alternatives that are—from the observer's point of view—all open.

A culture is not merely a congeries of customs. One cannot grasp the network of selective principles unless one understands the core values, the cognitive assumptions, and what the logicians call the "primitive categories." The way of life that is handed down as the social heritage of every people does more than supply a set of skills for making a living and a set of blueprints for human relations. Each different way of life makes its own assumptions about the ends and purposes of human existence, about ways by which knowledge may be obtained, about the organization of the pigeonholes in which each sense datum is filed, about what human beings have a right to expect from each other and from the gods, about what is "good" and "right" or "better" and "worse," about what constitutes fulfillment or frustration. Some of these assumptions are made explicit in the lore of the folk; others are tacit premises which the observer must infer by finding consistent trends in word and deed. The unstated assumptions (in particular) are ordinarily taken for granted as an ineradicable part of human nature, and naïve participants in one culture find it hard to understand that normal persons could possibly conceive life in other terms. In other words, many cultural premises and categories are nonrational, and defensive attitudes related to them may be decidedly irrational.

Anthropology in Today's World

The hybrid monster, anthropology, is lusty these days. In a world in which educated men and women now recognize that the ways of other tribes and nations cannot remain matters of indifference or antiquarian curiosity, anthropology suddenly finds itself fashionable. Anthropologists have returned from the natives and are thinking and talking about the wide contemporary world. In the present situation the constancies and variations between peoples, and the reasons for them, are a matter of the most intense practical as well as intellectual concern. Hence anthropology is taught in the Foreign Service Institute of the Department of State, lectured upon in the various war colleges, and studied—by requirement—by candidates for some sections of the British Civil Service.

The panorama of peoples and their ways constructed by recent anthropology has made a number of significant contributions to the modern temper, to the point of view held by educated men and women generally. The most specific is perhaps the demonstration, alike by physical and cultural anthropologists, that, although there may be meaningful biological differences between populations, "race," as judged by observation of a few outwardly visible features, is not a trustworthy guide. This conclusion rests, in part, on what is probably anthropology's broadest generalization: the necessity of taking into account the cultural dimensions in all understanding of human behavior. In generality and in explanatory power, "culture" is on a level with the categories of gravity in physics, disease in medicine, and gene in biology. Any particular culture of given locus in space or time is merely a specific manifestation of a greater phenomenon of which any one variant is only a temporary phase. For example, the culture of Classic Greece is seen as building upon prior civilizations of the Near East and the Mediterranean basin and also as one early climax in repeated strivings of men toward humanistic rationality. Thus, a dynamic conception of human social life replaces a static one.

But anthropological knowledge and the anthropological viewpoint are disturbing to many. In the first place, they seem to challenge "common sense" and threaten the stability of familiar, cherished values. They make enormously complex the question "What is human nature?"—to which the "practical" man and the traditional intellectual find it convenient to have a pat answer. In the second place, anthropology seems to some to open the way to a complete and chaotic relativism. The empirical data of anthropology do not warrant this fear. Yet it must be admitted that only recently have anthropologists begun to give the order and similarity in human cultures equal weight with their contrast and variability. In spite of this, anthropology has, directly and indirectly, made an important, if not the leading, contribution to the rebirth of a conception that was taken for granted by, say, Pascal and Burke—and perhaps Goethe—but which for a hundred years was obscured: namely, that the things all men hold in common bulk at least as large as those that separate them. Anthropology, as well as technology—especially in the realm of communication—has made physical appearance, language, and custom seem less relevant than humanity. The creation myths of the Polynesians take their place with those of the Hebrews. When T. S. Eliot juxtaposes Dante, Heraclitus, and a Sanscrit epic, or James Joyce draws words from a dozen languages and folklore from fifty cultures, when Igor Stravinsky and Karl Orff write music that is simultaneously "primitive" and Greek and Oriental, then we are living in an anthropologically sensitive world. The massive continuities of human experience blend and cumulate more and more, rather than remain isolated and disparate.

There are some, also, who are not happy that anthropologists are now working in international relations and industry and studying contemporary civilizations generally. Anthropologists feel that a science that sees institutions and values in cross-cultural perspective has its necessary place in all investigations of mid-twentieth century problems. But those who are troubled by anthropology's new look doubt the applicability of anthropological methods to complex, dynamic cultures. It is true that some anthropologists have been too hasty and far-reaching in entering the "modern" arena. And one can point to a few irresponsible pronouncements suggesting that anthropology has *the* answer rather than a useful but partial and limited contribution to make to *some* contemporary problems. There are anthropologists who are undoubtedly a bit intoxicated by the heady wine of a little power over the here and now, for, until recently, they had drunk only the austere nectar of detached contemplation of the long ago and far away. On the other hand, it is only factual to point out that the great bulk of anthropological publication remains descriptive, detailed, and rigorous within the limits of the theoretical framework. Against the few messianically tinged books of too-facile generalization that have caught the public eye, one can name hundreds of solid monographs produced in the same time period.

Finally, some theologians and philosophers reproach anthropology with *exalting* the irrational and nonrational aspects of human behavior. Actually, anthropology has very seldom been "vitalist" in tone, urging a surrender to the forces of chaos and unreason. Rather, anthropology has been steadily committed to the search for discoverable regularities. Regularities are the common responses of diverse persons to similar situations; in discovering them, one finds both rational and nonrational components underlying personal choices, however individualistic, erratic, and irrational such choices may appear to be in particular cases. In this way, anthropology seeks to extend the areas which reason can understand and perhaps to some extent control. This may help a little to halt the flight to the irrational, the terrified retreat to the older orthodoxies which we have seen on a mass scale in this century. The hallmark of the good anthropologist must be a curious mixture of passion and reserve.

The Anthropologist and His Informants

Ideally, the anthropologist's attitude toward his informants is that of "attached-detachment." That is to say, he studies his fellow men not solely as a dispassionate observer but also as a participant observer. He tries to feel with them, to see things as they see them, to experience some portion of their life with them. On the other hand, he tries to balance his identifications with detached objectivity (cf. Zelesnik, 1957). He must avoid the sentimental, the romantic, the conscious or unconscious attempt to "go native." As an anthropologist, he recognizes that no adult can—or should want—to shed his own culture completely. One great contribution of anthropology is that of supplying some emancipation from the values of any single culture. Yet the qualifier "some" must be emphasized. A person who views with complete detachment (emotional as well as intellectual) the designs for living of the group in which he was socialized is by definition rootless, disoriented, unhappy. He has lost the simple unself-conscious adhesion to those cognitive and moral norms that integrate the personality and constitute a necessary base for the understanding of other personalities and the comprehension of other norms that prevail in different social groups. An anthropologist who was truly and utterly free from his own culture would be no more competent to study other ways of life than an individual who has lost his memory is able to grasp all of what is going on around him.

Anthropologists, moreover, are aware that they are often unconsciously motivated by dislike of their own culture to escape into the exotic. Therefore the danger—which exists as a possibility for all men—of casting completely adrift from one's cultural moorings is particularly grave for the anthropologist, alike because of temperamental selectivity and because of training and experience. Anthropologists must, therefore, if they are to do successful scientific work, cling to their own cultural as well as personal identities. Their role as outsiders has other advantages comparable to those enjoyed by the psychiatrist with respect to his patients. What anthropologists refer to as "stranger value" means that the informant will be open to the outside investigator on matters on which he must preserve reticence with those who will be enduringly involved in the network of his life. But the anthropologist does not go as far as the psychoanalyst in presenting himself as an aloof and impersonal screen upon which subjects may project their problems and conflicts.[1] While remaining firmly a detached outsider in his total role, he nevertheless behaves with warmth and sympathy in immediate personal relations. Anthropological research demands that we not only observe our fellow men but also live with them. A tag from Walt Whitman could well serve as the motto of the anthropological field worker:

> Both in and out of the game, and watching and wondering at it.

In short, the anthropologist must behave and see and feel from within the foreign cultural context and, at the same time, withdraw and analyze.

This anthropological conception is quite distinct from that which is most typical of American sociologists. Bennett and Wolff (1955, p. 334) correctly say:

> Sociologists and anthropologists approach and perceive man differently; they have different *images of man*. In his search for laws and his interest in the abstract, the sociologist tends to view man as a technically "non-human" item, subject to many forces (including the sociologist's impersonal measurements). In this view, man is an element of nature, immersed in his environment—and the sociologist stands apart, observing and measuring man-in-environment.
>
> For the anthropologist, man is not a figure within a ground, but rather a figure against that ground; he is a *human* phenomenon, everlastingly variable, pre-

dictable only within broad limits if at all, and knowable only on a series of virtually infinite levels of understanding. . . . While the sociologist proposes to stand away, to perceive man "objectively," not to involve his own feelings and reactions, the cultural anthropologist has often striven to know man *through* his own feelings and reactions, to view the human beings he studies as "fellow men," not as "subjects."

The sociologist stresses distance, the anthropologist an equilibrium of involvement and detachment.

The anthropological premise is that (if I may paraphrase Zola) science is nature *vue à travers d'un tempérament.* The anthropologist deliberately uses his own feelings and reactions as one of his instruments of research.[2] This means that he must acquire some measure of understanding and control over this instrument whether by a personal psychoanalysis or simply through professional training and experience. Otherwise his work will be altogether at the mercy of unconscious pressures to select only certain kinds of informants, to be blind to much of what goes on about him, to be anaesthetized to sizable sectors of the culture. Self-understanding will not eliminate all distortions, though it will minimize some of them. Yet it will remain largely the case that we see things "not as they are, but as we are." All science is invention rather than discovery, as Bergson remarked in his introduction to the French translation of William James's *Pragmatism.*

However, so long as scientists face and take systematic account of the active role of the observer, these "inventions" are not disparate and irreconcilable monads created by the scientific imagination. No two anthropologists will ever see "the same" culture in identical terms any more than one can step twice into the same river. At the same time, science acquires wider and deeper knowledge of cultures precisely because of the variabilities in the natures and temperaments of different observers. Richness is gained at the sacrifice only of an illusion—namely, that cultural reality in its infinite variation can ever be completely captured and recorded with perfect objectivity. Nevertheless, most of what is essential and perduring can be reconstructed, given sufficient data from the culture in its own terms (artifacts, texts, accurate records of observed behavior), by doing a "triangulation" of views of the culture obtained from the different angles of vision supplied by the varying backgrounds and temperaments of independent investigators. This view presupposes *both* that there are varying perspectives *and* that there is a discoverable "objective reality." Father T. V. Moore (1933, p. viii) has put the matter well: "One might view a landscape from various mountain peaks and every height would give a different picture, but the lakes and rivers that stretched out beneath one's gaze could in no case be arbitrarily arranged in relation to the point of view."

The observed is no more passive and inert than the observer. This fact, in turn, supplies advantage as well as difficulty. Each unexpected reaction from a new informant is likely to reveal a fresh facet of the culture as well as an idiosyncratic response of personality. The anthropologist must systematically exploit the variabilities in interaction —to himself as representative of a foreign culture, to himself as an individual, between participants in the culture in terms of their individualities and their culturally specified roles—in order to factor out least-common denominators that give the culture its distinctive form. This he must do as well as be the patient student of his "native" teachers.

The difficulty—and I think it is one that cannot be completely resolved—arises primarily from the circumstance that the intervention of the observer instigates acts which otherwise would never have occurred. The presence of the anthropologist not only evokes sequences of behavior which lay bare cultural structure but also causes change. Cultures are, not closed, but open systems. Hence, the very process of field work may invalidate a well-conceived research design. This I know from experience. More than twenty years ago my associates and I began a longitudinal study of a carefully selected sample of Navaho Indian babies. These we observed and tested much more intensively than our control groups, who included siblings of the core sample. When, after an absence from the field for some months, I visited a little girl who had reached the age of ten, she become sulky and finally angry because for an hour or more I engaged in general conversation with her family. At last she screamed and struck her older sister, saying: "You know perfectly well he doesn't come here to see you and the others. He comes to see *me*. All the rest of you stop talking to him." Our research objective had been to discover the ordinary course of personality formation among the Navaho, but, obviously, the curse of this child's development had been altered to some degree by the research itself.

Perhaps the only cultural studies wherein the anthropologist does not alter somewhat by his very presence the materials that he is investigating are those of archaeology and linguistics. Nevertheless, if one conceives—as I do—of the ultimate aim of cultural anthropology as enquiry into the nature of human nature (with the depiction of the distinctive features of separate cultures as a means to this end and also an intrinsically worthwhile by-product), then changes brought about by the introduction of the observer are instructive even when they lead to the appreciable modification, or even the destruction, of the original culture.

The Limitations and Strengths
   of Anthropological Method

Anthropologists have been criticized frequently and severely for "subjectivity," lack of rigor and poor workmanship in detail, and insufficient attention to quantitative method and experiment.[3] Any anthropologist would grant that one or more of these strictures can be documented by reference to numerous publications. It is perfectly true that some monographs appear to reveal to the reader at least as much about the personality problems of the field worker as about the culture in question. Until recently anthropologists, even when they have recorded and interpreted with relatively little distortion due to personal bias, have more often than not been oriented to description rather than to problems and the testing of hypotheses. Anthropology has had some concepts of proven worth, but little systematic theory. Indeed, in only one branch of cultural anthropology (linguistics) can one up to the present claim even the beginnings of comprehensive theory of some rigor and elegance. It is likewise the case that anthropologists have frequently been cavalier about numbers. Readers have had no way of knowing whether a given generalization rested upon a single statement by one informant or a unique observation, or whether this cultural generalization was based upon many interviews and observations in the framework of at least an elementary consideration of the principles of sampling. Anthropologists have—at least implicitly—overestimated the homogeneity of nonliterate cultures, neglecting the facts that not only does personal idiosyncrasy always occur but also that variation in some form is always systematically built into the culture itself. Each culture exhibits deviant behavior, but this is only part of the story. In all cultures there are variant as well as dominant modalities.

On the other hand, critics—and not least colleagues in the neighboring fields of sociology and social psychology— have failed to see that certain limitations are inherent in the anthropological situation and in the task as conceived by members of the profession. Take, for example, work-manship on technical matters. The anthropological field worker has been by definition a jack-of-all-trades and a master of none. He has been—and to a considerable extent still is—expected to spend a year (two or three at most) among a people of a different culture and to bring back information on everything from music to the techniques of basket-making and weaning practices. He cannot possibly obtain and interpret data on economics, the plastic arts, and nutrition that will satisfy specialists who have devoted their lives exclusively to a single one of these subjects. On the other hand, he can probably say something significant about the linkages between subsistence, religion, and kinship that no specialist in one of these fields would be able to discern. In recent years "team research" has in part improved the level of workmanship on technical details. Yet most experienced anthropologists are of the opinion that loss as well as gain has resulted from the increasing division of labor.

This conclusion holds for most points, I believe. Cultural anthropology has been overwhelmingly an observational rather than an experimental science. The field anthropologist must follow events as they "naturally" develop in the cultural setting rather than (in most instances) trying to "control" them. This surely makes for loss of rigor, but anthropologists would reply that they are more interested in what happens in ordinary daily life than in the artificial situation of the laboratory. They would grant—indeed, insist—that some things essential to an understanding of human behavior can be learned only by controlled experiment. But they would argue that this method also has its limitations: that laboratory, clinical, and observational field studies are all necessary and that each alike provides and tests hypotheses for the others.

Rather than disputing about what is "the" best method, behavioral scientists, it seems to me, should examine dispassionately the advantages and disadvantages of every established technique in terms of the relevant situation and the specific questions that are being asked by one kind of investigator as against another. It is sometimes too easily assumed that the underlying assumptions are—or ought to be—the same. For instance, sociologists and social psychologists have on occasion taken it for granted that the "informants" of the anthropologist could be equated with their "respondents" and "subjects." Actually, the anthropologist often thinks of an informant much more as an historian thinks of a document in a period whose main outlines are already familiar, or as an art historian will treat a new specimen that fits into a series of recognized style. That is, the question is not that of incidence or distribution, but rather those of: what point in what pattern? or: in what slightly variant ways is a known pattern manifested? When anthropologists are addressing themselves—and they sometimes do—to questions of ranges of dispersion, or when they are trying to establish a statistically sound generalization, they can properly be asked for figures. But in questions of pattern analysis, the relevant point may be that of configuration or of abrupt alternation from one configuration to another. Figures may not only be beside the point; they may obscure the issue. For example, if I sedulously count the number of occasions on which American men arise when a woman enters a room where a social gathering is taking place, my data will simply blur the existence of a minor cultural pattern if part of my observations occur in upper middle-class families and part in lower-class families.

Even when the questions being asked are of the same general nature, different methods may complement each other. During my years of work with Navaho children, I sometimes envied my colleagues in psychology who could bring their subjects into an experimental room where noise and other distractions were eliminated, temperature and other variables perfectly controlled, etc. Nevertheless, I reflected, my psychological colleagues saw the children they were studying for a few hours a week at most and had to depend for an account of what went on the rest of the week upon an interview with the mother or, possibly, both parents. In contrast, my co-workers and I were able to live with a Navaho family in their one-room hut for virtually twenty-four hours a day. Not many family secrets can be concealed for more than a short period under those circumstances. What the psychologists learned, they learned —admittedly—in a more rigorous way. One knowledge, however, was richer, more ramified, and pertinent to behavior in ordinary daily life settings.

It has sometimes been asserted that when anthropologists analyze their materials they do so by "feel" or "appercep-tion" or "artistic insight." Instead of these epithets, certain critics might as well have said flatly: "Anthropologists are 'unscientific' or at any rate very sloppy workmen." Less unfriendly critics, however, use these terms, I believe, be-cause they sense that anthropologists are carrying out—or trying to carry out—a type of analysis which has little place in the repertory of some of the other varieties of behavioral science. This is the approach which anthropologists have variously referred to as that of "pattern," "configuration," "structure," or "contextualism."

Anthropologists are at fault for having made few attempts in print to specify the steps that in fact they take when they make this kind of analysis. Yet I can testify from almost daily contact with Ruth Benedict during the period when she was doing the research that led to *The Chrysanthemum and the Sword* that she did not evolve her ideas "mystically" from her inner consciousness, but worked very systematically. She saturated herself in Japanese materials of a carefully selected variety: literature, art, projective tests, interviews, etc. After she thought she had detected some highest common factors or least common denominators that constituted, so to speak, implicit premises cutting across bodies of culture content that were quite different, she then wrote down some hypotheses as to what she should find—and should not find—in as yet unexamined data if her initial formulations were correct. She then sought out fresh materials drawn from the same categories and validated, rejected, or reformulated her initial hypotheses and made at least one more trial run. Most American social psychologists, to be sure, would have been appalled at one aspect of her procedure. I once asked her: "But *how many* new novels, for instance, do you think you must read and analyze before you stop?" She told me plainly that this was a silly question.

I believe that the affiliation of many cultural anthropologists for pattern analysis has comparatively simple historical roots. In the first place, the field situation forced them to realize that the acts and thoughts of men and women do not remain dammed up in the neat little pools which the Western academic tradition has labeled "religion," "economics," and the like. They saw, with Dostoevsky, that "Reality is a thing of infinite diversity, and defies the most ingenious deductions and definitions of abstract thought, nay, abhors the clear and precise classifications we delight in: Reality tends to infinite subdivisions of things, and truth is a matter of infinite shadings and differentiations." At the same time, their unavoidable experience with the ramified context and with the abrupt alternations from one configuration to another compelled anthropologist to see that form and structure pervade human behavior and human cultures as much as they do molecules or crystals or organisms, and that the crucial structure points of one culture differ from those of another just as the planes of cleavage of one kind of crystal distinguish these from others, even others which to the eye appear rather similar.

Anthropological emphasis upon pattern and structure is, of course, unique only as regards intensity and certain details. In many ways, it is similar to the approach used by sophisticated students of art styles. All behavioral scientists must necessarily face problems of pattern analysis, and, as Whyte's (1951) volume shows, form is a central theme in almost all of the sciences at mid-twentieth century. But the distinctive aspects of the anthropological outlook derive primarily from the second historical factor: among behavioral scientists, only cultural anthropologists have been in sustained contact with the extraordinary developments in structural linguistics over the past generation.[4] This resulted—as so many things do—from a series of historical accidents. Comparative studies of culture really date from the discovery that Sanscrit was related to Greek and Latin. This finding was dramatic in the contemporary intellectual climate, partly because it cast doubt upon the customary assumption that Hebrew had been the original language of mankind. At any rate, the development of comparative Indo-European philology gave a tremendous impetus to many kinds of comparative investigation of which cultural anthropology was one. From its very beginnings, then, cultural anthropology had a kind of persistent tie to linguistics, and the subculture of the profession prescribed that the anthropologist would concern himself with the languages of the peoples he studied.

The philologists, however, showed little disposition to investigate the structures of "primitive" languages. They devoted their efforts first and foremost to the Indo-European tongues and, somewhat later, to the comparative philology of Semitic languages and those of the high civilizations of the Far East. Students trained in philology who did work with language families other than those just named had a strong propensity to force the data into the Procrustean bed of Indo-European phonological, grammatical, and syntactical categories. Anthropologists, and notably Franz Boas, speedily became aware that this brought about a ludicrous distortion of the materials. Boas forcefully argued that the first principle was that features both of sound and of morphology had to be seen "from within"—i.e., in terms of the principles governing the system in which they occurred in nature.

The insights of Boas were carried further by Edward Sapir, who was equally brilliant as linguist and as anthropologist. A series of papers by Sapir such as "Sound Patterns in Language" and "The Unconscious Patterning of Behavior in Society" had a profound impact upon cultural anthropologists and especially upon such "configurationalists" as Ruth Benedict. Sapir pointed out that ". . . the naïve Frenchman confounds the two sounds 's' of 'sick' and 'th' of 'thick' in a single pattern point—not because he is really unable to hear the difference, but because the setting up of such a difference disturbs his feeling for the necessary configuration of linguistic sounds." This statement constitutes a miniscule paradigm for a whole theory.

What is often decisive in the realms of culture (of which language is one) is not so and so much of something or whether or not phenomena have a random distribution (cultural phenomena, by definition, have other than a chance distribution) but rather the question of order and arrangement.

Moreover, a parsimonious description becomes possible only if the ordering principles are discovered. Speakers of English make sounds in which their vocal chords vibrate and others in which they do not. They also frequently make sounds which are—from the standpoint of an acoustics engineer—intermediate in type. However, the discrimination of shadings in this latter category is meaningless so far as language and culture are concerned, though it may have some interest for the biology or physics of speech sounds. The significant contrasts in English is between voiced and voiceless, and this contrast is used to make many distinctions vital to communication in that language. In the Algonkin Indian tongues, on the other hand, it is a matter indifferent to communication whether the stop series of sounds are voiced, voiceless, or intermediate. Every language employs between about five and eleven decisive contrasts which determine the discriminations between various classes of sounds. Exactly the same kind of thing applies in another realm of culture, kinship systems. As Radcliffe-Brown (1941, p. 17) has written, "We can 'find' beneath the diversities, a limited number of general principles applied and combined in various ways."

As Mead (1952, p. 655) says: "In dealing with culture, the anthropologist makes the same assumptions about the rest of culture that the linguist makes about the language—that he is dealing with a system which can be delineated by analysis of a small number of very highly specified samples."

There is no doubt that anthropologists must supply more quantitative data and become more sophisticated in mathematical analysis. And yet there is no necessary connection between measure and structure. For culture in general, there are many indications that one of its aspects (language) constitutes the best model. And, as B. L. Whorf (1940) has written:

In place of apparatus, linguistics uses and develops *techniques*. Experimental does not mean quantitative. Measuring, weighing, and pointer-reading devices are seldom needed in linguistics, for quantity and number play little part in the realm of pattern, where there are no variables but, instead, abrupt alternations from one configuration to another. The mathematical sciences require exact measurement, but what linguistics requires is, rather, exact "patternment"— an exactness of relation irrespective of dimensions. Quantity, dimension, magnitude are metaphors since they do not properly belong in this spaceless, relational world. I might use the simile: Exact measurement of lines and angles will be needed to draw exact squares or other regular polygons, but measurement, however precise, will not help us to draw an exact circle. Yet it is necessary only to discover the principle of the compass to reach by a leap the ability to draw perfect circles. Similarly, linguistics has developed techniques which, like compasses, enable it without any true measurement at all to specify *exactly* the patterns with which it is concerned. Or I might perhaps liken the case to the state of affairs within the atom, where also entities appear to alternate from configuration to configuration rather than to move in terms of measurable positions.[5] As alternants, quantum phenomena must be treated by a method of analysis that substitutes a point in a pattern under a set of conditions for a point in a pattern under another set of conditions—a method similar to that used in analysis of linguistic phenomena.

Students of human life who pride themselves on being "scientific" still tend, consciously or unconsciously to hold the view of "science" set forth in Karl Pearson's famous *Grammar*. They take as their model not only physics but specifically nineteenth century physics. Here problems of measurable incidence and intensity predominated. Such problems also have their importance in anthropology, but the most difficult and most essential problems about culture cannot be answered in these terms. As W. M. Wheeler remarked: "Form is the secretion of culture." Form is a matter of ordering, of arrangement, of emphasis. Measurement in and of itself is seldom the best instrument for recognizing and describing form. One can, yes, give a mathematical equation for a circle, but this form is more easily and immediately recognized by direct perception. Sometimes exactly the same entities—so far as measurement of their parts is concerned—differ; their configurations give rise to quite distinct properties.

Warren Weaver (1948) has pointed out that seventeenth-century science dealt largely with problems of organized simplicity and nineteenth-century science with problems of disorganized complexity where statistical techniques are most appropriate. But the crucial problems of present science generally are those of organized complexity. This is certainly true of anthropology, as Bateson (1947, p. 651) says:

> Another peculiarity of the data collected by cultural anthropologists is the extreme complexity of each

individual datum. The requirement that each datum include full identification of the individual and description of the context is perhaps never fully met in practice. The fact remains, however, that a very large number of circumstances are always relevant, in the sense that a small change in any one of them might reverse, or drastically change, the form of the behavior which we are recording. There is, therefore, almost no possibility of handling the data statistically. The contexts, the individuals, and the behaviors are too various for their combinations and permutations to be handled in this way.

In my opinion, the study of cultural phenomena will progress mainly along linguistic lines by distinguishing contrastive categories—rather than by measurement as such. We cannot master our knowledge until we have objectified it, and we cannot objectify it until we have found conventions to give it form. What is necessary is to discover the determinate organizations of various clusters of cultural features: an exactness and constancy of relationship irrespective of content and dimensions. The indispensable criterion is that of linguistics: significant discontinuities. The naïve adherents of "scientism" are actually disregarding the history of science which records that advance follows upon the isolation of the significant configurations. If operations are firmly and explicitly specified, "qualitative" judgments can be as systematic and as rigorous as quantitative ones. Edgar Anderson (1936) reminds us:

> Biology has advanced most rapidly when appropriate qualitative measures have been developed and used with precision. In genetics, for example, the fundamental data are qualitative. Once obtained they are treated with such precision that most geneticists prob-

ably think of their work as purely quantitative. But the fundamental categories, "vestigial" vs. "non-vestigal," "scute" vs. "non-scute," "forked" vs. "non-forked," etc. are quite as qualitative as the fundamental categories of taxonomy. . . . If the methods of Drosophila genetics were purely quantitative, the flies would not be classified in qualitative categories but their wing lengths, eye diameters, etc. would be laboriously measured. Imagine the difficulties of conducting a Drosophila experiment in which the only available data were the lengths and breadths of the wings! Genetics has been able to advance because it was willing to take the Mendelian recessive (a qualitative unit about whose ultimate significance relatively little was known) and to use that unknown but recognizable entity as a basic unit.

Recent investigations by Anderson (1954) represent, I believe, a dramatic warning to behavioral scientists who wish to measure without isolating elementary entities based upon significant discontinuities. Graphic representation of a few carefully selected features enabled biologists and many nonbiologists to differentiate two species correctly, even when they were not told the number of species involved. In contrast, analysis of variance and regression techniques yielded inconclusive or much less efficient results. He comments:

If one sets out to analyze the difference between two species, the actual data are individual plants or animals, each individual a multiple-sense-impression of size, shape, color, texture, etc. . . . To analyze the nature of these differences we need to make a selection among the thousands of sense-impressions which come to us from each specimen. . . . The two species may be completely separated by the resultant of seven variables even though any single variable would not suffice when used singly. . . . An impressive proportion of the multiple sense impressions, such as differences between species or varieties, where from each individual a seemingly infinite number of numerical facts could be derived . . . the customary methods of biometry are still inappropriate and ineffective. . . . Pointer readings are not more exact than any other kind of precise record . . . species are differentiated by combinations of characters more certainly than by single characters. . . .

Before I go on to enlarge the connection between the considerations we have been reviewing (especially the illustrations provided by Anderson) and the linguistic model, I want to recapitulate—briefly and plainly—what I regard as the essence of field method in cultural anthropology. It is primarily that of careful, continuous, theoretically pointed observation in the widest possible variety of context occurring in the life of that group. Personal observation and interview are supplemented and enriched by the collection of personal documents (including dreams), drawings, and other artifacts; by the use of projective and other tests; by objective recordings with still and moving pictures and sound scribers; by (today) simple "experiments." Yet first-hand observation (interviewing is really one form of direct observation) remains the backbone of anthropological method. Just as the anthropologist prefers ordinary life context to laboratory context, he prefers first-hand observation to the use of documents. He has the advantage over the historian of being able to make his own evaluation of the events in question. This coin has also, of course, its obverse in that the danger of personal implication is perhaps greater when the analyst has directly observed or even participated in the events he interprets. It is also true that anthropologists of this century have loved field work so much that they have, in general, neglected available and relevant documents. With some notable exceptions, recent anthropological research has been needlessly a-historical. Nevertheless—for better or for worse—contextual, observational field work has been the core.

Method: Linguistics and Values

It will have been noted that in speaking of genetics, Anderson referred to a number of complementary categories ("forked" vs. "non-forked," etc.). Similarly, linguists in their elegant analyses of one aspect of culture have found it extremely useful to set up a series of distinctive contrasts or oppositions, usually binary, which serve to identify each separate phoneme (sound class distinctive in that language). A "lump" or "bundle" of such "distinctive features" defines a phoneme. In its simplest form, the process is like a specialized version of the "twenty questions game." Thus one may ask, "Is the phoneme vocalic? Yes or no?" In Russian, eleven such questions will identify each phoneme uniquely. In the French phonemic system, the binary oppositions are the following: vowel-consonant, nasal-oral, saturated-diluted, grave-acute, tense-lax, and continuous-intercepted. While the particular principles or distinctive features and their combinations vary from one phonemic system to another, a total list of the oppositions utilized in known languages would not exceed twenty.

There are grounds, both empirical and theoretical, for supposing that a similar approach will yield good results with other aspects of culture, including cultural values. Human nature and the human situation are such that there are some fundamental questions of value upon which all cultures have felt compelled to take a position, explicit or implicit. As in the case of language, the foci or structure-points are largely supplied by the limits and potentialities given by the physical world, human biology, and social requirements. With language, the properties of sound waves, the anatomy and physiology of the speech organs, and social (communicative) needs constrain the range of variation. With values, such unavoidable facts as dependence upon the external environment, birth and death, and social relatedness make value "choices" in these areas inescapable. Nor, here again, is the range of loci for selection or indeed of possible selections at each locus unconstrained. Just as all phonemic systems include nasals, stops, and sibilants, so all value systems place their weightings, for instance, on the desirable relations to nature, other individuals, and the self within a describable set of alternatives.

The entities of value-culture may not have the all-or-none character of a simple physical event like the phonemes found in language-culture. Rather, they may have the character of weightings or emphases that are, on the whole, dominant in the culture. Even here there are parallels. A language or a phonemic system is, after all, a high-order abstraction. Concretely, each person's speech is an idio-dialect, and even this varies through time and between situations. Similarly, some individuals or groups may accept the variant rather than the dominant cultural values. They may reject some or many of the core values. To those values, whether dominant or variant, that they do accept each individual gives an interpretation and a coloring that is more or less private. It nevertheless remains meaningful to abstract common elements both in language and in values.

By proceeding as the geneticists have done so successfully with qualitative binary oppositions that represent

significant discontinuities and by using the linguistic technique (Bloch, 1953) of seeing which distributions are complementary, coincident, incorporating and overlapping, anthropologists may be able to answer the questions that are
at the heart of the principles of selectivity which determine
the distinctiveness of each culture. Which combinations of
value-emphases are "impossible?" Which are very rare and
probably due to exceptional circumstances? Which are so
frequent as to be predictable? On which is no guess justified
one way or the other? This particular task will indeed
involve counting, but the initial determination of the con-
trasting pairs is more likely to follow the linguistic experience. Once a linguist is certain that in one instance a
glottalized and a nonglottalized voiceless stop at the same
articulatory position are in complementary distribution—or
produce variation in the meaning of a morpheme—he
knows he has two distinct phonemes. In addition, he knows
that there is an overwhelming likelihood that glottalization
is one of the distinctive features of that language and is
decisive in a number of phonemic contrasts.

Dichotomies are very slippery, to be sure, and the use
of them often brings about a false simplification of the
phenomena. Yet they are not merely convenient. The fact
that human beings have two eyes, two hands, two feet; the
alternation of night and day; the existence of two sexes,
and other circumstances make it almost inevitable that
people tend strongly to think in terms of "either-or" and
"yes or no." In every culture there are many paired oppo-
sites: "love and hate," "friends and enemies," and the like.
Hence, however false to the complexity of the natural
world this anthropocentric two-valued logic may be, it
remains true that human behavior frequently takes place on
the binary basis, and this propensity introduces some regu-

larities useful for scientific analysis. No multivalued logic has thus far been very successful except at the level of formal mathematical notation.

Eventually anthropologists can, I believe, describe the compositional pattern of each culture and construct a comparative grammar and a comparative syntax of cultures. An anthropologist is interested in the grammar, a psychologist in the dialects. All grammars limit freedom and control choices. The function of linguistic grammar is to control the freedom of words so that there is no needless congestion of the communication traffic. The "grammar" of culture, in general, likewise makes for orderliness. A culture is a complex, yet unitary pattern.

A comparative grammar of cultures would delimit the necessities in cultural development: what features must precede or be associated with what others? Only the intensive and systematic study of variation—and variation through time—revealing the latent structures and latent concepts and incomplete paradigms, can make a grammar of cultures possible. The students of linguistic culture have pointed the way. Linguistics has proven the fallacy of radical reductionism. The unity of science is based not on reductionism but on perspectives—that is, the isomorphism of the concepts used throughout the sciences and especially those that investigate the same general sector of nature.

Cultural Constants and Variants

Anthropology—along with psychology and psychiatry—is building a model of "raw" human nature, a general conception of man, of human limits and potentialities. The anthropologist's special contribution is that of documenting empirically the constants and the variants in the human record. The constants presumably reflect our common humanity; they arise out of the biological nature of the species and the necessities imposed by the universal aspects of the human condition (generalities of the physical environment, helplessness of infants, family life, and the like). The variants[6] mirror cultural differences, for cultures in their uniqueness represent precipitates of the accidents of history, including the variations in the physical environments to which peoples have had to adapt. But the variants equally reveal at least a part of the range of the response potentialities of our species. If practitioners of the Yoga cult attain to voluntary control of their anal sphincters, then we can no longer say this is biologically impossible for men. Or, we can take Aztec human sacrifice or Hindu asceticism and introspection or Polynesian-Melanesian cannibalism and say: "Of these extremes, at least, human beings are capable."

But while a model of human nature is being constructed, anthropologists must work with a provisional theory which has developed from fact and analysis thus far available. These postulates, whether explicitly or implicitly held, enter in fact into all anthropological field work. I shall first list them briefly in a form to which I believe most anthropologists would give assent. I shall then explicate the grounds for holding them.

1. The logic (i.e., the fundamental processes of reasoning) of all peoples is the same, but the premises and basic categories are somewhat different. Different premises likewise lead to different epistemologies.

2. Human nature is in some sense the same throughout space and time. This does not signify, however, as common sense tends to assume, that similar stimuli will regularly produce similar responses.

Marcel Mauss has called the anthropologist "the astronomer of human constellations: *Il faut, avant tout, dresser le catalogue le plus grand possible de categories; il faut partir de toutes celles dont on peut savoir que les hommes se sont servis. On verra alors qu'il y a encore bien des lunes mortes, ou pales, ou obscures au firmament de la raison.* It was—and is—an indispensable scientific requirement that the gamut of human variability be explored exhaustively in order to know the empirically determinable range of human nature. But in their fascination—almost obsession—with the staggeringly extensive spectrum of actualized possibilities, anthropologists tended for long to see only the outward forms, the somewhat external trappings of custom. They lost sight of the likenesses. And yet the fact of a common human nature is demonstrated by an elementary and exceptionless induction from anthropological field experience. However masked the human beings of another culture may strike the observer at first, however much they may initially present themselves simply as players of unfamiliar roles defined by the new culture, the anthropologist eventually—but inevitably—recognizes similarities to personalities he has known elsewhere. As Robert Redfield (1947) has written:

> One must get beyond the culture to those elements in the behavior of the people which are, after all, the same as one's own. For as one comes to understand people who live by institutions and values different from one's own, at the same time one comes to see that these people are, nevertheless, like one's own people. The alien culture at first appears to us as a mask, enigmatic or repugnant. On closer acquaintance we see it as a garment for the spirit; we understand its harmonies and appreciate them. Finally, as ac-

quaintance goes deeper still, we do not see or for a time forget, the culture, but look only to the common humanity of the men and women underneath.

The investigator, even before he has learned the language, can "understand" much of what he observes because his subjects manifest hostility, altruism, pride, shame, sorrow, and need. It is true that when he learns the language he will discover that the terms for these are not minutely synonymous with those in his own tongue—the conceptual terrains will differ in extent, in relationships to other concepts, and in shadings. What will evoke these universal human feelings and the ways in which they are expressed may differ drastically. However, he will and must recognize their affinities, see that they are so many phenotypes of a prototypical, pan-human genotype. Field work would be possible under no other conditions. The stranger would either flee or be killed or quite literally go mad. If I may quote once again from the luminous writing of Redfield (1950):

> It may be asserted that all (normal) men and women have the same human nature. . . . But it cannot be asserted that all men have the same personality or that all groups have the same culture; although it is properly asserted that all men have personalities, and that all continuing groups of people who communicate with one another are characterized by culture. By human nature we mean that nature which everyone (after infancy) of our species has, if provided with the usual capacities, when he is brought up in a society characterized by culture. It is the nature we assume we shall meet in every man or woman, no matter where we meet him, or her. We assume, and rightly, that every human being has something of

which he may be proud, and something of which he may be ashamed. Before we have even tried to communicate with him, we know that if we hit upon what he finds amusing or shocking, he will be amused or shocked; that he will desire praise, and that he will give up present pleasures for some deferred good which he values highly. . . . The anthropologist demonstrates the existence of human nature whenever he finds out what an exotic people are thinking and feeling. He can do this only by supposing that they have in common with him certain acquired propensities of attitude; these are human nature. To be able to find out what it is that a Zuni Indian is ashamed of, one must first know what it is to be ashamed. Although anthropologists commonly make assertions to the effect that "human nature is infinitely malleable," or speak of "the refutation of human nature," as an achievement of their science, they in fact recognize its existence every day.

There is a generalized framework that underlies the more apparent and striking facts of cultural relativity. All cultures constitute so many somewhat different answers to essentially the same questions posed by human biology and by the generalities of the human situation. Every society's patterns for living must provide for approved and sanctioned ways of dealing with such universal circumstances as the existence of two sexes; the helplessness of infants; the need for satisfaction of the elementary requirements of food, warmth, and sex; the presence of individuals of different ages and of differing physical and other capacities. The basic similarities in human biology the world over are vastly more massive than the variations. Equally, there are certain necessities in social life for this kind of organism, regardless of where life is carried on or in what culture. Co-operation to obtain subsistence and for other ends requires a certain minimum of reciprocal behavior, a standard system of communication and indeed of mutually accepted values. The broad outlines of the ground plans of all cultures are and have to be about the same, because always and everywhere men are faced with certain unavoidable problems which arise out of the situation "given" by nature.

Some aspects of culture and some manifestations of human nature take their specific forms as a consequence of historical accidents; others are shaped by forces which can properly be regarded as universal. As Levi-Strauss (1945, p. 4) says:

> . . . enfin la récurrence, en des régions éloignés du monde et dans les sociétés profondement différentes, de formes de parenté, règles de mariage, attitudes pareillement prescrites entre certains types de parents, etc., donne a croire, que, dans un cas comme dans l'autre, les phénomènes observables résultent de jeu de lois générales, mais cachées.

Incest regulations contrasted with couvade and cannibalism serve as a good example. The essential psychological and behavioral possibilities for all three are present among humans. But the latter two present a sporadic occurrence, whereas the incest taboo (though the details differ) is absolutely universal. Nevertheless, it has its cultural dimensions. Highly similar stimuli and highly similar situations do not produce identical responses. The universality of incest avoidance is, as Freud and others have pointed out, related to the nuclear family and other ubiquitous factors. Yet this accounts neither for the extension of such taboos beyond the nuclear family nor for the diverse ways in which different cultures define the categories of prohibited relatives.

I have said that in a certain deep sense the logic (which means the modes of interpreting relationships between phenomena) of all members of the human species is the same. The differences in thinking and reacting arise from the value premises and existential conceptions about the nature of the external world and of human nature. These premises are learned as part of a cultural tradition. Such degree of synthesis as exists within a culture is achieved partly through the overt statements of dominant conceptions, assumptions, and aspirations of the group in its religious beliefs, secular thought, and ethical and legal codes, and partly through unconscious apperceptive habits —ways of perceiving and evaluating the stream of events that are so taken for granted as seldom or never to be verbalized explicitly except when challenged from without.

While the habits of men's minds, the habitual ways of begging certain questions that are distinctive of cultures influence or determine much differentiated behavior, some values, as well as some modes of thinking, characterize the species as a whole. Every culture has a concept of murder, distinguishing this from execution, killing in war, and other kinds of "justifiable homicide." Some societies are callous to suffering. Some justify suffering as a means to the ends of the society (e.g., punishment) or as a means to the ends of the individual (mystical exaltation or purification.) No society values human suffering as an end in itself. The notions of prohibitions upon untruth under defined circumstances,[7] of restitution and reciprocity, of mutual obligations between parents and children—these and many other moral concepts are altogether universal. And these values which are a part of human nature are as much "in" the organism as those standards of biological normality of which Canguilhem (1950, p. 143) writes: *S'il existe des normes biologiques c'est parce que la vie, étant non pas seulement soumission au milieu mais institution de son milieu propre, pose par là-même des valeurs non seulement dans le milieu mais aussi dans l'organisme même.*

In sum, cultures are distinct yet similar and comparable. The features that lend uniqueness are the secondary or variable ones. There is a proper analogy between cultures and personalities. Each human being is unique in his concrete totality, but he resembles all other human beings in certain respects and some particular human beings a great deal. Some similarities are the consequence of common learning experiences; others are the result of genetically controlled biological tendencies. It is no more correct to limit each way of life to its distinctive features and organization than to deny to each personality those aspects that derive from cultural heritage and from participation in common humanity. The common understandings between men of different cultures are very broad, very general, very easily obscured by languages and other immediately apparent symbols. True universals or near universals are apparently few in number. But they seem to be as deep-going as they are rare. Anthropology's facts attest that the phrase "a common humanity" is in no sense meaningless. Indeed, it is an essential pre-condition of our being able to study each other.

To discover something about the limits and potentialities of human nature, to see how this universal nature is molded by varying cultures, and especially to learn something about those nonrational cultural responses which appear to the naive view to possess almost the automatic character of "instinctive" reactions—this is no mere academic query. The fate of our Western civilization and perhaps of civilization in general may hang upon humanity's gaining some orderly and systematic insight into the non-rational and irrational factors in human behavior. E. R. Dodds (1951, pp. 254-5), Regius Professor of Greek in the University of Oxford, has expressed all this more eloquently than I can:

> We . . . have experienced a great age of rationalism, marked by scientific advances beyond anything that earlier times had thought possible, and confronting mankind with the prospect of a society more open than any it has ever known. And in the last forty years we have also experienced something else—the unmistakable symptoms of a recoil from that prospect. It would appear that, in the words used recently by Andre Malraux, "Western civilisation has begun to doubt its own credentials."
>
> What is the meaning of this recoil, this doubt? Is it the hesitation before the jump, or the beginning of a panic flight? I do not know. On such a matter a simple professor of Greek is in no position to offer an opinion. But he can do one thing. He can remind his readers that once before a civilised people rode to this jump—rode to it and refused it. And he can beg them to examine all the circumstances of that refusal.
>
> Was it the horse that refused, or the rider? That is really the crucial question. Personally, I believe it was the horse—in other words, those irrational elements in human nature which govern without our knowledge so much of our behaviour and so much of what we think is our thinking. And if I am right about this, I can see in it grounds for hope . . . the men who created the first European rationalism were never

—until the Hellenistic Age—"mere" rationalists: that is to say, they were deeply and imaginatively aware of the power, the wonder, and the peril of the Irrational. But they could describe what went on below the threshold of consciousness only in mythological or symbolic language; they had no instrument for understanding it, still less for controlling it; and in the Hellenistic Age too many of them made the fatal mistake of thinking they could ignore it. Modern man, on the other hand, is beginning to acquire such an instrument. It is still very far from perfect, nor is it always skilfully handled; in many fields, including that of history, its possibilities and its limitations have still to be tested. Yet it seems to offer the hope that if we use it wisely we shall eventually understand our horse better; that, understanding him better, we shall be able by better training to overcome his fears; and that through the overcoming of fear horse and rider will one day take that decisive jump, and take it successfully.

REFERENCES CITED

ANDERSON, EDGAR: Hybridization in American Tradescantias. *Annals of the Missouri Botanical Garden,* 23: 511-25, 1936
———: Efficient and Inefficient Methods of Measuring Species Differences. In: *Statistics and Mathematics in Biology,* (Kempthorne, O., *et al.,* eds.), 1954.

BATESON, GREGORY: Sex and Culture. *Annals of the New York Academy of Sciences,* 47: 647-60, 1947.

BENNETT, JOHN W. and WOLFF, KURT, H.: Toward Communication Between Sociology and Anthropology. In: *Yearbook of Anthropology, 1955* (Thomas, William, ed.), New York:

The Wenner-Gren Foundation for Anthropological Research, 1955, 329-51.

BLOCH, BERNARD: Contrast. *Language,* 29: 59-61, 1953.

BOHR, NIELS: Natural Philosophy and Human Cultures. *Nature,* 143: 268-72, 1939.

CANGUILHEM, GEORGES: Essai sur Quelques Problémes Concernant le Normal et le Pathologique. *Publications de la Faculté des Lettres de l'Universite de Strasbourg,* Fasicule 100, 1950.

DODDS, E. R.: *The Greeks and the Irrational,* 1951.

LÉVI-STRAUSS, CLAUDE: L'Analyse Structurale en Linguistique et en Anthropologie. *Word* 1: 1-21, 1945.

MEAD, MARGARET: *Studies in Soviet Communication.* Center for International Studies, Massachusetts Institute of Technology, Duplicated, 1952.

MOORE, T. V.: The Essential Psychoses and Their Fundamental Syndromes. *Studies in Psychology and Psychiatry,* Catholic University of America, Vol. 3, No. 3, 1933.

MURDOCK, G. P.: Anthropology as a Comparative Science. *Behavioral Science,* Vol. 2, No. 4, pp. 249-54.

RADCLIFFE-BROWN, A. R.: The Study of Kinship Systems. *Journal of the Royal Anthropological Institute,* 71: 1-17, 1941.

REDFIELD, ROBERT: The Study of Culture in General Education. *Social Education.* 11: 259-64, 1947.

————: Social Science Among the Humanities. *Measure,* 1: 60-74, 1950.

STAVRIANOS, BERTHA K.: Research Methods in Cultural Anthropology in Relation to Scientific Criteria. *Psychological Review,* 57: 334-44, 1950.

WEAVER, WARREN: Science and Complexity. *American Scientist,* 36: 536-44, 1948.

WHORF, B. L.: Linguistics as an Exact Science. *Technology Review,* December 1940.

WHYTE, LAUNCELOT (ed.): *Aspects of Form,* 1951.

ZELESNIK, CARTER: The Role of Empathy in Science: Measurement and Control. *Kyklos,* 2: 172-84, 1957.

NOTES

[1] And yet the anthropologist recognizes that some projection is a necessary condition for empathy; which is a prerequisite of good field work.

[2] There is some disagreement here. Some anthropologists hold that one should hold up a mirror to the culture from one's personally chosen angle, others that one should let the picture fall on a ground glass placed in standard position.

[3] For a criticism that deals with these points, but attempts to be fair, see Stavrianos (1950).

[4] For about five years now, some psychologists have been influenced by linguists.

[5] It is interesting that Niels Bohr (1939) has independently suggested the relevance of the principle of complementarity to the understanding of human cultures.

[6] One must not, of course, underestimate the variation. Even among closely related cultures such as those of the United States and of Western Europe, Murdock (1958) reports that of 30 basic cultural categories there was 39 per cent of variation between the two groups. The European sample showed 30 per cent identity with an Asian and only 22 per cent with an African. "Moreover, almost 50 per cent of the items listed for the 50 randomly selected non-European societies fell into categories which were completely unrepresented in any of the European cultures. . . . Note that the reference here is to purely classificatory categories, not to specific items of cultural content. For these the differences between European and non-European cultures would be infinitely more numerous."

[7] For some purposes the "defined circumstances" become, of course, interesting and highly important. Nevertheless, my point here remains: "truth" (however limited and defined) is a universal human value.

CHANGING CULTURE: SOME OBSERVA-
TIONS IN PRIMITIVE SOCIETIES

Margaret Mead

The use of studies of primitive cultures to provide models for the consideration of the processes of reflective change is necessarily limited by the nature of the primitive societies themselves and the conditions under which they have been observed.[1] In only a handful of cases have primitive societies, already subject to some culture contact at the moment of observation, been restudied over time by the same investigators or within the same framework of investigation.[2] As a result we deal almost always with a single study made at a given period in history, which incorporates to a greater or lesser degree the memories of the living as to what the past was like. These memories may be supplemented by the accounts of other types of observers, explorers, traders, missionaries, and the existence of physical objects left over from the past—weapons, building sites, modes of orna-mentation.

Because the science of cultural anthropology is so young,

restudies of previously well-described primitive societies in later stages of transition are just becoming feasible. In the use of these materials it is important to distinguish those cases where data have been collected over time within the same conceptual scheme and by the same methods from restudies from another point of view.[3] With regard to modern societies with extensive documentation on some, but not all, parts of the culture, references in this discussion may be considered diagnostic extensions of the models provided by studies of primitive cultures.

One of the most fundamental prerequisites for conscious or self-reflective change would seem to be the knowledge that members of other societies behave in a different way—for example, live in tents in winter instead of snow houses, eat a different kind of food, wear different clothes, and speak a different language. If, however, the members of a group conceive of themselves as following the particular customs they follow because they are who they are—members of the Oqomiut Eskimo group, or of the Manus village of Mok—knowledge of this sort, may not be any more functional than the knowledge that other creatures do other things—beavers build dams, birds build nests—Any piece, or all pieces, of behavior may be viewed as innate and even the fact that they have to be taught may make no difference. Birds, for example, obviously have to learn to fly, but this does not necessarily indicate to the observer that flying is not peculiar and natural to birds, in comparison to squirrels. In examining history—from the simplest primitive people of whom we have any record to the most sophisticated members of modern societies, with full access to all our knowledge of the way in which culture is learned—we find those who treat at least certain parts of their cultural behavior, in which they are known to differ from members of other societies, other classes, the other sex, or even other families, as completely innate and not subject to modification.

But such a belief obviously forms an effective barrier against any attempt at reflective change. It may be all-embracing, so that a people feel that everything they do is innate and not subject to change, or it may refer only to parts of life—language may be regarded as more primary than material things, beliefs than objects, religion than economics, etc. Or it may be limited in other ways; distinctions may be made between those persons who look most like the group that claims some innate cultural possession—such as the "sense of social justice" sometimes claimed by Eastern European Jews, or an innate sense of fair play sometimes claimed for the English, or clear-headedness for the French—and those individuals who either actually do deviate in physique or appear to do so because of other deviant attitudes affecting their posture, etc., who may then be regarded as non-Jewish, or un-English, or un-French, in some subtle and unspecified way.

The ineradicable innateness of a type of behavior may be regarded as limited to a single generation, as in the Soviet view of the *kulaks* who were believed to be incapable of learning behavior appropriate to the new society. Here also there was a subtle differentiation of view in the belief that the type of attitude toward acquisition found among peasants could be eradicated in the next generation, but that higher-class origin was even harder to deal with so that the first generation of young people with middle- and upper-class origin were debarred from the full benefits of the new education.

It is interesting to compare here the way the Chinese belief that Chinese culture has always triumphed over the invader can now be seen in the belief of Chinese Communists that adults—of any origin or occupation, including

European Christian missionaries—can be altered by proper forms of "struggle." [4] American culture, based upon the activities of innovating and revolutionary Europeans, remains consistently apprehensive that existing forms will be subverted by the arrival of new ideas of European origin—socialism and communism.

These varied and limited ways of handling innateness carry with them certain expectable complications—the fear of change, in all of its ramifications, or the Soviet preoccupation lest some small bit of the past should somehow survive,[5] grow again and overwhelm the new social structure. It is also probable that, wherever change has been conspicuously introduced by a single individual or a small group, fear of this order of change may become part of the whole expectation of change if this process is remembered either overtly or covertly.

Another dimension may be found in the valuation placed upon a society's own behavior as simply something that they as themselves have always done, as something that they at sometime began doing, or as something that is the essential basis of their superiority, real or imagined, over other peoples or of their inferiority, real or imagined, to other peoples. If the language is regarded as more difficult or more elegant than that which is spoken by neighbors, and the fact plays a larger role in the self-esteem of a group, such as some of the attitudes toward Arabic, this may then become less subject to reflection and change. On the other hand, a vanishing society, sunk in despair and close to annihilation, may also cling stubbornly to a language spoken by only as few as a hundred people, as has been the case with many North American Indian tribes.

There are also wide differences in the extent to which people are able to label a part of their behavior and see it as separate from a whole sequence of behaviors or, in some instances, even as separable from the mass of behavior characteristic of their group. If a deer hunter is a man who carries a certain kind of bow when he hunts, and the bow itself is seen as an extension of that kind of hunter, as his stance might be, it may be labeled and conceptualized in such a way that only if he stops being a deer hunter could he use some other weapon for what would then be a quite different activity. It is more usual for material objects—which can themselves be physically separated from their users and passed, at least temporarily, into the hands of other people (or another sex or tribe or race)—to be conceptualized as something that can be adopted from the culture of others or diffused into another society than to consider such forms of behavior as marriage as susceptible of such transmission.

The order of behaviors that are borrowed or transmitted to others differs, however, from one area of the world to another, and itself constitutes a definition of possible change. The primitive peoples of New Guinea are an example of a hypertrophy of fragmentation of culture for export and import purposes.[6] Not only pots and spears, puppies and seeds, but also forms of magic, ways of organizing the group into dual or quaternary sets, forms of marriage (e.g., marriage with father's sister's daughter, or brother and sister exchange), and types of initiation can be bought and sold between villages or between linguistic groups. This area is characterized by an enormous number of languages, vaguely defined boundaries, rapid social change, and low political organization. Selections from the available supply of new artifacts, social customs, beliefs and practices, are made on the basis of ethnological emphasis.

The Mountain Arapesh would reject an item of love magic which looked disruptive of their contemporary premium on placid domesticity. The Iatmul of the Sepik River[7] would superimpose still another dual organization on an existing dual organization, as multiple realignments were a tolerable device in preserving their precarious social equilibrium, which itself depended on people shifting partisanship from one membership category to another whenever a conflict approached a breaking point—e.g., no longer acting as part of the initiatory moiety system but acting instead in terms of ceremonial linkages between clans. But a capacity to criticize and reject incompatible elements of culture was lacking, so a people with one form of marriage would cheerfully import an incompatible form. Where incompatibility could be handled, as among the Iatmul, as alternative forms of insult, additional elements did little harm. So in a quarrel a Iatmul might say, "You are the sort of useless creature whom even your *iai* wouldn't marry"—the *iai* being one form of enjoined marriage, to a woman of father's mother's clan. But one could also say, "You are the sort of man who couldn't get anyone to marry you *except a iai.*"

In a culture where confusion of marriage patterns led to sorcery, however, the incompatibilities were much less manageable. In general, it might be said that the people of New Guinea had many of the necessary ideas for self-reflective social change—the knowledge that culture was learned, that items of culture could be identified, named, separated from their surrounding matrix, and transmitted from one group to another without immediate mediation of persons, and that once accepted they could be abandoned —by transmission to another group or through disuse—but they lacked the structural criteria for appropriateness, any idea of progression or evolution, and any articulate recognition of the relationship between a practice and the practitioner. This meant, concretely, that individuals would attempt to copy imported objects such as pots, carvings, ornaments, with no knowledge of the particular technique with which they had been made.

Another sort of awareness of the possibility of change is found in Polynesia, where ideas of rank and breeding are of great importance. Here the practitioner, the carver, the dancer, the bard, the tattooer, the housebuilder, and the canoe builder were treated with honor, as if their skills were tantamount to rank. Thus, in Samoa, when a house builder—without rank—worked for a man of high rank, his employer had to treat him as if he had rank—seat him as an honored guest and address him in honorific language.[8]

If the Polynesians particularly admired the canoe building skill of another group, rather than import objects and copy them, they would try to import the builders in person, or, among the Maori, capture them in war to work for their captors as slaves.[9] Here the idea of change was definitely tied to the fact of breeding, in the aristocratic sense that high rank must be developed through high breeding which then becomes inalienable, with the idea that such aristocratic skills could only be exercised by those so taught. This concept of possible change involved a respect for the delicate processes of nonverbal apprenticeship,[10] and the intimate relationships between the way a thing is done and what it is—whether it be a dance or a piece of carving—was limited by the existence of distinctions among peoples of different rank.

Whether such respect for apprenticeship is found in a professional group—as in the practice of medicine or the law—or in a social class, the emphasis is upon the long association of the tutor and the pupil while the learning is going on. In such an association many aspects of the process could be left unverbalized and the contribution of the learner could be absorbed inarticulately without challenging the status of the teacher. When, however, the techniques of a craft become articulately recognized as "secrets" and the property of a particular craft group, the apprenticeship position can become a rigid barrier to change.

The association between any skill—or even the ability to learn—and a particular status may become a vehicle for cross-cultural learning. It seems to be a characteristic of peoples or classes or castes who see themselves in the superior role in a hierarchy, that this superiority gives them a high facility in taking on almost any of the behavior of members of other groups whom they see as members of the same high status.[11] So the savage king builds a palace with modern plumbing, fur and feathers are doffed for a top hat, a little-known and isolated language is replaced by elegant French or English, and eating with the fingers easily passes over into the use of the most beautiful table silver. But contretemps can occur when the culture contact situation is ambiguous and the equivalences between members of the donor and receiving cultures are not clear— when, for example, a chief's daughter marries a sailor before the mast, or an American Indian with land to lease classifies himself in a leisure-class role. Then all the possibilities of the dignified acquisition of comparable skills in the other group—through the mechanisms of tutoring, modeling, and role playing—are lost.

This sort of easy identification according to rank has also a negative correlate, for what is easy for chiefs and kings and members of priestly castes may be comparably difficult for commoners, whose self-identification includes their low social status. If access to the strange and the new, the possession of beautiful objects from abroad, foreign languages taught by foreign tutors, and various foreign airs and graces are seen as the attributes of the aristocratic groups—by whom they are in fact most often first exercised—then the inability or unwillingness to acquire any foreign ways may become a continuing and intractable part of the identity structure of peasants, commoners, urban proletarians, etc. Once established, acceptance or rejection of new forms of highly valued, prestige-giving behavior—cosmopolitanism or provincialism—may become entrenched within the society, becoming a differentiating element between classes and a significant factor in the society's ability to initiate or carry through change. Something of this sort seems to lie at the roots of much of the behavior that is usually attributed to the unwillingness of the peasant sector of a society to change in any way. Mine workers who have accepted the definition of themselves as hereditary miners may show a related type of behavior, simply refusing to learn a new occupation when the old one disappears.[12]

An excessive disregard of the differences within the own society—or the initiating group within a society, or a loosely integrated group of related societies—may at first facilitate self-conscious change but, in the end, become a factor in breakdown of the very change that was inaugurated. This seems to have been the case with African kingdoms such as that of the Ashanti tribe on the Gold Coast —now part of Ghana. Reconstruction from comparative material and early records suggests[13] that the Ashanti kingdom was elaborated from simple clusters of lineages, living in forest clearings into which they had been driven, into a complex bureaucracy governing hundreds of thousands of people. The simple pattern of choice of lineage leader—by nomination of the senior female in the matrilineage, assent by all lineage leaders, agreement by peers, possible institutionalized opposition by untitled juniors—was re-enacted with little modification for leaders of higher

levels and finally for the king himself. While the great kingdom was being elaborated through the incorporation of
peoples of comparable cultural patterns, this mechanism,
which included more and more legal fictions based on kinship patterns—as new groups were incorporated—worked
well; but one of the factors in the loss of political integration and eventual defeat of the Ashanti seems to have been
their decreasing success in dealing with the coastal peoples
whose cultural patterns differed.

In the United States, the failure of southern European
immigrants to respond to the conditions of immigration as
northern European immigrants had done led to a type of
stigmatizing of particular immigrant groups in immigration
laws of the 20's and the perpetuation of myths of inferiority derived from a failure to take cultural differences
correctly into account.

One of the great sources of the kind of self-consciousness that leads to recognition of cultural learning as learning rather than as the unfolding of instinct is division of
labor. As soon as one group in a culture can and does do
something which is regarded as inappropriate for another
group, the opportunity for awareness is introduced.

Relative willingness to change behavior appropriate to
one sex or one age group may also contribute, positively or
negatively, to the eventual powers of self-revision and self-
criticism of a society. If a shift in sex roles has been accomplished with, for example, a change in terrain, the
adoption of herding, immigration to another country, etc.,
the new role adoption may have occurred with considerable
tension, and the shift, originally accomplished with what
looked like reasonable celerity and lack of conflict, may
nevertheless establish a new rigidity which may be much
more difficult to shift again. There will, of course, be many
other complicating factors; if the males are already uncer-

tain of their status, they may handle the newly adopted roles—such as milking cows or carrying parcels or pushing baby carriages—very differently than males who have a different order of investment in their masculinity. It has been reported, for example, that in Puerto Rican families in New York, where men are adopting modern American habits of baby care by fathers, the Puerto Rican males impose a kind of *machismo* flourish on the details of infant care; if done by them it is a male act.[14]

Any change in the personnel of any activity is, therefore, bound to introduce an element of further self-consciousness and recognition of the degree to which that occupation or role is not bound by sex, age, class, caste, or race. If the new officiants come from a group previously defined as unable to perform a certain act—such as manning a canoe alone, handling a blowtorch, flying a plane, presiding in a law court, officiating in a religious service, driving a taxi, or serving in the senate—the new arrangements not only may contribute to greater awareness but also are likely to permit those new officiants to channel a greater amount of energy into the activity.[15] Consequently, the first group of women to be allowed to enter medical school, or do welding in a shipyard, or drive railroad engines, may do extraordinarily well. This very high achievement may, however, harden the resistance against them and so lower the possibility of the occupation being seen as interchangeably appropriate for either sex, or it may result in the whole activity being turned over to the new group, who will no longer have the original incentive to validate themselves by superior performance and will, in addition, very likely depress the status of the occupation in which they are now the sole performers or lower the potential contribution of those few members of the original performer group who have remained in the invaded occupation.

What holds for women here holds also for other visible and disadvantaged groups, and may be generalized by the dangers to capacity for reflective change which are provided when the change involves reversals in the status positions of hierarchically arranged groups within a society. As scar tissue is less flexible than unscarred skin, accomplished but traumatic change of any sort may become a precursor of resistance to self-initiated change in the future.

The rigidity of small cult groups such as the various nonconformist Christian sects of the sixteenth and seventeenth centuries offers a good illustration of how changes involving a complete break with the past, inaugurated against great opposition and maintained with enormous dedication and sacrifice, may induce extraordinarily rigid structuring. Doctrinaire communism, originally dependent upon a complete break with every element of the past, also retains traces of the trauma of repudiating both persons and practices with high previous emotional value.[16]

As, in New Guinea, the very ease and fluidity of the culture was actually one component in the lack of any sort of progression within the aboriginal culture, so other forms of apparent ease of learning and ability to innovate may actually be conservative rather than facilitative of change. The Eskimo are notoriously conservative, with a highly stable culture and a language that can be understood from Greenland to Alaska, and they are also exceedingly ingenious in improvising changes in mechanism or in using different materials.[17] This apparent contradiction seems to be related to a double self-definition. On the one hand, one is a member of small, fully-defined group of people who belong in a particular bay or inlet and know every detail of life there—what the indicators are of when the snow will break up, how to follow the directions by the way the wind blows, when and where the fish will run, or where the polar bears wander.[18] As such a people, they also have special myths, their own distinctive version of widespread tales. But, on the other hand, they have a self-definition of themselves as capable of traveling far and wide, of staying away for months or years or half a lifetime, returning only in their old age. And these two self-definitions are not incompatible, for the culture itself is built both for hospitality and for visiting. The visitor is received and helped in understanding the local situation—our bears, our deer, our fish—and there are adequate rituals that govern how he is to be offered a wife, when he may set up a separate cooking fire (if he comes fully equipped for hunting), and how his initial strength is to be tried out so that he may be placed in the strength-order of the group he is visiting. And while he visits, he tells his version of the widespread mythology, and others listen. So the ability to learn, temporarily, and adapt to new situations, without losing or altering one's primary adaptation—which one will use again at home when one is host instead of guest—co-exist, each as part of being an Eskimo.

Definitions of whether one learns only from friends and allies or from rivals and enemies also play a part. The Indians of the North American Plains, whose culture flowered after they obtained the horse and the gun, had, as part of their war-making pattern, the practice of taking captives alive and incorporating them into the group, which provided for a continuous flow of information about the developing institutions of a whole series of warring tribes who were responding with lively creativity to the new freedom given them by the horse and the gun. Longstanding positions of rivalry and hostility—as between France and Germany, Christianity and Judaism, the United States and Russia—may also become conditions within which a great deal of cultural exchange may develop with possibilities either for greater standardization—as when competition is too narrowly defined—or greater variation. But, here again, a tendency to see every contemplated act within a framework of competitiveness may inhibit a society's ability to change in a specified direction,[19] as the advocates and opponents of change manipulate deeply ingrained attitudes of rivalry. So in American civic communities, the knowledge that the town of A is behind the town of B, which is about the same size, in some activity—such as Red Cross, schools, or hospitals—will act as a stimulant to change in town A.[20] But meanwhile, the citizens of town B, with the same information, will relax, and citizens' groups armed with statistics on the need for blood banks or the rising rate of delinquency will be unable to effect a change.

The present situation between the Arab countries and Israel contains elements of this dilemma; as long as the hostility remains overt, Israeli accomplishments, in agriculture and industry, act as stimuli to the members of Arab states to step up their industry and modernize their agriculture; a relaxation of the tension carries with it the possibilities of a lowering of intensity, so that available energy may be reduced in both Arab and Israeli groups.

Another type of capacity for reflective change is found in the nature of the continuities and discontinuities between one chronological stage and another and the roles that are played by members of one age group in orienting another age group. If the basic cultural attitudes are laid down very early in such a way that they simply unfold in later life, intervention by changed forms purposefully introduced at a later stage may fail. For example, an English upper- or upper-middle class child is reared as an infant in a way that is a precursor of a public school education; if later the public school education is not forthcoming, the result is likely to be mutilation rather than growth in some other direction.

American children are reared with the expectation of occupational choice; if, later, through illness or death of the parent or dominance of the parent, a son is forced into his father's business against his consent, this also becomes a traumatic experience. Cultures differ in the degree to which the first year or the first two or first six years lay down a pattern which unfolds, in contradistinction to laying down the first stage in a sequence in which it is not the pattern of any stage but the place in the sequence—in a series of indulgences, deprivations, restrictions, privileges —that is determinative. A quite different order of conscious reorientation is possible in the latter type than in the former.

The same sort of situation obtains as to whether the cultural transmission process is carried on by near age mates, by parents, or by grandparents. Where grandparents are the principal surrogates of the culture, the child receives an image of the completion of the sequence of life which the grandparent has experienced which, when it is not interrupted, is conspicuously resistant to change.[21] But when the grandparent generation is removed, as by the influenza epidemic of 1918 in the Southwest Pacific or by immigration in which the grandparents are left behind—in Europe, or Puerto Rico, or in the American South—this provides an interruption in the process of cultural transmission which makes conscious change more possible. Transmission by child nurses, or by their analogues, the peasant nurses in a stratified society, also provides an intractable resistance to change, since the learning is likely to. be inarticulate or formulated in terms of bogies, threats, or magical penalties for disobedience—whether they are, "If you step on a crack you'll break your mother's back," or threats of a mythical monster. Where the transmission process is in the hands of young adults whose own lives lie before them, as learned from young adults, the possibilities of self-conscious change would seem to be higher.

Furthermore, cultural theories of learning play an important part. Human societies differ very sharply in whether they believe that "you can't teach an old dog new tricks" or that new skills can be learned at any age. The assumption that childhood is a time for learning and adulthood the period for which the learning was done is deeply engrained in our own society and is, indeed, a feature of most civilizations with a weighty classical tradition that, by its very nature, is regarded as something which, once learned, is a permanent and unchangeable possession. A kind of partial counterpoint to such a view of learning is found in highly mobile societies, or societies dependent upon adult immigration and new adaptations, such as the United States and Australia, but in this case the emphasis may shift from a belief that all important skills are learned in childhood to a decrease in the complexity of skills demanded from adults. The skilled task becomes just a job; an adult becomes not a person with great possibilities of transformation within a new situation, but a person who can hold many lightly differentiated jobs.

In closing, I should like to describe briefly, in the terms of this analysis, the transformation of the culture of the Manus people of the Admiralty Islands whom I studied in 1928 [22] and in 1953. [23]

In the Trust Territory of New Guinea, the village of Peri, of the Manus tribe of the Admiralty Islands, is our only case in which a community of completely identified individuals—including adults and children—has been studied before (in 1928) and after a major change (in

1953). In 1928 this group of primitive fishermen and traders, without a written language or knowledge of the use of metals, had undergone about a quarter of a century of culture contact—first with the Germans who were mainly interested in crushing warfare and in recruiting an occasional native for the police force and in obtaining a few work boys, then with the Australians who instituted, under a League of Nations Mandate, a form of government in which recruiting of endentured labor, a head tax, and compulsory resort to government-maintained courts were instituted.

In 1928, when we could study adult men who had taken part in internecine strife and headhunting raids, it was possible to form a fairly clear picture of what the conditions had been immediately previous to culture contact with Europeans. The course of contact such as this is very well known; it has occurred in hundreds of well-documented cases. After warfare and other practices repugnant to either the convenience or the moral sense of the conquering power are suppressed, missionization sets in, the local culture becomes attenuated and unbalanced, there is great cultural loss, and an expectation arises of a restabilization of the group as a dependent and depressed proletariat in a permanently inferior role vis-à-vis the donor culture. Depending upon the period of history and the available techniques and ethics, the size of the group, and the degree of stratification within it—from rank or caste, or due to education introduced by the donor culture—there may develop in time various sorts of protest movements, nativistic cults, demands for "national status," etc.

In the case of some 2200 Manus natives living in eleven villages (part of some 13,000 Admiralty Island natives), their small numbers, relatively stratified cultures, poor land, and absence of resources appeared, in the late 20's, to set a very low political and economic role for them in the generations ahead. Instead, a series of unique historical circumstances, in which some particular flexibilities and disharmonies in their own culture played an important part, permitted this small group of people to conceive the possibility of a major cultural shift, an across-the-board transformation of the old and traditional into a twentieth-century version of a democratic community modeled on American and Australian political practices. The determining conditions in the old culture seem to have been (1) a way of life keyed to events (such as birth and marriage) rather than to a calendar, accompanied by little sense of history; (2) a short life span and social provisions for apprenticeship in terms of function rather than status (an entrepreneur was succeeded not by a son but by the member of his lineage with suitable ability); (3) a trading psychology which permitted the stating of traits as well as objects in articulate cost terms; (4) a dislike of the old system which required boys, after a carefree childhood, to become the driven dependents of their economic backers, a system incorporated in turn by each generation of growing children; (5) a high recognition, due to close contact with neighbors who spoke other languages and had other customs, of the possibility of cultural differences; and (6) an invincible sense of their own superiority over the members of other language groups around them. (It should be remembered that all of these aspects of their culture might, under different conditions, have become drawbacks rather than facilitators of change.) To these cultural conditions were added the events of World War II: (1) many of the young men who would otherwise have been assuming leadership and acquiring vested interests were caught behind enemy lines and left free to plan and to dream; (2) a highly gifted leader of a nearby small tribe, with a capacity for programing change, was able to utilize a nativistic cult, thus preventing the cult from fizzling out into despair; (3) the climate of opinion in the world of metropolitan powers permitted the Australian Trust administration to take a constructive attitude toward the native desire to remodel their society.

Under these complex conditions, they reorganized their entire way of life and abolished those aspects of the old forms of kinship which they considered incompatible with the new: arranged marriages, long chains of affinal indebtedness, avoidance between affinal kin, consanguinous partisanship in quarrels, heavy investment in rites-de-passage, male power over adult female kin, a father's power over adult children, etc. They designed a new type of village on land and set up new officials, town meetings, forms of banking and taxation, types of travel and hospitality, and wider political cooperation which now included about five thousand people—the whole Manus-speaking group and parts of other linguistic groups.

In considering the conditions under which this tremendous skip was made from a Stone Age type of culture to one whose members could comprehend economic and social planning and the role of the United Nations, discuss the need for governmental sanctions and the relationship between ethical norms and the acquisition of modern technology, the following facilitations of self-consciousness may be indicated. Their ability to recognize cultural difference became operative in adopting European models only when contact with the Americans, not used to the caste distinctions operative in another culture, suggested that they might regard themselves as human beings of the same order as the white people, and therefore able to learn the same things. They also had an ability to analyze and abstract, to take an idea such as "all men are brothers" and apply it to emancipating women and children, prodded also by their experience of the behavior of Australian officials toward their wives.

Vividly observed concrete experience was translated, through the mediation of higher level abstractions—such as the virtues of a universal currency, of labor-saving devices which prevented premature aging, of a system of education which would ensure literacy, of economic planning for community goals—into well-devised patterns which were explicit and also detailed and congruent with existing materials. A new village plan was devised in which the positions of honor were given not to the members of the old ranking lineages but to newly elected officials. Boundary marks were invented to mark the newly bounded political organization. Devices for the handling of money and goods were developed to meet the danger of incessant borrowing which arises when there is a breakdown in old traditional and respected types of savings for ceremonies.

The principal failures, up to 1954, had come from an inability to devise methods of keeping morale high when there was no crisis—a difficulty they shared with the democracies on which they were modeling their society— a lack of sources of new models—they eagerly seized on magazines that suggested new forms of architecture or clothing—an inability to include fully women as partners in innovation—which came from an earlier imbalance combined with work experience for males alone—and a lack of technical skill for changing their economic base to a commercially viable one.

The detailed analysis of this one case suggests that very rapid and complete transformations may be more viable than slow and piecemeal change in which the maladjustments and resistances of generations become part of the culture, and also suggests the value of models which a people feel they themselves seize upon spontaneously as against models which are imposed by small reforming segments of another society.

The Manus transformation did not, however, essentially go beyond existing models, and does not solve the question of how societies are to develop models for a type of life which no one has yet attempted. Here the dilemma seems to be that any vivid picture of an unrealized future tends to become a blueprint in the name of which human beings, born and unborn, can be coerced.[24] It suggests that our present task is to determine models of direction rather than of fixed goals. To the extent that the Manus leaders recognized that new inventions were necessary, they kept their system open against a continuing danger of attempts to restore the past, now pictured as intense moments of high morale when a level of completed transformation had really been attained. Primitive models necessarily end at this point.

NOTES

[1] Margaret Mead, "Professional Problems of Education in Dependent Countries," *Journal of Negro Education,* Vol. 40, no. 3, 1946, pp. 346-357; Margaret Mead (Ed.), *Cultural Patterns and Technical Change,* Unesco, 1953 (New York: Mentor Books, 1955).

[2] O. Lewis, "Controls and Experiments in Field Work," in A. L. Kroeber (Ed.), *Anthropology Today* (Chicago: University of Chicago Press, 1953), pp. 430-451.

[3] Margaret Mead, *New Lives for Old* (New York: Wiliam Morrow, 1955), p. 1.

[4] R. Lifton, "Chinese Communist Thought Reform," in B.

Schaffner (Ed.), *Group Processes*, Transcript of the 3rd Conference, 1956 (New York: Josiah Macy Foundation, 1957), pp. 219-311.

[5] N. Leites, *A Study of Bolshevism* (Glencoe, Illinois: Free Press, 1957).

[6] Margaret Mead, "The Mountain Arapesh I An Importing Culture," *Anthropological Papers*, Vol. 36, part 3 (New York: The American Museum of Natural History, 1938), pp. 139-340.

[7] G. Bateson, *Naven: A Survey of the Problems suggested by a Composite Picture of the Culture of a New Guinea Tribe Drawn from Three Points of View*, Cambridge University Press, 1936; 2nd ed. (Stanford, Calif.: Stanford University Press, 1958).

[8] Te Rangi Hiroa (Peter Buck), *Samoan Material Culture*, Bulletin 75 (Honolulu: Bernice P. Bishop Museum, 1930).

[9] H. G. Robley, *Moko or Maori Tattooing* (London: 1896).

[10] Te Rangi Hiroa (Peter Buck), "On the Maori Art of Weaving Cloaks, Capes and Kilys," *Dominion Museum Bulletin*, No. 3, 1911, pp. 69-90. Wellington.

[11] Margaret Mead, "Professional Problems of Education in Dependent Countries," *Journal of Negro Education*, Vol. 40, no. 3, 1946, pp. 346-357.

[12] H. R. Lantz, *People of Coal Town* (New York: Columbia University Press, 1958).

[13] T. E. Bowditch, *Mission from Cape Coast Castle to Ashanti* (London: Murray, 1819); K. A. Busia, "The Ashanti of the Gold Coast," in D. Forde (Ed.), *African Worlds* (London & New York: Oxford University Press), pp. 190-209; R. S. Rattray, *Ashanti* (Oxford: Clarendon Press, 1923) and *Ashanti Law and Constitution* (Oxford: Clarendon Press, 1929).

[14] Joan Mencher, Child Rearing and Family Organization Among Puerto Ricans in Eastville: el Barrio del Nueva York, Ph.D. Thesis, Columbia University, Department of Anthropology, 1958.

[15] Margaret Mead, "Energy Changes under Conditions of Cul-

tural Change," *Sociometry and the Science of Man,* Vol. XVIII, no. 4, December 1955, pp. 201-211.

[16] Margaret Mead and Elena Calas, "Child Training Ideals in Post-revolutionary Context: Soviet Russia," in Margaret Mead, and Martha Wolfenstein, *Childhood in Contemporary Cultures* (Chicago: University of Chicago Press, 1955), pp. 179-203.

[17] Edmund Carpenter, "Eskimo Space Concepts," *Explorations V,* 1955, pp. 131-145.

[18] F. Boas, "The Central Eskimo," *Sixth Annual Report* (Washington, D. C.: Bureau of American Ethnology, 1888).

[19] L. K. Frank, "The Cost of Competition," in *Society as the Patient* (New Brunswick: Rutgers University Press, 1948), pp. 21-36; Margaret Mead, *Social Organization of Manu'a,* Bulletin 76 (Honolulu: Bernice P. Bishop Museum, 1930).

[20] Margaret Mead, "Methods of Implementing a National Morale Program," *Applied Anthropology.* Vol. 1, no. 1, Oct.-Dec. 1941, pp. 20-24.

[21] Margaret Mead, *The School in American Culture, Inglis Lecture* (Cambridge: Harvard University Press, 1951).

[22] Margaret Mead, "Growing Up in New Guinea, 1930," included in *From the South Seas* (New York: Morrow, 1939).

[23] Margaret Mead, "Cultural Discontinuities and Personality Transformation," *Journal of Social Issues,* Kurt Lewin Memorial Award Issue, Sup. Series, no. 8, 1954.

[24] Margaret Mead, "Towards More Vivid Utopias," *Science,* Vol. 126, no. 3280, 1957, pp. 957-961.

SUGGESTED READINGS

CHAPTER 1

The place and prospects of social science in the American and world scene have not yet been systematically investigated. Useful insights and information are given in D. Lerner and H. D. Lasswell, eds., *The Policy Sciences: Recent Developments in Scope and Method* (Stanford University Press, 1951), which reviewed the state of inquiry as of the early postwar period. On the specific development of attitude research, see the Twentieth Anniversary Issue of *Public Opinion Quarterly,* vol. XXI (1957), ed. W. P. Davison. R. A. Bauer judiciously assesses the role of social science in the bipolarized current world arena in "The Social Sciences: Our Big Advantage," *Harvard Business Review,* vol. XXXVI (1958). The extension of social science to the modernizing areas is exemplified in M. Mead, *New Lives for Old* (Morrow, 1957) and D. Lerner, *The Passing of Traditional Society* (Free Press, 1958).

CHAPTER 2

The history of social science remains to be written. An interesting synopsis is B. F. Hoselitz. "The Social Sciences in the Last Two Hundred Years," *Journal of General Education*, vol. IV (1950). Social science in France, on the eve of the historic expansion, is competently surveyed in R. Hubert, *Les Sciences Sociales dans l'Encyclopédie* (Félix Alcan, 1923) and the British background is given in L. Stephen, *The English Utilitarians*, 2v. (John Murray, 1900). Summaries of growth by disciplines in 19th century Europe are given in the "100 Years Series" published by Duckworth (London), notably on psychology by J. C. Flugel and on anthropology by T. K. Penniman. A vivid account of the group that gave social research, in turn-of-century Britain, its distinctively empirical, quantitative, policy-related character is B. Webb, *My Apprenticeship* (Penguin, 1938). The more recent scene is put in historical setting by E. A. Shils, *The Present State of American Sociology* (Free Press, 1948).

CHAPTER 3

The organization and utilization of American social science today needs close study. Useful information is given in: National Science Foundation, *Government Sponsored and Government Supported Research, Social Sciences and Interdisciplinary Areas*, a semi-annual listing of unclassified, extramural social science research sponsored by government agencies. Russell Sage Foundation, *Effective Use of Social Science Research in the Federal Services* (1950) describes the social sciences and shows how they can serve the needs of federal government agencies. M. D. Graham, *Federal Utilization of Social Science Research: Exploration of the Problems* (The Brookings Institution, 1954) provides background data on government social science programs and stresses difficulties in effective utilization of social science research. F. Emerson Andrews, *Philanthropic Foundations* (Russell Sage Foundation,

1956) describes organization and activities of philanthropic foundations, including their support of scientific research.

CHAPTER 4

A grand strategy of social inquiry has been articulated most clearly in H. D. Lasswell's conception of "the policy sciences of democracy." See: *The Political Writings of H. D. Lasswell* (Free Press, 1951). A strong case for "theories of the middle range" is made in R. K. Merton, Social Theory and Social Structure (Free Press, 1949).

CHAPTER 5

The impingement of inquiry upon the autonomy of the private sphere was stated in modern form by L. D. Brandeis and S. D. Warren, "The Right of Privacy," *Harvard Law Review*, vol. IV (1890-91). Contemporary statements are E. A. Shils, *The Torment of Secrecy* (Free Press, 1956); R. H. Rovere, "The Invasion of Privacy," *The American Scholar*, vol. XXVII (1958); H. D. Lasswell, "The Threat to Privacy," in *Conflict of Loyalties*, ed. R. MacIver (Harper & Bros., 1952).

CHAPTER 6

The complex relations between social science and social policy in America today have been formulated by Roger Hilsman, *Strategic Intelligence and National Decisions* (Free Press, 1956). A good exemplification of wartime attitude research in the service of government policy is S. A. Stouffer *et al*, *The American Soldier*, 2v. (Princeton University Press, 1949). *The Policy Sciences*, edited by Lerner and Lasswell, examines the policy relevance of several strategic research areas. Recent studies of the "decision-making process" contain many useful clarifications of the contemporary relationship between knowledge and power.

CHAPTER 7

Arthur F. Burns, *Prosperity Without Inflation* (Fordham University Press, 1957) is an excellent appraisal of the problems of the current American economy written by Eisenhower's former Economic Adviser, Columbia's expert on business cycles. Benjamin Graham, *The Intelligent Investor* (Harper & Bros., 1954) is a good statement of the problems that face the individual who wants to invest his money, by a successful financial analyst and thoughtful student. Robert Heilbroner, *Worldly Philosophers* (Simon and Schuster, 1953) is a readable account of past economists and of the historical schools of political economy. John Maynard Keynes, *General Theory of Employment, Interest, and Money* (Harcourt Brace, 1936) is a modern classic difficult for the non-economist to read but particularly in its initial chapters a rewarding book. Paul A. Samuelson, *Economics: An Introductory Analysis* (McGraw-Hill, 1958) is the widest used elementary text book in economics here and abroad, designed for the student who wants to know what economics is all about. Adam Smith, *The Wealth of Nations* (Modern Library, 1937) is a first rate book on economics from which all the rest has stemmed. It is well worth dipping into.

CHAPTER 8

Edward W. Bakke, *Bonds of Organization* (Harper & Bros., 1950) examines individual group relations in business and industry and how these are being altered today. Carl A. L. Binger, *The Doctor's Job* (Norton, 1948) analyzes the physician's role and ways of thinking, acting, and treating patients as personalities whose feelings and emotions cannot be ignored in illness. Albert Deutsch, *The Mentally Ill in America* (Columbia University Press, 1949) presents a history of the care and treatment of mental illness from colonial times, with insight into the impact of our changing conception of men upon our institutions. Erik H. Erikson, *Childhood and Society* (Norton, 1950) shows how each culture trains its children to develop the kind of personality or character-structure required by its social order and mode of living, with discussion of the processes involved and interpretation of some historic figures. Lawrence K. Frank, *Society as the Patient* (Rutgers University Press, 1948) formulates a psychocultural approach to an understanding of contemporary society and an interpretation of its problems and modes of operations. Iago Galdston, ed., *Ministry and Medicine in Human Relations* (International University Press, 1955) is a symposium on overlapping fields of religion and medicine as presented by psychiatrists, anthropologists and ministers, discussing their contributions to human living, and their different approaches to problems of morals and moralism. Dewey B. Stuit, *Personnel Research and Test Development* (Princeton University Press, 1947) shows the application of work in personnel psychology, under the Bureau of Naval Personnel, to business and industry public administration, educational and military institutions.

CHAPTER 9

A. L. Kroeber, *Anthropology* (Harcourt Brace, 1948) is a treatise in which, insofar as it can be done between the covers of a single book and by one man, Kroeber has synthesized the total theoretical and substantive content of anthropology. In A. L. Kroeber, *Anthropology Today* (University of Chicago Press, 1953), fifty specialists survey the state of existing knowledge in most, but not all, of the principal fields. Many of the chapters are highly technical, but this is an authoritative compendium of present anthropological knowledge. Sol Tax, ed., *An Appraisal of Anthro-*

pology Today (University of Chicago Press, 1953) is a discussion at an international conference of the papers printed in *Anthropology Today*. This record gives a good idea of the frontiers of anthropology, of agreement and disagreement and of issues that are just beginning to be explored. William Thomas, ed., *Current Anthropology* (University of Chicago Press, 1956) in effect carries forward a few years the topics dealt with in the preceding books. Felix Keesing, *Cultural Anthropology* (Rinehart & Co., 1958) is the best text book on cultural anthropology thus far available. John Honigmann, *Culture and Personality* (Harper & Bros., 1954) is a clear synthesis of this new and controversial field, with a valuable bibliography.

CHAPTER 10

See the following articles and books by Margaret Mead: *New Lives for Old* (William Morrow, 1955); *From the South Seas* (William Morrow, 1939); *The School in American Culture* (Harvard University Press, 1951); "The Mountain Arapesh . . . ," *Anthropological Papers*, Vol. 36, part 3 (The American Museum of Natural History, 1938); "Professional Problems of Education in Dependent Countries," *Journal of Negro Education*, Vol. 40, no. 3, 1946; "Energy Changes under Conditions of Cultural Change," *Sociometry and the Science of Man*, Vol. 18, no. 4, 1955; "Towards More Vivid Utopias," *Science*, Vol. 126, no. 3280, 1957. See also these books edited by Margaret Mead: *Childhood in Contemporary Cultures* (University of Chicago Press, 1955), co-edited by Martha Wolfenstein; *Cultural Patterns and Technical Change* (Mentor Books, 1955). Other relevant books are N. Leites, *A Study of Bolshevism* (Free Press, 1957), and H. R. Lantz, *People of Coal Town* (Columbia University Press, 1958).

NOTES ON CONTRIBUTORS

DANIEL LERNER

is Professor of Sociology and International Communication at M.I.T., where he is on the senior research staff of its Center for International Studies. In 1954 he founded the Institut d'Etudes Européennes in Paris, and he has lectured on social research at universities throughout Europe and the Middle East. His books include *Propaganda in War and Crisis, The Nazi Elite, France Defeats EDC* (with Raymond Aron), and most recently *The Passing of Traditional Society: Modernizing the Middle East.*

NATHAN GLAZER

is consulting editor at Random House. As an editor of *Commentary* Magazine (1945-53) and of Doubleday Anchor Books (1953-58), his special concern was to focus critical public attention on contemporary social science. Subsequently, as Guggenheim Fellow, Walgreen Lecturer at the University of Chicago, and Lecturer in Sociology at the University of California (Berkeley), he has explored the historical roots of empirical social research. His books include *American Judaism,* and (with David Riesman and Reuel Denney) *The Lonely Crowd* and *Faces in the Crowd.*

HARRY ALPERT

is Dean of the Graduate School and Professor of Sociology at the University of Oregon. As Program Director for Social Science Research at the National Science Foundation, Vice-President of the American Sociological Society, and past president of the American Association of Public Opinion Research, he has played a large role in relating the social sciences to their policy function. He has also served in various government agencies, including the Office of War Information, Office of Price Administration, Department of the Air Force, and Bureau of the Budget. He is the author of *Emile Durkheim and His Sociology.*

HAROLD D. LASSWELL

is Professor of Law and Political Science at Yale University. A past president of the American Political Science Association, his work is known wherever political behavior is systematically studied. His books include *Psychopathology and Politics, World Politics and Personal Insecurity, National Security and Individual Freedom,* and *The Policy Sciences* (with Daniel Lerner). His classic *Politics: Who Gets What, When, How* is now published by Meridian Books.

EDWARD A. SHILS

is Professor of Social Thought and Sociology at the University of Chicago. His books include *The Structure of Social Action* (with Talcott Parsons *et al.*) *The Present*

State of American Sociology and, most recently, *The Torment of Secrecy*.

MAX F. MILLIKAN

is Professor of Economics at M.I.T., where he is also Director of the Center for International Studies. He has held important executive posts in government and contributed much to the efficient linkage of knowledge and policy, his topic in this volume. He edited *Income Stabilization for a Developing Democracy* and his most recent book, *A Proposal* (with W. W. Rostow), grew out of expert testimony before a Senate committee on foreign aid.

PAUL A. SAMUELSON

is Professor of Economics at M.I.T. A member of the Society of Fellows at Harvard (1937-40), he was awarded the David A. Wells prize of Harvard and the John Bates Clark medal of the American Economic Association, of which he later became vice-president. He is also a past president of the Econometric Society. His textbook *Economics* has given their basic training to many thousands of students in the postwar decade and his journalistic essays have enlightened readers around the world, most often those of the *London Financial Times*.

LAWRENCE K. FRANK

the intellectual godfather of projective testing, has retired from a distinguished career as foundation executive with the Laura Spelman Rockefeller Memorial, General Education Board, Josiah Macy Jr. Foundation. He received the Lasker Award in Mental Health (1947) and the Kurt Lewin Award (1957). His books include *Society as the Patient, Projective Methods, Nature and Human Nature;*

and (with Mary K. Frank) *How to Help Your Child in School* and *Your Adolescent at Home and at School.*

CLYDE KLUCKHOHN

had been chairman of the Department of Anthropology and a member of the Department of Social Relations at Harvard University, where from 1947 to 1954 he was director of the Russian Research Centre. Past President of the American Anthropological Association, he was also a member of the American Philosophical Society and the National Academy of Sciences. His books include *To the Foot of the Rainbow, Beyond the Rainbow, The Navaho* (with D. C. Leighton) and *Mirror for Man.* He died in 1960.

MARGARET MEAD

is Curator of Ethnology at the American Museum of Natural History. As an officer of the American Association for the Advancement of Science, she has done much to define the role of social science on the national scene. Among her many books are *Growing Up in New Guinea, Male and Female, Soviet Attitudes to Authority,* and her recent restudy of the Admiralty Islands (25 years after her original work there) entitled *New Lives for Old.*

DANIEL LERNER

Daniel Lerner is Professor of Sociology and International Communication at M.I.T., where he is on the senior research staff of its Center for International Studies. He has taught the human meaning of the social sciences at universities in Europe and the Middle East. In 1954, he founded the Institut d'Etudes Européennes in Paris. His books include The Policy Sciences, Propaganda in War and Crisis, The Nazi Elite, *and most recently,* The Passing of Traditional Society: Modernizing the Middle East.